"A remarkably fine tribute to C.S. Le[...]
-**Walter Hooper**, literary advisor t[...]

"A fine survey of the many aspects of this perennially interesting topic, any book that brings together the voices of Don W. King, Crystal L. Downing, Andrew Lazo, and Malcolm Guite is worth the read. I find myself with an even deeper appreciation for the roles Dorothy L. Sayers and Joy Davidman played in Lewis' life and their influence on him as a writer and thinker."
- **Janet Brennan Croft**, Editor of *Mythlore: A Journal of J.R.R. Tolkien, C.S. Lewis, Charles Williams, and Mythopoeic Literature*. Rutgers University, New Jersey.

"The stellar cast of thinkers assembled for this unique anthology delivers an astonishing array of insightful essays written with erudition and nuance. This is a substantial, original work of great merit; the editors, Curtis and Key, are to be commended for their inclusion of multiple viewpoints that grapple with Lewis' stated beliefs, rendering them with clarity and diligence."
- **Dr Bruce L. Edwards**, Professor Emeritus, English and Africana Studies, Bowling Green State University (Ohio); Editor of *C.S. Lewis: Life, Works, Legacy*; Online Editor of *The C.S. Lewis Review*, www.cslewisreview.org. Willow, Alaska.

"In Women and C.S. Lewis *we do not meet 'Jack' Lewis the Feminist – there are no attempts to smooth over beliefs unacceptable today. Who we do meet is a Lewis who lived, corresponded, and collaborated with women, valuing, edifying, and enjoying their company. A remarkable melding of quick pace and ample information.*"
- **Dr Charlie W. Starr**, Professor, English and Humanities, and Program Chair, Humanities, Kentucky Christian University; author of *Light: C.S. Lewis' First and Final Short Story*.

"Thought-provoking from the very first page, this collection brings together a wide variety of perspectives on a single, significant question: Was Lewis sexist? It's a lively conversation, and there's plenty to enjoy."
- **Dr Diana Pavlac Glyer**, Professor of English, Azusa Pacific University, California; author of *Bandersnatch: C.S. Lewis, J.R.R. Tolkien, and the Creative Collaboration of the Inklings* and *The Company They Keep*.

"Excellent for both fans of Lewis and for scholars. Rich in truth and wisdom for the twenty-first century. A most welcome contribution to closure on the vital question of Lewis' views on gender."
- **Dr J. Stanley Mattson**, Founder and President, The C.S. Lewis Foundation, Redlands, California.

"Thanks! Someone needed to write this book."
- **Eric Metaxas**, *New York Times* best-selling author of *Miracles, Bonhoeffer, 7 Men*, and others.

"In reading Women and C.S. Lewis *we are invited to be part of an important conversation. Attitudes and resulting actions towards others matter greatly, and this is certainly no less so, when they are informed by understanding based on gender. In this book, we find a variety of voices 'pursuing truth in the company of friends' as they thoughtfully reflect upon Lewis' response to women in both his life and in his writings. Not all contributors in this volume agree, but all take seriously the significance of the issue of gender, and we should as well.* Women and C.S. Lewis *is a very good place to begin to deepen our understanding, and to help us frame our own considered questions."*
– **Marjorie Lamp Mead**, Interim Director, Marion E. Wade Center, Wheaton College, Illinois.

"This book brings new light, thought, and perception to the subject of women in C.S. Lewis' life and writings. These essays are full of shared wisdom and cogent argument that will challenge your perceptions of Lewis and his world."
– **Brian Sibley**, writer and broadcaster known for his highly acclaimed BBC serializations of The Chronicles of Narnia and The Lord of the Rings.

"It's about time! Many seem to think C.S. Lewis was a misogynist, who lived in a stuffy, male dominated, academic world, and we finally have a book that addresses this. The matter is far more complex than some have charged. The judgments against Lewis are generally made by people who have not read him deeply and certainly not for any great length of time. Curtis and Key have put together a cadre of some of the best Lewis thinkers who know the material and can write authoritatively on the matter. The judgments in this book are fair-minded, nuanced, and have no ax to grind. The editors simply desire to set the record straight, and, it's about time."
– **Jerry Root**, Ph.D., Wheaton College, Illinois, co-editor (with Wayne Martindale) of *The Quotable C.S. Lewis* and co-author (with Mark Neal) of *The Surprising Imagination of C.S. Lewis.*

"Controversy about the women in Jack's life and literature has often left a cloud of controversy over his life and writings. Finally, here is a book that properly places Lewis in his socio-cultural setting for a thorough and positive examination of nearly every aspect in which women touched his life – from created literary characters, professional acquaintances, familial relationships, literary references, to the deep marital love that so blessed his life with Joy. This collective work of prominent Lewis scholars is an extraordinary and vital read for any Lewis enthusiast."
– **Deborah Higgens**, PhD, former Director of the C.S. Lewis Study Centre, Oxford; Professor of Medieval Literature, La Sierra University, California; author of *Anglo-Saxon Community in J.R.R. Tolkien's The Lord of the Rings.*

"This collection of voices makes the point so solidly – that C.S. Lewis was emphatically not a woman-hater but ahead of his time in his attitudes toward them – with such variety of experience, eloquence of expression, and annotated proof, that I felt a sadness at turning the last page. Like saying goodbye to a motley collection of old friends after a long anticipated, stimulating, memory-making reunion and wondering if we would ever again gather in the same way."
– **Connie Cavanaugh**, Lewis admirer, speaker, author. Hear her speak and see her books at www.conniecavanaugh.com. Alberta, Canada.

"What a great read! Women and C.S. Lewis takes readers on a carefully curated journey through his life and literature. Nimble editing by Curtis and Key weaves together a tapestry of voices that clearly depicts Lewis' high regard and respect for women, refuting critics who try to discredit Lewis because of his effectiveness in explaining the life of Christian faith."
– **Carol Pipes**, Editor of Facts & Trends magazine, LifeWay, Nashville.

"Written for laypeople and academics alike, this collection of essays would likely have pleased Lewis himself. Rather than respond to the charge that Lewis was sexist by merely assigning its own pejorative label to those responsible for the accusation, which occurs all too frequently in what passes for intellectual exchange these days, it rejects mere shibboleth for honest engagement with the issues themselves, drawing on a diverse array of authors who consider the evidence from both Lewis' writings and life. Curtis and Key are to be commended for this valuable contribution to a crucial discussion."
– **Dr Stephen Dunning**, Associate Professor of English, Trinity Western University, Langley, British Columbia; author of The Crisis and the Quest: A Kierkegaardian Reading of Charles Williams; co-founder and co-director of the Inklings Institute of Canada, housed at TWU.

"How refreshing and encouraging to be reminded that Lewis' fictional heroines were brave, feisty, and thoughtful. I love that they could be anything their male counterparts could be, both good or bad."
– **Gayle Roper**, award-winning, Pennsylvania-based novelist of a wide range of fiction from Allah's Fire to Lost and Found.

"I am indeed very supportive of Women and C.S. Lewis, a worthwhile contribution that a wide range of readers will enjoy and find most helpful."
– **Mark A. Pike**, BA (Hons), PGCE, MA (Ed), PhD, Professor of Education and Head of the School of Education, University of Leeds, England. Author of C.S. Lewis as Teacher for our Time (Lutterworth Press, Cambridge, 2013).

"Curtis and Key have assembled wonderfully varied voices yielding high scholarship that is yet readily accessible to address the question of C.S Lewis' attitude toward women. Does misogyny exist in Lewis' writings, or in the eye of the beholder? No contributor to this fine volume shies away from that question. What an engaging, delightful read!"
– **D. Joy Riley**, MD, MA (Bioethics), Executive Director of The Tennessee Center for Bioethics & Culture. Co-author (with C. Ben Mitchell) of *Christian Bioethics: A Guide for Pastors, Health Care Professionals, and Families* (B&H Academic, 2014).

"In this work you will find a thorough and honest exploration into the role of women in the life of C.S. Lewis. Its great strength is found in the diversity, depth, and breadth of perspectives, the range of which offers valuable insight into the nuances of his writing and his growth as a person. Given the frequent criticism directed toward Lewis in regard to women, this book is a much-needed voice and essential resource: an excellent read."
– **Lisa Coutras**, author of the forthcoming *Tolkien's Theology of Beauty*; PhD Candidate, Kings College London.

"This balanced, irenic collection takes up a vital issue in the study of C.S. Lewis; lovers of Lewis will want to join the conversation."
– **Louis Markos**, Ph.D., Professor in English and Scholar in Residence, Houston Baptist University, Texas; author of *Restoring Beauty: The Good, the True, and the Beautiful in the Writings of C.S. Lewis.*

"I am convinced that C.S. Lewis well understood women because he took seriously the theology that before God we are all feminine."
– **Dr Paul F. Ford**, author of *Companion to Narnia*; Professor of Theology and Liturgy, St. John Seminary, Camarillo, California.

"Are you a woman who loves to think and create? You will find in these pages a brilliant scholar who honors your depth and complexity, who engages women like you in his personal correspondence and writes women of reason and imagination into his strong, winsome, female characters. Are you a man who wants to encourage women? You will learn from a man who not only engages women but learns from them. The book offers depth of scholarship and breadth of analysis of Lewis' life and writings – all in an accessible style that will change the way you think about thinking women."
– **Lael Arrington**, author of *Faith and Culture: The Guide to a Culture Shaped by Faith* (Zondervan, 2011). Columbia, South Carolina.

Women and
C.S. Lewis

What his life and literature reveal for today's culture

Edited by
Carolyn Curtis and Mary Pomroy Key

Text copyright © 2015 Carolyn Curtis and Mary Pomroy Key
This edition copyright © 2015 Lion Hudson

The right of Carolyn Curtis and Mary Pomroy Key to be identified as the
authors of this work has been asserted by them in accordance with the
Copyright, Designs and Patents Act 1988.

All rights reserved. No part of this publication may be reproduced or
transmitted in any form or by any means, electronic or mechanical, including
photocopy, recording, or any information storage and retrieval system, without
permission in writing from the publisher.

Published by Lion Books
an imprint of
Lion Hudson plc
Wilkinson House, Jordan Hill Road,
Oxford OX2 8DR, England
www.lionhudson.com/lion

ISBN 978 0 7459 5694 7
e-ISBN 978 0 7459 5695 4

First edition 2015

Acknowledgments
Inside images: pp. 18, 23, 38, 82, 90, 117, 141, 165, 188, 196, 230 copyright ©
Lancia E. Smith, lanciaesmith.com; p. 70 courtesy Montreat College; p. 212 by
Godwell Chan, courtesy Redeemer Presbyterian Church, Manhattan; p. 157
by Gloria Moore; p. 184 by Wendy Delamont Lees; p. 220 courtesy Michael
Timms; p. 230 by Elizabeth Panzachi

Extracts by C.S. Lewis copyright © C.S. Lewis Pte Ltd. Reprinted by permission.
Extract p. 57 taken from "The Longest Way Round", in Don W. King (ed.),
Out of My Bone: The Letters of Joy Davidman, copyright © Joy Davidman.
Extract p. 69 taken from *Collected Poems* by Ruther Pitter copyright © Ruth
Pitter. Reprinted by permission of Enitharmon Press Ltd.
Extract p. 71 taken from "Yet One More Spring", in *Letter to a Comrade* by Joy
Davidman, copyright © 1938 Joy Davidman. Reprinted by permission of Yale
University Press Ltd.

A catalogue record for this book is available from the British Library

Printed and bound in the UK, May 2015, LH26

Contents

Chapter Seven

C.S. Lewis and the friends who apparently couldn't really have been his friends, but actually were

SECTION TWO

Lewis, the fiction author – how girls and women are

Chapter One

Are The Chronicles of Narnia sexist?

Chapter Two

"The Abolition of Woman": gender and hierarchy in Lewis'
Space Trilogy

Chapter Three

"She is one of the great ones." The radical world of *The Great Divorce*

Chapter Four

The Pilgrim's Paradox: female characters in *The Pilgrim's Regress*

Chapter Five

New perspectives: *Till We Have Faces*, *The Four Loves*, and other works

SECTION THREE

Chapter One

Setting the man–woman thing to rights

Acknowledgments

Heartfelt thanks to our wonderful team at Lion Hudson in Oxford, England (Ali, Jess, Andrew, Tony, Emma, Rachel, Jude, and Jonathan); literary agent (Steve Laube); family, friends, prayer partners (Tom, Gale, Nancy, Melanie, Ann, Lanier, Mark, Cindy, Roschelle, Joan, Lancia, Scott, Jonathan, Jordan, Emily – and others we love).

A note on style: we have kept the appropriate usage – American, British, or Canadian English – based on nationalities of our contributors, to whom we are extremely grateful for their energetic discussions and enthusiasm for the project. We think our readers will be pleased by the variety of insights, approaches, and – often – engaging wit.

Special thanks to Doug Gresham, son of Joy and stepson of Jack, for his gracious loan of our cover photo, which he snapped at the age of eleven with his trusty Kodak. And thanks to our brilliant cover designer, Jonathan, for converting it to color.

Carolyn Curtis, in Texas

Mary Pomroy Key, in California

Was C.S. Lewis sexist?
Is he relevant today?

Carolyn Curtis

Why read a book on *Women and C.S. Lewis*? The hottest question on Lewis today is whether or not he was sexist, says a contributor to this book, Monika Hilder, who has written three volumes examining this accusation. What do other respected thinkers, such as Alister McGrath and Randy Alcorn, plus more than two dozen others we have gathered, say about Lewis' treatment of women in his life and literature and, thus, his relevance in the twenty-first century?

Whether you are new to C.S. Lewis or already among the millions of readers of his books – *Mere Christianity, The Screwtape Letters, Surprised by Joy, Miracles, The Problem of Pain, The Allegory of Love, The Great Divorce, A Grief Observed, Till We Have Faces*, his Space Trilogy, and, of course, The Chronicles of Narnia, to name a few – accusations of personal or literary ill-treatment of women by such a famous, well-regarded British scholar and author may come as a shock. You may wonder why some critics even call Lewis a misogynist, a harsher term suggesting a man is a woman-hater, has no respect for women in general, or holds little if any regard for intelligent, successful women.

Excellent books analyze these claims, mostly written by scholars – and, frankly, *for* scholars. We wanted a book that's valuable to scholars yet accessible to a wider range of people, thoughtful readers who might want to dog-ear pages yet can't because the book belongs to a library.

Who are our readers?

C.S. Lewis and his friend, J.R.R. Tolkien, resolved to write books *they* would enjoy reading, confirmation that even prominent academics like those two beloved authors actively sought to find pleasure in their work.

For *Women and C.S. Lewis: What his life and literature reveal for today's culture*, we chose to include contributors who range from noted Lewis scholars to newer Lewis thinkers, a blend we hope accomplishes several goals: 1) bringing to new and long-time readers many of the authoritative voices on Lewis; 2) allowing those authorities to debate the sexism charges within the pages of one volume; 3) mirroring Lewis' admirable efforts to support and give light to many newer, up-and-coming thinkers; 4) providing answers to readers who consider themselves fans of Lewis but who are mystified when they stumble across words like "sexist" in the same sentence as his name; 5) giving direction to people who are new to Lewis or who have avoided reading him because they were put off by critics who cried "misogynist."

So, in addition to scholar friends, we anticipate that our readers will be people raised on Narnia but who find themselves conflicted or puzzled over claims that Lewis did not write his female characters with the strong, courageous characteristics of his males. Other readers may love fantasy/science fiction but have avoided Lewis because of a nagging feeling that a "religious author" might have made his sci fi lame with gender stereotypes. Some readers may wonder if his poetry insults half the population. Others might be suspicious of an Oxford scholar known for his radical turn from atheism to Christianity and wonder if it meant he had abandoned his intellect. (Yet Cambridge created a prominent position for Lewis *after* he became known for his faith and his ability to explain it. He did this so effectively that both laypeople and theologians still quote him fifty years after his death.)

What are today's issues?

As for Lewis' relevance, what are today's women's issues? And do they affect only women? (Quick answer to the latter: No.) I'll share from my personal perspective.

My coming of age was after Lewis' death. The late 1960s through the next decades were times of great change for women. I earned undergraduate and graduate degrees in journalism, entered the workforce and enjoyed a fulfilling career which moved me from Arizona to New Hampshire and found me in settings ranging from Capitol Hill in Washington D.C. to communications management in three Fortune 50 companies, plus the corporate offices of two of America's most influential church denominations. I taught journalism at a college. I covered top newsmakers; wrote speeches for corporate executives; managed groups of employees; spoke at conferences; wrote for, edited, even launched publications; authored books and assisted other authors with theirs; helped newer writers develop their skills and find their voices. I also travelled, eventually to twenty-five countries – the ultimate adventure for a culture watcher.

In most ways, it's been a wonderful ride, but I'd be lying if I claimed I never observed or experienced some sexism along the way. However, when I consider attitudes that deny basic rights to girls and women or force them into unspeakable situations of degradation, my experiences as a student and a career woman seem minor. No one shot me for going to school. No one whisked me away to be their sex slave. However, the underlying attitudes of such outrageous actions occasionally showed their ugly faces, even in civilized corporate cultures – a lack of respect, a desire to humiliate, inflated (or fragile) egos denying professional opportunities to qualified women.

To be fair, many fine men provided me with a generous hand-up, especially men with the intelligence and integrity I saw in C.S. Lewis, whose non-fiction books I began reading in my twenties. As an older adult, I discovered Narnia, then realized

I wouldn't have understood Lewis' deeper meanings as a child, making me appreciate his opinion that any book worth reading only in childhood is not worth reading even then. I required more life experiences and maturity to benefit from the deep truths revealed in the land of Narnia. Maybe that's just me.

As a thinker, Lewis was God's powerful instrument in my life's journey. I read him voraciously, learning and growing with each book as he dealt so effectively with themes such as sin, humanity's fall from grace, and redemption. His observation in "The Weight of Glory" that God finds our desires too weak rather than too strong resonated in me. Even with my heady professional opportunities, I recognized myself in his description of the half-hearted creature "fooling about with... ambition" when God's grace was offered to me. I remained content to make "mud pies in a slum," because, before experiencing God's redemption, I could not envision "the infinite joy of a seaside holiday." Now I saw myself as having the dignity of a free moral agent made in God's image to live a life worthy of my creator. And I began the journey of understanding what that meant.

In short, Lewis baptized my intellect. Before reading Lewis, I did not seem to know many intellectual Christians. Then I discovered they were all around me, and I began outgrowing my childish understanding of how God works in the world and in my life. Also, Lewis made me laugh. His wit was so original and fun to discover that I found myself laughing out loud while I was alone reading him. So now I had two new points of view: faith could be intellectual, and faith could be fun. Plus, the more I read, the more I discovered about Lewis himself. His life story became as fascinating to me as his literature.

And so, with my personal and professional perspective, imagine how startled I was to discover that some critics have called Lewis "sexist." I was spending a week at The Kilns, the author's home in Oxford, England, when I heard a conversation exploring this claim. The idea shook my world. I was acutely aware of what I'd seen as Lewis' high view of women – in his books and personal life choices. My "antenna" for sexist attitudes was well developed, so I resolved to check out the theory that a thinker whose ability to communicate effectively such truths would have intended them for (or been influenced by) only the male half of the population. I braced myself for disappointment.

The publisher for my first book, back in the 1980s, had described me in marketing literature as a research journalist. At the time, I thought with amusement, *Is there any other kind?* In retrospect, the description fits my personality. So, armed with this new and disturbing claim about Lewis, I read and met more Lewis thinkers, picking their mighty brains for answers. Eventually, I realized the idea of Lewis as sexist or misogynist needed to be addressed in a book (result: *Women and C.S. Lewis*). Lewis' influence is even more widespread than during his lifetime and attitudes about women continue to be relevant. It's not a stretch to say such attitudes provide fuel for wars being fought. When I was younger, I thought the wars were in corporate boardrooms; now I see they're on actual battlefields. Cultures are fighting one another – with ideas, bombs, and bullets. We are influenced by what we read, even by a thinker/writer dead for more than half a century.

Should today's readers care?

Cultural attitudes, "women's issues," what are they? Today's female college graduates still might say lack of leadership opportunities or disparity in pay. Women in some cultures might refer to a denial of education or forced prostitution. Readers may wonder if a writer of C.S. Lewis' stature wove messages into his literature that disrespect women and girls and are therefore "out of touch" (even embarrassing or dangerous) for twenty-first century readers. And that's a fair and relevant concern, given what some critics have said about Lewis, including claims we quote in this book. Today's generation, after all, is redefining many cultural values, such as marriage – and we can't be too careful of our reading.

One so-called women's issue is abortion, back in the news. My writing partner, **Mary Pomroy Key**, reminds me that abortion has been newsworthy throughout her lifetime. Is abortion a cultural issue? Perhaps. Is it strictly a women's issue? No, it affects both women and men. Is this book about abortion? No, although an insightful thinker, **Mary Poplin**, addresses it in these pages from personal experience. Do we know the views of C.S. Lewis on this topic and others regarding sexual practices and results (degradation of women individually and as a group through pornography; sex trafficking)? Perhaps not for certain, although writers on both sides of the pond, **Holly Ordway** and **Michael Ward**, provide their thoughts based on Lewis' works, specifically on sexual intercourse (Ordway) and contraception (Ward), topics that may sound quaint – and yet these terrific writers plumb Lewis' thinking and ponder: is Lewis relevant in the twenty-first century?

To tackle that question, we invited contributors from beyond the halls of academia, though many in *Women and C.S. Lewis* do teach, research, and write. We wanted thinkers and writers you might not know, but should. So we have **Crystal Hurd**, who writes on the very first woman who loved Jack Lewis; **Brett McCracken**, a young blogger and book author with a growing following and impressive journalism credits; **Kelly Belmonte**, a newer poet winning awards; and **Kasey Macsenti**, who imagines Lewis and Dorothy L. Sayers meeting for a pint of beer and their trademark deep but witty conversation.

If you want people *known* as scholars, you'll find them too, and we've asked them to share from their hearts as well as their minds. They include **Randy Alcorn**, who tells how Lewis inspires him to stand up for women; **Alister McGrath**, who writes in this book on the Inklings; **Devin Brown**, on sexism in Narnia; Canadian author **Monika Hilder,** who discusses masculine and feminine, or classical and spiritual, principles in history and culture as guides to heroism. (She "names the names" of several who accuse Lewis of sexism or misogyny such as J.K. Rowling, Philip Pullman, and Kath Filmer. Brown and others do that too, refuting their claims.)

Did we shy away from controversy? We invited writers with views that differ in certain ways including **Jeanette Sears** in the United Kingdom and **Kathy Keller** in the United States of America with contributions on Lewis' views about women in the pulpit and other leadership issues, based on their personal experiences.

We invited writers to use their own delightful voices: beloved British expert on all-things-Lewis, **Colin Duriez**; award-winning novelist, **Joy Jordan-Lake**; author and playwright **Paul McCusker**, who takes you into the Jack Lewis/Janie Moore household; **Andrew Lazo**, on *Till We Have Faces*; **Steven Elmore**, who breaks down Lewis' sci fi as it relates to the author's view of women; **Brad Davis**, a poet with a refreshing take on Lewis; and **John Stonestreet**, who looks to Lewis for advice as a father to his daughters.

Women and C.S. Lewis also includes deep, insightful, satisfying contributions from well-established Lewis experts and authors **Lyle Dorsett**, **Don W. King**, **Crystal Downing**, **Malcolm Guite**, **Christin Ditchfield**, and **David C. Downing**, people with wisdom whose books are cherished.

Read, learn, enjoy.

Make up your own mind. In our book's Conclusion, we provide applications from people inspired by Lewis whose life examples are worth remembering, even emulating: **Carol W. Swain**, **Randy Singer**, **Lancia E. Smith**, **David Holland,** and **Lisa Ledri-Aguilar**. That's because we are serious about our book's subtitle: *What his life and literature reveal for today's culture.* Would C.S. Lewis write or speak on issues in today's headlines (throughout history, if we are honest), atrocities including brutality to women, and humiliation (or even death) for speaking up? Jack would call such a question a "supposal."

We invite readers to look at Lewis' values, the principles which undergirded his life and work, and the choices he made as a man and as an author. Perhaps Lewis would remind us of his opinion from an essay, "Christian Apologetics," that readers don't need more books about Christianity but more written by people applying their faith to the characters they develop, the words they write, the ideas they share. Perhaps you will come to the conclusion I did during my work on this book that people trying to discredit Lewis with charges like sexism are really attacking him for his effectiveness in explaining the life of faith.

Throughout the contributors' chapters and in our Conclusion, you will meet people whom Lewis inspired to take action. At the end we provide Questions for Reflection and Discussion for group or personal study.

• •

 **Carolyn Curtis** *is the author or collaborator of seven books, and a veteran journalist with awards from* The Wall Street Journal, *Evangelical Press Association, Society of Professional Journalists, etc. She has been published in* On Mission, Christianity Today, By Faith, Sports Illustrated, The Saturday Evening Post *and many others. She worked in communications management for three Fortune 50 companies and at corporate headquarters for two major church denominations. She has reported from daily newsrooms and from Capitol Hill in Washington D.C. She has taught journalism at a college and been a speaker at numerous conferences. She has a BA in journalism from The University of Texas at Austin and an MA in communication from Stephen F. Austin State University. She lives in Fort Worth, Texas.*

Not mere mortals

Dr Mary Pomroy Key

"Child," said the Lion, "I am telling you your story, not hers.
No one is told any story but their own."
– C.S. Lewis, *The Horse and His Boy*

Each of us has our own unique story of discovery and surprise, challenge and indebtedness to one of the most insightful and creative, intelligent and sometimes puzzling thinkers of the twentieth century, Clive Staples Lewis. As a college student in the 1970s, Lewis opened up for me a precise language for relationships and friendship in *The Four Loves*. The command to trust, resting only on the floating islands in *Perelandra*, gave me comfort and courage in the 1980s as I drifted through advanced degrees and new career opportunities. Reading Narnia for the first time as a young mother and lecturer in Children's Literature in the 1990s challenged my concepts of education, imagination and reality. And so it was, entering the twenty-first century, I set aside for a season the roles expected of a professional counselor, college professor and licensed minister for the privilege of raising and schooling our children at home. Once again, Lewis, both in *The Great Divorce* and in the complex character of Jane Studdock, offered perspective in giving up the things that once seemed so important. With that, a door opened into a new world.

I became involved with the C.S. Lewis Foundation; "Living the Legacy," as our tagline proclaims. Spirited discussions revolve around just that. What exactly is Lewis' legacy? Is it the specific, timeless topics he addressed – love and friendship, faith and truth, life and death, and what it is to be human, male and female?

Is it the genres he used in conveying simple, yet profound, truths – through essay and poetry, fantasy and science fiction, myth and apologetics? Is it the very life he lived – truth-telling through lectures and correspondence, grace-giving through sponsoring refugees and caring for family?

The trajectory of his ideas and writings is, in fact, the legacy that is being lived out – through this collection of essays and the other myriad of works of literature, music and art inspired by Lewis. James Como, Professor Emeritus of Rhetoric and Public Communication at York College, New York, and a founding member of the New York C.S. Lewis Society in 1969, in his *Remembering C.S. Lewis*, notes that the key to Lewis' enduring literary and spiritual achievement rests in his adherence to the vibrant, living faith. As poet, philosopher and apologist, Lewis wrestled with and sought to articulate his faith, offering hope in an ever-changing post-Christian world. It was precisely the honest wrestling with the significant, and sometimes very dark, issues of life and death and after-life that gave Lewis' work its peculiar power to penetrate the reader's deepest questions. "As a concept, personhood, I think, interested him as much as God... [and] more than ever, (I believe) we should be paying attention to his views of the masculine and feminine, which (he reminds us) are not quite the same as male and female."[1]

We, too, struggle with deep questions and longings, with the tensions of tradition, modernism and post-modernism, with questions that strike at the very core of our being... What does it mean to be an immortal, a woman or a man, feminine or masculine, in this age, and how do we reconcile these struggles with a living faith? How can we hope to honor and live out so rich a legacy as Lewis inspires? In *Women and C.S. Lewis*, we seek to participate in the conversation – with an informed, yet informal voice – to encourage lively and respectful debate, and to consider new perspectives as we join together in "pursuing truth in the company of friends." [2] Along this journey, we hear scholarly voices speaking, cup of tea in hand, from their easy chair for all to enjoy; we see children, wide-eyed and incredulous, pouring out their woes to attentive ears; we are surprised by a turn of phrase that unlocks a new world of ideas; we are alarmed by the pain and suffering inflicted by our darkened world; we are quickened, made hopeful by a roar.

We delight in the merriment which exists, as Lewis points out, "between people who have, from the outset, taken each other seriously – no flippancy, no superiority, no presumption."[3] Our collection of essays and personal reflections is the result of a community, a "Sprinkling"[4] of sincere, thoughtful and inquisitive scholars, artists, writers, parents, business executives, poets, actors, webmasters, ministers, musicians, high school mentors and college professors, a fencer and a change-ringer – all of whom seek truth and its creative expression, and all of whom Lewis would have welcomed as "everlasting splendors." Does everyone agree? No. Is there room (or perhaps a hallway?) for debate and interpretation? Of course.

This mosaic, composed of both seasoned thinkers and young millennials, reflects Lewis' own practice of encouraging and mentoring the next generation, not all of whom were on a rigorous academic track. Lewis often took an interest in the up-and-coming, offering financial assistance, letters of recommendation and words of encouragement. Colin Duriez, recollecting Lewis' breadth of friendships, includes in his essay June Flewett (later "Jill Freud"), a young wartime refugee turned actress, who billeted at The Kilns and was later provided with a scholarship by Lewis to the Royal Academy of Dramatic Art. Laurence Harwood, who sheepishly admitted to his godfather/Oxford don his failure of university preliminary exams, found a remarkable source of encouragement in Lewis. "The world is full of capable and useful people who began life by ploughing in exams... so don't think either that you are no good or that you are a victim. Write the whole thing off and get on."[5] And so Laurence did "get on" – with

Lewis' financial backing and whole-hearted support – to a very fulfilling career with the National Trust.

In keeping with the legacy of mentoring, Carolyn Curtis, an accomplished journalist, author, and speaker, generously offered to me the opportunity of not only co-editing this collection as my entrance into the world of publication, but also allowing me to glean from her own personal and professional life the wisdom of experience. For that, I am truly grateful. We met as a result of my responsibilities with the C.S. Lewis Foundation, assisting with the writers track at the C.S. Lewis Conference at Camp Allen, Texas. Two years later, we are handing in a manuscript. One of the strengths of the C.S. Lewis Foundation over the past twenty-seven years has been its emphasis on *making connections* – offering a variety of venues at which creative and imaginative artists and other professionals may be inspired, as Lewis was, to be in company with those creating new, meaningful presentations of the incarnate Christ, thereby building bridges with the secular world. A living faith, connection, inspiration, respect, joy – these are the heart of the Foundation; this book is a result of living Lewis' legacy.

But that is my story, and not another's, as will be evident throughout this particular collection of essays highlighting the women, both real and fictional, in Lewis' life. Are his writings still relevant today? The fact is that Lewis continues to fascinate. He continues to matter. Readers continue to look at the details of his life and the meanings behind his body of work. Lewis' ability to enthrall, woo, and captivate the keen imaginations of both the intellect and the heart will draw you in, no matter if you've lived with Lewis for decades, or are a new friend of Narnia. These essayists are pursuing truth in the company of friends – and contributing to building modern bridges through media and social networking venues. The "radio broadcasts" of the 1940s have morphed into podcasts and YouTube videos; letter writing has been transformed into emails, Instagrams, and tweets. You'll find evidence of these new realms coexisting with the timeless truths of the old tales. Aslan is on the move. Hold on tight!

"Aslan," said Lucy, "you're bigger."
"That is because you are older, little one," answered he.
"Not because you are?"
"I am not. But every year you grow, you will find me bigger."
– C.S. Lewis, *Prince Caspian*

. . . .

Dr Mary Pomroy Key *serves as Director of Special Programs for the C.S. Lewis Foundation, which has a goal to establish C.S. Lewis College, a four-year accredited Great Books and "Mere Christian" college. Contributing strategically to the fulfillment of this goal, as the Director of the newly established C.S. Lewis Study Center in Northfield, Massachusetts, she oversees renovations and programming at the Study Center, housed in an historic Victorian home known as "Green Pastures" and located adjacent to the former Northfield Seminary for Girls established by Dwight L. Moody. An experienced educator and administrator at the college level, Mary has held several student life positions and taught psychology, education and literature at California Baptist University, where she earned her BSc and MSc degrees in Psychology. She earned her PhD in Counseling Psychology through the University of Southern California, specializing in College Student Development. She also holds a Marriage and Family Therapist license. She and her husband, a professor of philosophy, have home educated their three children for seventeen years.*

SECTION ONE

Lewis, the man – and the women in his life

In *Lenten Lands, My Childhood with Joy Davidman and C.S. Lewis*, Douglas Gresham describes the time leading up to the marriage of his mother and stepfather. As her British visa expired, Jack did not want to part with Joy and her "two small, active satellites who hurtled around her in wildly divergent, though equally eccentric orbits," referencing himself and David, his older brother. With pride, Gresham describes the date of their civil ceremony, 23 April 1956, as the day "I became a British Citizen." He sensed the deep love between Jack and Joy, affection that spilled over to include the boys. In admiration, Gresham describes Warnie as a wise fox, sensing that this kind, gentle brother of his new stepfather considered moving from The Kilns but decided first to "try out the new regime." The author reminds *Lenten Lands* readers that Warnie later would write, "What Jack's marriage meant to me was that our home was enriched and enlivened."

As time passed and Joy's cancer surfaced, the civil marriage was supplemented by an ecclesiastical ceremony, and Joy was brought home to The Kilns from the hospital. Meantime, Jack had accepted a position at Cambridge created for him. Doug, full of schoolboy loyalty to Oxford blue, plucked up his courage to ask why Jack had moved from one university to the other. Jack's answer taught young Doug an early lesson about the responsibility a loving father, even a stepfather, takes toward marriage "and acquiring two children into the bargain." Gresham's memoir also describes the timeline he understands of when friendship blossomed into romance and romance into commitment – a credible and revealing explanation by one who knew. Readers of this book and others, even blogs, might conclude that Jack's love for Joy was the culmination of his growing appreciation for women as equals. It was a comfort level honed by life lessons Jack learned from other relationships, some healthier than others.

* * *

Section One examines key women in C.S. Lewis' life, beginning with his mother, the brilliant Flora Hamilton Lewis, whose intellect, influence, and untimely death set the stage for his relationships with women for the rest of his life. Chapter one is "The enduring influence of Flora Lewis" by Dr Crystal Hurd. It also provides glimpses into Lewis' sometimes misunderstood father Albert, acknowledging that parenting is a joint effort that's difficult to accomplish even in a Christ-focused home and finding new insights about Lewis' complicated relationship with his father. Jack, as he became known, and brother Warnie responded to regrets about their treatment of Albert after his passing and as they embraced Christianity with its emphasis on grace, forgiveness, and reconciliation.

Chapter two introduces Mrs Jane King Moore, a complex woman and a controversial influence in Jack's life. "What do we make of Lewis' relationship with Mrs Moore?" by Paul McCusker will provoke new thoughts about Lewis and his life with her.

Dr Lyle W. Dorsett provides our third chapter's portrait of Lewis' wife Joy Davidman Gresham, whom Jack described as having "a mind like a leopard... lithe and quick and muscular," and tells their great love story. To fully appreciate and understand Lewis' attitudes toward women, readers must know Joy, who was his soulmate, his writing partner and, for too short a time, the romantic love of his life.

Chapter four is "Fire and Ice," by Dr Don W. King, a fascinating examination of Lewis' close friendship with acclaimed poet Ruth Pitter, contrasting her with Joy, whom he eventually married, by looking at the women's poetry for clues to their methods of drawing him to themselves, not just as poets but as women desiring his love.

One of Lewis' closest friendships was with his author friend, Dorothy L. Sayers, whose influence on him was so complex and interesting we have devoted two chapters to her. In the first, Dr Crystal L. Downing, an expert on *The Divine Comedy*, compares Sayers to Dante's Beatrice as the one who directed Lewis' eyes to the Light through whom both male and female were created in the image of God.

If Lewis maintained close friendships with literary women, why did he not make a point to include them in the Inklings? Dr Alister McGrath describes this lively group and provides satisfying answers in chapter six, "On Tolkien, the Inklings – and Lewis' blindness to gender."

Section One ends with chapter seven, the delightfully titled "C.S. Lewis and the friends who apparently couldn't really have been his friends, but actually were" by Colin Duriez, who summarizes several key women in Lewis' life and their influences on him. It explores women chronologically from Janie Moore to Joy Davidman, and provides an initial glimpse of the trajectory of his life – the direction or path his relationships, his attitudes, his work, and his influence would take – which we explore deeper in our Conclusion, "What do Lewis' life and literature reveal for today's culture?"

CHAPTER ONE

The enduring influence of Flora Lewis

Dr Crystal Hurd

The dining room of the sprawling house known as Little Lea on the edge of Belfast is abuzz with activity. Stretched limply upon the family's table is a surgical patient, beloved mother of two, Flora Lewis, undergoing exploratory surgery for what will be diagnosed as abdominal cancer. She is young – only forty-six.

As the murmur of discussion drifts ominously through the house, the patient's nine-year-old son listens intently, hearing endless footsteps as nurses and surgeon circle the table in a stoic march. Clive Staples "Jack" Lewis prays fervently for healing. Although Flora will survive the surgery, she will succumb to cancer six months later, creating an unrelenting wound in her sons. The younger – Jack, as he will be known – suffers silently but will use the emotion derived from these memories in his great apologetic and fiction classics such as *The Problem of Pain*, The Chronicles of Narnia and more than thirty other titles read by millions.

Florence Augusta Hamilton was born to a third-generation clergyman, Thomas Hamilton, and wife, Mary Warren, on 18 May 1862. Although Flora, as she was called, was the fourth and youngest, she was not the most adored. In fact, Flora and her brother Augustus acknowledged that they were not their parents' favorites and formed a lifelong alliance. Perhaps this encouraged Flora's desire to achieve academic success, apart from the traditional expectations of motherhood.

The Hamiltons were not extremely wealthy, but they descended from Scottish royalty. Thomas Hamilton's ancestor was the daughter of King James II, himself descended from other Scottish kings, dating back to Robert the Bruce.[1] Also, Flora's mother traced her lineage to William de Warenne, first Earl of Surrey and one of the loyal soldiers who accompanied William the Conqueror at the Battle of Hastings in 1066.[2]

For some time, Flora's parents and siblings resided in County Cork, but in 1870 moved to Rome when Revd Thomas Hamilton became Curate at Holy Trinity Church. Revd Hamilton had previously studied in Italy, and some suggest that's where the idea of naming a daughter "Florence" originated.[3] After four years in Italy, the family returned to Ireland, but this time they migrated to the influential city of Belfast, in the north. Flora, a bright and impressionable twelve-year-old, had been greatly influenced by her time in Italy, gaining a knowledge of languages and an appreciation for history and other cultural interests which she eventually passed along to her sons.

Also residing in Belfast was the prominent Lewis family. Like the Hamiltons, the Lewises had moved from County Cork in the south to the northern city of Belfast, location of the final residences of the two families and their long-lasting roots. For the Hamiltons this meant Flora's father becoming rector of a prominent church, St Mark's. For Albert's father, the move meant establishing a successful shipbuilding business. Richard Lewis and his partner John H. MacIlwaine operated the engineering and iron shipbuilding firm which built, among other ships, a freight named the *SS Titanic*. MacIlwaine and Lewis was located near another shipbuilder operated by Harland and Wolff which eventually constructed the luxurious *RMS Titanic*, whose maiden voyage ended in tragedy. Unlike the passenger ship, the freight ship *SS Titanic* had a long, successful career.[4]

Flora marries Albert Lewis

Had Flora met Albert, her future husband, years earlier in County Cork? In a letter to Albert shortly after their engagement, Flora wrote that his affection since "childhood" convinced her to accept his proposal. Records indicate that Flora and Albert lived in County Cork at roughly the same time.[5] Once both families settled in the north of Ireland, Flora's brother Augustus accepted an apprenticeship in engineering with Richard Lewis' company in the shipyards of Belfast.[6] Educated in the law, Albert became a court solicitor in 1885 while Flora earned a college degree.

Albert, in his early courtship letters, poured out his heart to Flora, claiming deep love and devotion. Flora, however, initially rejected his advances. (Five years earlier, Flora had a courtship with Albert's brother, William, who ended the relationship, yet Flora struggled with residual feelings.) In letter after letter, Flora admitted that she did not reciprocate Albert's love. She included self-effacing comments, criticizing what she considered her lack of beauty and absence of connections.[7]

However, Albert was not one to be deterred; he simply changed his approach. After reading a copy of Flora's short story "The Princess Rosetta" in *Home Journal*, he extolled her writing capabilities, requesting more stories. Flora hesitated, feeling that Albert would find her writing too simple for one of his vast intellect. Reluctantly, she sent him other work which, to her surprise and delight, he highly praised. In exchange, Albert shared his short stories with Flora. Not only did he provide assurance for her writing, Albert lovingly improved Flora's self-confidence. She disposed of the negative self-talk in her correspondence and began exuding optimism. Despite Flora's initial disinclination, a romance blossomed.

Flora and Albert married in 1894 and welcomed sons Warren Hamilton (Warnie) on 16 June 1895 and Clive Staples (Jack) on 29 November 1898. How appropriate that a couple united by a passion for writing and an appetite for good literature should produce two exceedingly talented authors. Jack's scholarly works are still respected and used as texts. His many popular works both in fiction and non-fiction genres, ranging from *Mere Christianity* to *The Screwtape Letters*, continue to sell in the millions. Warnie, after retiring as a major in the British Army, became a scholar and book author on the history of seventeenth-century France.

Who was Flora's husband?

With his resonant voice, quick wit, and towering intellect, Albert quickly rose to popularity in Belfast, even before his marriage to Flora when both were in their thirties. His stirring speeches provided evidence of his power of persuasion. According to George Sayer's biography, *Jack*, and documents at the Marion E. Wade Center of Wheaton College, Illinois, Albert spoke passionately about the complexities of Irish independence, urging his fellow citizens to remain loyal to the United Kingdom. He was a promising talent, a rising star among the movers and shakers but too humble to consider himself among the elite. Albert's warm countenance and sense of humor made him easy to admire. Newspapers often showcased his persuasive talent, capturing images and impressions of him in cartoons and editorials.

Albert's law career as a court solicitor often prevented his accompanying Flora and the boys on seaside holidays, a disappointment that caused bitterness, even laying the groundwork for ridicule by the boys and worsening the grief which followed their mother's death. Jack and Warnie later experienced remorse for portraying their father as a boring workaholic (especially after each – independently and in different parts of the world but at nearly the same time – made their strong and lasting returns to faith in Christ).

A careful reading of family correspondence paints a nuanced picture of Albert. He adored his family, as illustrated through his correspondence, compiled after Albert's death by Warnie into *The Lewis Papers* and now housed at the Wade Center. Both sons remembered their family home of Little Lea as filled with political chatter but also with whimsy and laughter provided by both parents. Their adolescent and young adult impressions seem overshadowed by their experiences after Flora's death, among them Albert's decision to send Jack to boarding school in England only weeks after she passed away. The decision appeared to be Albert's way of escaping parental duties, but as his correspondence demonstrates, Albert was, surprisingly, an attentive, loving, and generous father.[8] We must remember that Albert lost his father, wife, and brother all within the span of a few weeks during 1908, a catastrophic pattern of loss. Most feel that Albert never recovered from his grief.

After Albert's death and while Warnie was posted overseas, Jack took responsibility for commissioning a stained-glass window honoring Albert and Flora in St Mark's Church, Dundela (their grandfather Hamilton's parish). The window features intricate and symbolic designs which capture the essence of both parents and serve as a reminder of the love and gratitude the Lewis brothers felt in adulthood, particularly toward their father. They came to appreciate him more as they matured into men, especially after they returned to Christianity with its emphasis on grace, forgiveness, and reconciliation.[9]

Flora's intellectual and imaginative influence

Flora was not a "conventional" nineteenth-century woman. While others were marrying and establishing families, she attended college, enduring intense criticism for her untraditional choice.[10] However, her aspirations were not diminished by this censure. Flora's superior knowledge of mathematics earned her top honors at the prestigious Queen's University (then known as the Royal University of Ireland), first class honors in Geometry and Algebra in 1881, and first class honors in Logic with second class honors in Mathematics in 1885. She graduated as a Bachelor of Arts in 1886, one of a few women to receive a degree. Scholars call Flora a pioneer among women for thriving in co-educational higher education institutions.[11]

Flora's academic background richly profited her sons. Before her final illness, she trained them in Latin, French, and mathematics. Ironically, mathematics proved a difficult subject for Jack when he sought admittance to Oxford. She aimed to nurture her sons personally, spiritually, and intellectually.

Fond of seaside locations, Flora traveled often with the boys, spending time in Ballycastle, County Antrim, in 1900, and Castlerock, County Londonderry, during the summers of 1901, 1903, 1904, and 1906. Other favorite destinations included Killough, County Down, on the Irish Sea, and Berneval, on the coast of northern France.

During these extended holidays, Flora continued to shape her sons to become great men of intellect and character. She encouraged her boys to explore the surrounding territory and its history, cultivating an interest in historical narratives. These experiences would echo throughout her sons' works, including their fictional worlds of Animal-Land and India (known as Boxen) and the books of both as scholars and authors in adulthood. (In addition to Jack's prolific writing, Warnie was one of the Inklings, sharing his writings on French history and contributing his ideas on works in progress by the others, in that storied literary group who today are household names.)

It was perhaps on such an excursion – or at home in Belfast – that Flora recalled a small Italian village from her childhood named Narni, located fifty miles north of Rome. The name is thought to be the inspiration for "Narnia."[12] Surely the stories of her family's adventures in Italy were a subject of fascination to the boys.

Albert Lewis also contributed to his sons' intellectual development. He was a connoisseur of literature, appreciating and discussing great books with Flora and the boys. It was at his insistence that Little Lea was overflowing with books. Albert was a prominent member of several literary societies, and his political speeches often alluded to influential literary works.[13] C.S. Lewis writes in *Surprised by Joy* that he matured in an environment surrounded by endless books – his family exhibited a perpetual thirst for knowledge. No doubt Flora and Albert, who both dabbled in writing, led their sons to continue a family tradition of appreciating and practicing the written word. In short, Jack and Warnie had "good literary genes."

Flora's spiritual inspiration

As a clergyman's daughter, faith was an important aspect of Flora Lewis' life. Her childhood was saturated by truths and Christian stories, by the enduring archetypes of the church, by the swelling hymns echoing through vast sanctuaries. When Flora's illness worsened, she was determined to provide one last gift to her children. Too weak to leave Little Lea, she asked Albert's brother Joseph to purchase two Bibles, one for each son.[14] The Bibles were presented to Warnie and Jack as Flora's final gifts, lasting reminders of the significance of faith.

This legacy, coupled with her final words, created a lasting impression. According to Albert's copious notes recorded during his diligent, loving vigil at Flora's deathbed, her final words, in response to his comment on the goodness of God, were, "What have we done for Him?"[15]

Flora's question, perhaps rhetorical yet substantial, echoes throughout Lewis' post-conversion work, prompting him to address faith and spirituality through fiction and non-fiction. Lewis desired to untangle the spiritual mysteries which plagued his generation, devoting some of his best work to Christian fiction and apologetics. His influential book, *The Problem of Pain*, earned him a weekly spot on BBC radio during World War II, where he gave insightful talks which eventually became his best-selling book *Mere Christianity*. Soon after these popular broadcasts, Lewis was invited to give talks and sermons to captivated audiences, following in the footsteps of his grandfather, Revd Thomas Hamilton.

By his death on 22 November 1963, what had C.S. Lewis done for Christ? The answer: much indeed.

Flora's impact on Lewis' perspective of women

Flora was the first woman in C.S. Lewis' life to successfully model a domestic yet intellectual female. Over the years, Lewis endured criticism for being misogynistic, mainly stemming from what some perceived as his unflattering depictions of women, such as Susan in The Chronicles of Narnia. Yet, Lewis' earliest encounters with females, including aunts, nurses and governesses, were positive experiences; his grandmothers were both strong-willed and accomplished women.

Flora was determined to be an intellectual influence by tutoring her boys in scholarly subjects and exposing them to travel. In fact, it was during travel that the nickname "Jack" originated. Flora often took her sons to seaside locations. She suffered from headaches and little Jack from a "weak chest." Both parents felt that the northern coast was more medically beneficial than the climate in Belfast. On an excursion when Flora and the boys were accompanied by their nurse Lizzie Endicott – Lewis speaks fondly of Endicott in *Surprised by Joy* – Lizzie took a fancy to a train conductor named "Jack." (As a boy, C.S. Lewis was fascinated by trains. Flora even bought a wooden train for him while on holiday.) Soon after this summer journey little Clive declared that he would now be called "Jacksie," later shortened to Jack.[16]

Flora had been a nurturing and encouraging presence. Perhaps it was the absence of a mother which set an unrealistic expectation for the Lewis brothers concerning relationships with females. (It is noteworthy that his brother Warnie never married.) It is conceivable that Jack possessed a lingering sense of inadequacy that fueled his reluctance to engage in romantic relationships. Ironically, Flora experienced similar emotions before marriage. Her premature death may have encouraged an "arrested development" in Jack's understanding of and interactions with women, perhaps one explanation for his later attachment to Mrs Janie Moore. A hospitable but spiritually ambivalent woman, she became a mother figure for the young Lewis during his years as a self-declared atheist. However, as Lewis matured, he seemed more attracted to women modeled like his mother – loving, intelligent, sensitive, observant.

Flora's death contributed to Lewis' sense of longing, of *sehnsucht,* a German term Lewis used in reference to thoughts and feelings which describe an intense "yearning." Lewis mentions that his mother's death extracted all joy from his early life; he refers to it as "the sinking of Atlantis." Lewis often recalled his search for what he termed "Joy," a lifelong attempt to retrace steps into Eden, into unfiltered glory. Until his conversion, he discovered shadows of this Joy in a toy garden, in the poignant lines of Beatrix Potter's *Squirrel Nutkin* and Longfellow's *Saga of King Olaf,* and in the pale figures of Wagner's *Ring* as depicted by prolific illustrator Arthur Rackham. After he committed himself to Christ, Lewis realized that these encounters and their subsequent emotions were shallow substitutes for something greater, of a truth expounded from his grandfather's pulpit and recorded in the beloved Bible his mother left him.

Although Flora Lewis was physically present for just a few years, the impact on her sons, especially the youngest, Jack, is continually evident. Flora's intellectual achievements and literary instincts helped shape her sons' creative dispositions, nurturing them into lifelong learners, thinkers, and writers. Early adventures by the Irish coast had a formidable impact on Jack's imaginative development, while her warm temperament and faithful obedience left a strong spiritual legacy. He wrote years later to Phyllis Elinor Sandeman on 31 December 1953 that his first encounter with lingering insecurity occurred with the death of his mother and that there was much of "Mammy's little lost boy" which yet remained in him.[17]

Flora was the first woman to love C.S. Lewis and her influence left a lasting impression, both intellectually and artistically, on the rest of his life.

· ·

Dr Crystal Hurd *is an educator, writer, poet, and scholar in Virginia. She holds a BA in English Literature, an MA in English, and a PhD in Educational Leadership. She enjoys exploring aspects of C.S. Lewis, J.R.R. Tolkien, and Dorothy L. Sayers, while also examining the role of artists as leaders and the rhetoric of power. She has published articles and reviews in* Inklings Forever, Mythlore, The Englewood Review of Books, *and* Sehnsucht: the C.S. Lewis Journal, *with poetry published in* Neon Ink, *a literary magazine. She is a monthly contributor to the art/faith site All Nine Muses (www.allninemuses.wordpress.com) and a staff writer for the sci-fi/fantasy news site Legendarium. She and her husband Aaron have three dogs. www.crystalhurd.com.*

CHAPTER TWO

What do we make of Lewis' relationship with Mrs Moore?

Paul McCusker

Few would argue it was a puzzling, even disturbing, set-up. A young man living with a woman twice his age? No. It wasn't done that way.

Admittedly, the woman's daughter lived there, too. Later a gardener joined them. But something wasn't right about the arrangement.

The young man's father, hundreds of miles away, worried about the woman's emotional hold over his son. The young man's older brother was perplexed and later, after moving in with them, admitted how much he disliked the woman's control over his brother.

Colleagues wondered and whispered. Good friends took the relationship in their stride, dismissing it as a makeshift family agreement born of necessity.

For Clive Staples Lewis, there was nothing to say about his unorthodox domestic lifestyle. Those who knew him understood that once he made a decision, he would see it through, no matter what. The presence of Mrs Moore, this woman in his life, was not merely the result of a decision. Lewis was keeping a promise.

A new family

In 1917 C.S. Lewis – Jack, as intimates called him – was a student at the University of Oxford (at that time studying at University College). Born in Northern Ireland in 1898, Lewis was the right nationality and age to be enlisted in the University Officer Training Corps for what would become known as the First World War, then raging in France. He wound up at Keble College Oxford as a cadet, with expectation of an officer's commission.

Jack's roommate was Paddy Moore, another Irishman. They hit it off. Paddy invited Lewis to meet his family – Paddy's mother, Mrs Janie Moore, and Paddy's eleven-year-old sister, Maureen. Separated from her husband in Ireland, Mrs Moore had found lodgings in Oxford to be near Paddy before he was sent to France.

Mrs Moore was forty-five. She was an amiable hostess, who enjoyed feeding and entertaining the students and would-be soldiers. She was anxious for them, knowing they might be called at any time to battle.

For Lewis – who had an absent much-loved older brother serving in France and a father with whom the relationship was uneven at the best of times – the Moores became the surrogate family he craved.

Lewis wrote to his father, Albert Lewis, that he liked Mrs Moore immensely. In a private letter to a friend, Lewis wrote about an infatuation with an unnamed woman. It is easy to suppose Lewis was writing about Mrs Moore.

And so began Lewis' complex attachment to a woman who may have been the recipient of a crush, perhaps a lover (a matter of some debate), but primarily a mother to replace the one he'd lost.

The unforgettable loss

On 23 August 1908 Flora Hamilton Lewis had died at home near Belfast after a battle with cancer. That day was her husband Albert's forty-fifth birthday. Her eldest son Warren was thirteen and home from boarding school in England to be with her before she died. Her precocious son Jack was only nine.

Flora doted on her two boys, in part from fear she might lose them to one of the sicknesses increasing the mortality rate among Irish children. She had been a great source of stability thanks to her keen intelligence and sunny disposition. She and Jack became very close, especially after Warren went away to school. Jack relied on his mother for everything.

Albert, on the other hand, was a passionate and emotionally volatile Irishman who was obsessively dedicated to his job as a solicitor. From all accounts, he understood the duties of fatherhood but little of its heart. After Flora's death, he decided it would be best to send Jack, sooner rather than later, to Warren's English boarding school.

It was the first of many missteps that would impair their relationship. The school, as it turned out, was run by a brutal and certifiably insane headmaster who delighted in torturing his students – especially more sensitive boys like Jack, vulnerable because of his recent bereavement.

Lewis would never forget the loss of his mother and the sense of being cruelly thrust from the security of home. Readers of his Narnia classic, *The Magician's Nephew*, will recognize in Digory the emotions young Lewis must have felt during her illness – the whispers in the hallway, the refusal to be allowed into her room – which impacted him in many ways for the rest of his life.

The Great War

Lewis completed officer's training and, in September 1917, became a second lieutenant in the Third Battalion of the Somerset Light Infantry. Given a month's leave before shipping off to France, it's noteworthy that, rather than going straight home to see his father in Belfast, he spent half of his leave with the Moores. Albert was hurt by Lewis' choice. Then a series of telegram miscommunications kept Albert from seeing his son one last time before Lewis was sent to France.

Before Paddy Moore shipped off with the Rifle Brigade in October 1917, his sister overheard Paddy and Jack promise to care for the other's family if the worst happened in battle.

Lewis arrived in France in mid-November 1917. His experience was typical: he dug trenches, he dealt with water-logged boots, he learned to ignore the dead bodies around him, he slept standing up and even while marching. In February, he was hospitalized with trench fever, recovering in time to return to the battlefield for Germany's final offensive on the Western Front.

In April, Lewis was with friend and mentor Sergeant Harry Ayres. A shell exploded nearby, killing the sergeant and wounding Lewis in his chest, leg, and hand. He was taken to a field hospital.

No one seemed to know the fate of Paddy Moore. Last seen in battle at Pargny, France, in March, he fought heroically against superior numbers of Germans. His death was confirmed by a letter sent in April to the estranged husband of Mrs Moore. Indicative of the antipathy of their relationship, he didn't tell her. She learned the terrible news after months of inquiries to officials – in September.

Meanwhile, Lewis was hospitalized in London. He wrote begging his father to visit. For reasons unknown, Albert didn't. But Mrs Moore did. Their relationship quickened. And, from that time until Mrs Moore's death in 1951, Lewis was bound to her. At first he acted out of a sense of affection and honor. Later, he would act from an abiding sense of duty.

Setting up house

Lewis finished his education and became a tutor at Magdalen College Oxford. He lived with Mrs Moore and Maureen in rented accommodations until they put their money together to buy a house outside Oxford on a large property with a pond and structures of kilns that had been part of a quarry. That became the name of the house, The Kilns, and it was where Lewis, Mrs Moore, and, after his army retirement, Major Warren Lewis, would spend the rest of their lives. Maureen left after getting married.

The domestic arrangement was kept discreet to avoid scandal – but it was an open secret. Mrs Moore's hospitality – and Lewis' sociability – turned The Kilns into a house where friends, scholars, and even strangers were welcomed.

Lewis taught and lectured. Mrs Moore became the matriarch, taking care of everything to do with the house. It might have been ideal and quaint. But it wasn't.

Behind the scenes, Mrs Moore resented anything that took Lewis away from her. She was demanding. Based on observations by his brother and several friends, it appears she was pathologically selfish and manipulative. Warren chronicled the ways she put Lewis to work or created a crisis to claim attention away from his writing. Warren later speculated about how much more great work Lewis might have created if Mrs Moore hadn't been around.

Their relationship suffered even greater tension when Lewis made a life-changing decision about his beliefs.

The journey

Lewis chronicled his spiritual journey in his autobiography, *Surprised by Joy*, explaining his withdrawal from a conventional Protestant sense of faith after childhood prayers for his mother's recovery seemingly went unanswered. At boarding school, he found church-going tedious and irrelevant. He determined that God didn't exist – later admitting that he became angry with God for not existing. Through the sharp-minded teaching of tutor W.T. Kirkpatrick, Lewis learned to articulate and argue his disbelief in God (though Kirkpatrick insisted Lewis attend church in deference to Albert Lewis' wishes). Lewis even toyed with forms of occultism. He was articulate in his case against God and held firmly to his views until his late twenties.

But Lewis' intellect and sensibilities would not leave him alone. He had a nagging sense of an attraction he called "Joy" – a deep and abiding yearning for a transcendent connectedness to something greater than himself, yet the desire was evasive and unattainable. No philosophical explanation could satisfy it. Christian writers like George MacDonald and G.K. Chesterton, along with good friends J.R.R. Tolkien and Hugo Dyson, fed his understanding of "Joy."

Over time, Lewis re-examined the assumptions that had made him skeptical – modern psychology and self-indulgent introspection – and abandoned his hardcore atheism for an acceptance of a Supreme Being. Wrestling in the intersection of intellect and imagination, he became a theist.

As time passed, he found the case for Christianity more compelling through objective reasoning. Eventually, he embraced Christ personally and Christianity wholeheartedly.

Warren Lewis took this same journey with his brother. Mrs Moore did not. Her spiritual sensibilities seemed to be of no fixed position. At times she was caustic and derisive about Lewis' faith, sometimes conceding to its possibility, occasionally attending church. But Lewis' new and all-out commitment to Christianity had to be troubling for someone who wanted to be the center of his devotion.

Worse, his public writing and speaking about faith meant more time away from The Kilns. Lewis did all he could to minimize the impact on their domestic life. But Mrs Moore resented it and continued to interfere with his productivity by requiring his help with household chores.

A portrait of Mrs Moore may appear in *The Screwtape Letters*. Some biographers believe she was the model for the "patient's" mother, a woman who believes that everything she does is for her son – whether he wants it or not. A devoted tyrant, she resents his faith – the source of any happiness apart from her.

Lewis rarely argued with Mrs Moore, patiently enduring her complaints and endless tests of his loyalty. In letters, he wrote of her graciously, acknowledging the good she contributed to his life. As her physical and mental health declined, his letters reflected the anguish of an attentive son. In her last years, he visited her daily in a nursing facility, despite her dementia. Only after her death did he concede, in careful terms, the difficulty she had been. Yet he never expressed regret for carrying out his promise to Paddy.

Duty and service

The question of "why?" has bothered Lewis biographers and readers for years. While it's understandable that Lewis found in Mrs Moore a mother figure, why did he persevere in such a difficult relationship for so many years?

It's ironic that Lewis – the great debater – would prove to be conflict-aversive in his personal relationships. For example, there's scant evidence that Lewis directly confronted his brother about his binge-drinking. Instead Jack was attentive and caring when Warren needed help with recovery. We find stories of Lewis' sharp skills in academic arguments, but fewer in his personal relationships. To understand Lewis' relationship with Mrs Moore, we must look carefully at recurring themes in his personal and public writings. Lewis wrote about duty and service.

Once Lewis embraced Christianity, he believed that serving God and one's neighbors was a primary duty – faith in Christ was empty unless a Christian took that faith beyond the confines of his heart. That meant service to others even when he felt tired or irritable or desirous of something else. Is doing one's duty by serving others easy? Not at all. Lewis' letters and writings give a glimpse of the fatigue, impatience and self-pity he sometimes felt. But, for him, those weren't acceptable excuses. It was nobler to push those feelings aside and carry on. All seven Chronicles of Narnia carry this theme, plus other books, such as *The Screwtape Letters* and *Mere Christianity*.

Showing Christ's love to Mrs Moore, even when she was being extremely difficult, was a tangible way to demonstrate the reality of Jesus whom she didn't want to accept. When any feelings of familial affection had deserted Lewis, he still did his duty by her. Whatever sacrifice he was tempted to think he'd made for her, he recalled how their relationship brought out Christ's sacrificial love in him.

In short, Lewis was living out a faith lesson upon which he would write and speak to explain the life of faith in Christ. In the context of his growing understanding of men's relationships with women, it is interesting to note that during his time with Mrs Moore – though he was neither a married man nor a father – Lewis came to believe that women often serve as initiators for men to rise to nobler ambitions, drawing men away from selfishness to do their duty in service to others. He pointed out in *Mere Christianity* that any claim men might have to being the head of a family, or over women, must be modeled after Christ. Any crown a man might claim had to be a crown of thorns.

During World War II and at Mrs Moore's encouragement, The Kilns became home to children evacuated from London during the Nazi bombings. Imagine the bachelor brothers adjusting to such a chaotic, if cheerful, living arrangement. Mrs Moore made that generosity possible in a way that Lewis and his brother could not. Biographers note that the creation of Narnia might not have happened without Lewis' first-hand interactions with those children. So Lewis' duty led to service which led to far greater outcomes.

Remorse and shame

Likewise, Lewis' time with Mrs Moore led to another significant part of his personal growth – his eventual resolution of the remorse and shame he experienced because of his father. Lewis believed he had treated the man poorly.

When Albert's health began failing, a time when Warren was still stationed in Shanghai, Jack used holidays to visit their father in Belfast – even though time together was awkward and often contentious. He visited in August, running errands, taking care of meals, helping with baths and shaving. The next month Albert had an operation that revealed cancer. The memories of his mother Flora – taken by cancer twenty years earlier – must have weighed heavily. But doctors were encouraging, even stating that Albert might live another few years.

Lewis returned to Oxford on 22 September. Two days later he was summoned back to Belfast. When he arrived on 25 September, he learned that his father had died the previous afternoon.

Albert's death stirred feelings of remorse and shame. Jack recognized how regularly he had deceived his father when it came to Mrs Moore, diminishing the extent of their relationship even while using his father's money to subsidize their peculiar and sometimes secretive living arrangement. His private taunts and mockery of his father over the years echoed back to him as accusations. His father's death led him to remedy the flaws in his character that had fostered such selfish behavior.

Remarkably, Jack felt his father's presence after his death. He believed Albert was somehow helping him to reform his character – providing Jack a glimpse of the immortality of the soul as a personal reality beyond some vague idea. It's another example of how his unconventional and even troubling relationship with Mrs Moore spun him around – for good.

Mrs Moore, sexual partner or not?

A generation in the sex-saturated twenty-first century can hardly be expected to know the nuances of being raised in the early part of the last century – specifically, a boy from Ireland who reached manhood in England. How would he view his role as a man, his sexuality or the role and sexuality of a woman?

We could be led to believe, by modern standards, that there was something wrong with Jack if he did *not* have a sexual relationship with Mrs Moore. Or we might believe there was something wrong with him if he did. Or we may want to believe that he later chose abstinence as part of his conversion to Christianity, public prominence and success in explaining how to live out one's faith in Christ.

Let's examine their relationship more deeply.

Friends and biographers have noted that, no matter how personable C.S. Lewis could be, he was careful about being too personal. He had the keen ability to reveal a lot about himself – utilizing a particular kind of transparency – while actually revealing very little. He knew how to create empathy and affinity, speaking candidly about common foibles and temptations, without exposing his deepest struggles. It's noteworthy that *Surprised by Joy* is exclusively a spiritual autobiography with that limited focus. He made clear that it would not cover his relationship with Mrs Moore, suggesting that she was not relevant to his spiritual journey or that discussing their arrangement was not appropriate.

If there was impropriety, no one reported evidence of it. Lewis and Mrs Moore had separate bedrooms. Surviving letters and accounts suggest the two were as they portrayed themselves – a surrogate mother and son.

Yet some biographers look at references in some of Lewis' letters – and the domestic arrangement at The Kilns – and conclude that there was a sexual basis to their relationship. Others conclude that there may have been a sexual encounter early on but that it ended quickly – or that any sex within their relationship stopped when Lewis became a Christian. Others are resolute in their arguments that neither Lewis nor Mrs Moore would have allowed a sexual dalliance to take place. She was a legally married woman, after all, with her honor to protect. Lewis, apart from being somewhat awkward and shy, would have struggled with participating in adultery even before his conversion to Christianity – and it would have been a betrayal of the familial feelings that drew him into the Moore circle to begin with. The inherent conflict between being a trusted member of the family and engaging in a sexual relationship with the matriarch would not have sat well with a young man of Lewis' Edwardian moral code.

What about claims of misogyny?

It's worth examining this question in the timeframe of Lewis' three-decade relationship with Mrs Moore during which he became an outspoken Christian, a somewhat controversial decision in the scholarly environment of the University of Oxford. Today we might say his career was limited by "workplace discrimination," although this situation was reversed in 1954 when Magdalene College Cambridge offered Lewis the newly founded chair of Mediaeval and Renaissance Literature, where he finished his career.

Some argue that there is evidence of misogyny in his writings. Others argue for or against the legitimacy of those interpretations, especially if modern post-feminist thinking becomes the filter through which Lewis is read. However, isolating it to his domestic relationship with Mrs Moore, we find – from diaries, letters and other evidence – that he did not care for sloppy thinking in either gender. Foolish women bothered him no more or less than foolish men. He could be equally tender or terse with both.

When the chaos with Mrs Moore or her daughter Maureen or their battles with housekeepers at The Kilns reached a feverish pitch, Lewis preferred the relative sanity of his male friends – often the group known as the Inklings. There he found an understandable degree of comfort and relaxation, as most men and women do with their own gender.

Some critics point to the absence of women in the Inklings as suggesting that Jack possessed an inherent disregard for women – despite the numerous individual friendships he maintained with them elsewhere. This argument fails too when we realize that the Inklings wanted to talk freely, drink and tell jokes perhaps considered inappropriate in "mixed" company. The loosely knit group was based on the desire by those particular men to enjoy the company of other like-minded men in social, cultural and literary discourse – avoiding the complexities of having women present and during a time that was decades before political correctness. Also, because some of the Inklings were married men, it would have been considered questionable, if not reckless, to include women in that environment.

Prudence and misogyny should not be confused.

Paul McCusker *is an author and dramatist. His books include* The Screwtape Letters Annotated Edition *and* C.S. Lewis & Mere Christianity: The Crisis that Created a Classic, *plus more than twenty novels and non-fiction works. His scriptwriting includes the multiple award-winning audio dramatizations of* The Chronicles of Narnia, The Screwtape Letters, C.S. Lewis at War *and the Peabody Award-winning* Bonhoeffer: The Cost of Freedom. *He is also a writer and director for the popular children's program,* Adventures in Odyssey. *Paul lives in Colorado Springs with his wife, son and daughter.*

Chapter Three

Helen Joy Davidman (Mrs C.S. Lewis) 1915–1960: a portrait

Dr Lyle W. Dorsett

After C.S. Lewis went public with his conversion and commitment to Jesus Christ, controversy hounded him until his death. Fashionable agnostics dubbed him "Heavy Lewis," liberal Christians reviled him for what they perceived as his lack of theological sophistication, and fundamentalist Christians attacked his interpretation of Scripture and ecumenical charity towards most Christian traditions. But neither these issues nor others stirred up anything like the furor that surrounded his marriage to Helen Joy Davidman. In the minds of many of Lewis' friends, it was bad enough that a bachelor nearly sixty years old married a woman of forty. To make matters worse, they reasoned, she was an American who was raised Jewish and the divorced mother of two boys.

The brilliant and attractive woman Lewis married in 1956 possessed a well-deserved literary reputation in her own right years before she met the celebrated Oxford don. Joy Davidman was born in New York City to well-educated Jewish parents in 1915 and raised in a middle-class Bronx neighborhood. She attended public schools, then earned a BA at Hunter College and an MA from Columbia University. Joy had exhibited intellectual prowess since childhood, breaking the scale on an IQ test in elementary school. As a youngster she loved books, reading numerous volumes each week.

Obviously a prodigy, Joy manifested unusual critical and analytical skills, and musical talent. She amazed her brilliant and demanding father by reading a Chopin score once, then playing it on the piano without another glance at the score. At school, she could memorize her lines after the first reading for her roles in Shakespearean plays.

Howard Davidman, Joy's brother and her junior by four years, recalled that her intellectual powers and aggressive personality elicited his devoted admiration, yet also inhibited him. Howard was no intellectual slouch, excelling at the University of Virginia and becoming a medical doctor who practiced psychiatry in Manhattan after serving in World War II. Yet he confessed to me that he was so intimidated by Joy's writing that he never attempted to publish anything until his sister died.

Joy graduated from a demanding high school at age fourteen, then read books at home for a year before matriculating at Hunter College when she was fifteen. Clipping through Hunter as an English major and French Literature minor with honors at age nineteen, she became a high school teacher after graduation. While teaching during her first year out of college, she earned an MA from Columbia in only three semesters.

Joy exuded a passion for writing: publishing poems, several of which were purchased by *Poetry*, a prestigious magazine edited by the venerable Harriet Monroe. Monroe published more, then asked Joy to serve as a reader and editor. Joy resigned from teaching after one year, and devoted herself full time to writing and editing.

Her choice to write turned out to be wise. By age twenty-three her poetry caught the attention of Stephen Vincent Benet, who published her volume, *Letters to a Comrade*, in the Younger Poet Series he edited for Yale University Press. Joy's volume of forty-five poems was celebrated by Benet and received excellent reviews. Thanks to her successes and connection with the eastern literary establishment, she became a client of Brandt and Brandt, one of New York's finest literary agencies, and Macmillan brought her into its stable of writers. *Anya*, her first novel, was published in 1940 and well received. She spent four summers at the MacDowell Colony for writers in New Hampshire, writing articles and poetry, and editing.

Radical choices

Joy was considered a radical with a somewhat obsessive personality. Like many intellectuals in the 1930s and 1940s, she claimed disillusionment with capitalism and the "American system." Flirting with Communism, she never became a doctrinaire Marxist, but she advocated socialism over capitalism, since the latter system, in her opinion, had failed and caused the Great Depression. Joy joined the Communist Party but found meetings and many members quite boring. Although she never advocated or expected the overthrow of capitalism, she enjoyed criticizing both Democrats and Republicans whom she considered less enlightened than the supposedly heroic socialists who led the USSR.

Ultimately Joy Davidman was too intelligent to buy into the Soviet Union's romanticized notions circulating among the American intelligentsia pre-World War II. Basically what Joy got from her brief affair with Communism was part-time employment as a film critic, book reviewer and poetry editor for the Communist newspaper, *New Masses*. She also met and fell in love with another left-wing writer who would become her husband and father of their two bright and healthy boys.

By 1942 twenty-seven-year-old Joy observed that the American Communist Party had only one valid reason for being: "...a great matchmaker." In August, Joy married William Lindsay Gresham, novelist, journalist, Spanish Civil War veteran, charming story teller, and sometime guitar player and vocalist in Greenwich Village drinking establishments. Bill had grown disillusioned with Communists and their lofty speeches during his time in Spain. His dim view of the leftist movement hurried Joy out of the Party, especially when she gave birth to David in early 1944, and Douglas less than a year and a half later.

By her own admission, she had been searching for fulfillment for years. College and graduate school, writing and editing, and socializing with New York's most celebrated editors and authors, as well as political activism, were good in their place, but she was empty inside. So with the highest expectations she entered family life with her husband, who wrote and sold novels, including one (*Nightmare Alley*) that became a motion picture starring Tyrone Power. Joy stayed home, did freelance writing, and cared for their little boys, and the house and garden.

Bill had a serious problem with alcohol and the Gresham marriage was in trouble from the outset. Binges and hangovers cut into his writing – just when the growing family needed more time and money. Bill not only wasted time and earned little money, he embarked upon a series of extra-marital affairs that broke Joy's heart and drove her to fits of anger and despair. During this time, she had few friends and no religion to turn to for strength.

C.S. Lewis once remarked that "every story of conversion is a story of blessed defeat." In 1945 large cracks began to appear in Joy's protective armor. Better educated and more intelligent than most, well published and highly respected for a person only thirty, she had seldom entertained weakness or failure. But Bill's long absences and apparent lack of concern for her and the boys left her devastated.

God comes in

One evening in spring 1946 Bill called from Manhattan and told Joy he was having a nervous breakdown. Whether true or just another story to cover his escapades is beside the point. He was not coming home and could not promise when or if he would be back. Bill hung up, and Joy entered the nursery where her babies slept. In her words, she was alone with her fears and the quiet. Later recalling that "for the first time my pride was forced to admit that I was not, after all, 'the master of my fate'… All my defenses – all the walls of arrogance and cocksureness and self-love behind which I had hid from God – went down momentarily – and God came in." She described her perception of the mystical encounter:

It is infinite, unique; there are no words, there are no comparisons... Those who have known God will understand me... There was a Person with me in that room, directly present to my consciousness – a Person so real that all my precious life was by comparison a mere shadow play. And I myself was more alive than I had ever been; it was like waking from sleep. So intense a life cannot be endured long by flesh and blood; we must ordinarily take our life watered down, diluted as it were, by time and space and matter. My perception of God lasted perhaps half a minute.

Joy concluded that since God apparently exists, there's nothing more important than learning who God is and what he requires of us. The former atheist embarked on a journey to know more of God. First Joy explored Reformed Judaism but found no inner peace. Always the reader, she devoured books on spirituality, including Francis Thompson's poem "The Hound of Heaven." It was first Thompson's poetry, then three books by C.S. Lewis – *The Great Divorce, Miracles,* and *The Screwtape Letters* – that led her to read the Bible. According to her testimony, when she got into the Gospels, the One who had come to her appeared again: "He was Jesus."

Joy was nourished by the spiritual food she found in the Bible and the writings of Lewis. Because of her interest in Lewis, she noticed the publications of a college professor and poet, Chad Walsh, who also was a mid-life convert and writer of an article on Lewis for *The New York Times* in 1948. Later Walsh penned the first biography of Lewis, *C.S. Lewis: Apostle to the Skeptics.* Joy corresponded with Walsh about her many questions related to Lewis' books and her new-found faith. Because he understood and respected Joy's pilgrimage, he and his wife began entertaining Joy and her sons at their summer cottage in Vermont.

The Lewis–Walsh connection provided the right tonic for Joy's thirsty soul. She read everything Lewis wrote plus books by Charles Williams, George MacDonald, G. K. Chesterton, and Dorothy Sayers. By 1948 Joy pursued instruction in a Presbyterian church near her upstate New York home. Soon she and the boys were baptized. Between the New York pastor and her mentor, Chad Walsh, Joy grew in faith and began manifesting signs of genuine conversion and repentance.

At Walsh's urging, Joy wrote to Lewis about her thoughts on his books. Although Walsh assured her that Lewis answered his correspondence, it took her two years to find the courage to write. She finally did so in January 1950, and Lewis' brother Warren (Warnie) noted that Jack received a fascinating letter from a most interesting American woman, Mrs Gresham.

For the next two and a half years Joy and C.S. Lewis enjoyed a rich correspondence that intellectually and spiritually encouraged each of them. Finally, Joy's health and family problems opened the way for the famous author and his talented American pen friend to meet.

Joy's health declines

During the late 1940s Joy suffered from nervous exhaustion while trying to raise the boys and write enough to pay the bills. Bill Gresham sobered up for brief periods, but he was in and out of the house depending on his moods.

Joy finished several writing projects, including a novel, *Weeping Bay*, published by Macmillan in 1950. A *New York Post* reporter interviewed Joy for a multi-part series dubbed "Girl Communist" about her faith journey. While writing a Jewish–Christian interpretation of the Ten Commandments, Joy became gravely ill with jaundice. The doctor ordered rest – preferably away from her chaotic house and family.

During this turmoil Joy received a cry for help from her cousin, Renée Pierce, who had two children, an alcoholic husband, and a desperate need to live apart from him until a divorce could be finalized. Lacking money and alternatives, she threw herself on the Greshams for mercy. Joy took her in, and Renée enthusiastically agreed to oversee the household so Joy could get away for rest.

With financial help from her parents, Joy sailed for England in August 1950. She found a room in London, rested, and finished *Smoke on the Mountain: An Interpretation of the Ten Commandments*. During her four-month stay in London, the Lewis brothers invited her to Oxford, followed by more visits where Joy Gresham and Jack Lewis had the opportunity to get better acquainted. Joy laid out her problems to Jack. He listened, grieved for her, and said a sad farewell when she returned to New York in January 1951.

During Joy's time in London, Bill wrote with news about the boys. Just before her return, he announced that he and Renée were in love and having an affair. He asked if Joy would consider living under the same roof despite the circumstances. Joy had no intention of doing so, but she returned anyway with hope that the mess could be redeemed.

Months of wrangling failed to bring reconciliation. Nine months later Bill sued Joy for divorce on grounds of desertion for travelling to England. Meantime, Jack Lewis and Warnie – both extremely fond of Joy – urged her to return and bring the boys. She was back in England with David and Douglas by Christmas.

They lived in London for nearly two years, with Joy supporting them through freelance typing and writing to supplement Bill's erratic child support checks. The boys were placed in private schools thanks to Lewis' generosity. Joy and Jack visited one another regularly. When Joy's financial situation worsened in August 1955, Lewis secured a place for her in Oxford, not far from his home. Jack paid the rent, and the brothers plied her with manuscripts to edit.

Love comes in

By Christmas 1955 it was apparent to all who knew them that friendship had become love. Lewis visited Joy almost daily. She and the boys spent holidays and special occasions with Warnie and Jack at The Kilns. Joy was now a divorced woman, so there was no impropriety – at least to their minds – in seeing one another regularly. But Joy told close friends that, although they frequently walked and held hands, marriage was out of the question. Because she was divorced, even their friendship was scandalous to some people.

In April 1956 the British government, perhaps because of Joy's previous Communist Party affiliation, refused to renew her visa. Lewis was devastated. How could she return to America where her boys might be abused by their alcoholic father who more than once had done them physical harm? And how could he manage without Joy nearby? She was his equal if not superior in intellect, and they were the epitome of two people who truly were iron sharpening iron.

Eventually, C.S. Lewis realized he could not imagine living apart from Joy Davidman. Throwing caution and appearances to the wind, they married quietly in a civil ceremony on 23 April 1956. Now Joy could legally remain in England with her boys as long as she wished.

Lewis inquired about a sacramental marriage in the Anglican church; to his mind a civil marriage was a legal convenience but not a real marriage. He sought the church's blessing, arguing that Joy had legal grounds to be divorced and remarried due to Bill's infidelity, and because Bill had been married before his marriage to Joy. Also, Lewis argued, neither Joy nor Bill were Christians when joined in a civil service years earlier. The Bishop of Oxford refused, saying the church did not condone divorce and he would not give his blessing.

The couple lived apart but continued to see one another, despite criticism from some people who could not understand why Jack and Joy continued to honor the church's guidance.

Everything changed in October 1956. Joy was standing in her kitchen when her leg broke. In excruciating pain, she dragged herself to call for help. Hospital X-rays and tests revealed that her body was full of cancer. Lewis' doctor, who tended her at the hospital, told me in the 1980s that she was dreadfully ill – malignant tumors in her breast, and bones riddled with cancer. Dr Humphrey Havard told Jack to prepare for her death, believing Joy would live for only days or weeks.

Finally, Christian marriage

Months passed. Joy rallied, but then became worse and returned to the hospital. Professor Lewis called in a favor from a man he'd helped after the war. Father Peter Bide, an Anglican priest with a parish south of London, was purported to have the spiritual gift of healing. Lewis asked if he would come up to Oxford, anoint Joy with oil, and pray for her.

Father Bide arrived at night. He and Jack talked at length about Joy's situation, and Lewis shared Joy's dying wish to be married in the church. Father Bide recalled that he did not feel he could in good conscience deny this poor soul her wish, even though she was not in his diocese. The next day, 21 March 1957, he anointed her with oil, prayed for healing, and in the presence of Warren Lewis and one of the sisters at the hospital, he administered the sacraments of Holy Matrimony and Holy Communion. Within minutes an apparently dying Joy Davidman became Mrs C.S. Lewis.

Christian marriage was only the first unexpected aftermath of Joy's illness. To the amazement of doctors and nurses, she made a rapid recovery after going home to die. She went into a remission of nearly three years. She and Jack traveled to Ireland and Wales, and took a memorable trip to Greece with friends June and Roger Lancelyn Green. The Greens plus George and Moira Sayers all said Joy showed no signs of poor health except edema.

Joy and Jack were like two school-aged sweethearts being silly and having a wonderful time. That Joy brought great happiness to Jack became evident by what he wrote to a friend: "it's funny having at fifty-nine the sort of happiness most men have in their twenties… [ellipses his] 'Thou has kept the good wine till now.'"

Their relationship lasted only a decade. She first wrote to Jack in January 1950, and the cancer returned with a vengeance in spring 1960. Joy died in July and her ashes (she requested cremation) were scattered over the crematorium's rose garden. Although it's impossible to quantify the impact of any loving relationship, massive evidence demonstrates these two pilgrims were unusually important to one another.

On Jack's part, his early books helped Joy come to faith in Christ. Letters and their personal relationship helped her mature spiritually, and he helped her development as a writer, including sharpening *Smoke on the Mountain*. He wrote a Foreword for the British edition, helped promote the book and intervened to secure her a good contract with a British publisher.

For her part, Joy had an impact on C.S. Lewis that should be recognized. Lewis admitted that when she, David and Douglas came into his life it was difficult for an aging bachelor to have an instant family in his home. The result surprised both Jack and Warnie: they were forced outside of themselves, precisely what these self-centered bachelors needed.

Beyond such intangible benefits, Joy helped Lewis with his writing. She wrote to one person that she increasingly felt called to give up her own writing to assist Jack with his. Lewis abandoned non-fiction and apologetics books after publishing *Miracles* in 1947. (Some argue it was because Elizabeth Anscombe attacked a part of the book.) Joy Davidman encouraged him to take up non-fiction again, especially to explain the Christian faith, helping him produce *Reflections on the Psalms* (1958). Also, she talked him through writer's block so he could move forward with his *Letters to Malcolm, Chiefly on Prayer*.

Lewis believed his best book was *Till We Have Faces*, and most students of his books agree. He unabashedly dedicated this classic to Joy, and many saw her in the novel's character Orual. To the point, Lewis said Joy helped complete him as a person; she acknowledged that he did the same for her. A careful reader will find Joy's fingerprints on several of his other works, from the double-meaning title of *Surprised by Joy* to some words and phrases in later books of The Chronicles of Narnia.

I think the clearest evidence of her impact on his thinking and writing is in *The Four Loves* and *A Grief Observed*. Lewis might have written *The Four Loves* without Joy as his wife, but it would have been much less profound and certainly more theoretical than experiential. *A Grief Observed* never could have been written without the love and pain of Jack's life with Joy.

Those of us who thank God for the way C.S. Lewis has been our teacher through his books must also be grateful for Joy Davidman Lewis. Without her the Lewis collection would be smaller and poorer.

· ·

Dr Lyle W. Dorsett *is Billy Graham Professor of Evangelism at Beeson Divinity School, Samford University, Birmingham, Alabama. He is the author of twenty books – histories and biographies, several on Lewis and Davidman, including* And God Came In; *and others, plus articles for the C.S. Lewis Institute, Washington D.C., including "Helen Joy Davidman (Mrs C.S. Lewis) 1915-1960: A Portrait." His most recent book is* Serving God and Country: U.S. Military Chaplains of World War II *(Berkley, 2013). Lyle is former Curator of the Marion E. Wade Center at Wheaton College, Illinois, housing papers, memorabilia and effects of Lewis and other British authors. Lyle and wife Mary Dorsett, deacon in PEARUSA/ ACNA, founded Christ the King Anglican, Birmingham, where he is pastor.*

CHAPTER FOUR

Fire and Ice: why did Lewis marry Joy Davidman rather than Ruth Pitter?

Dr Don W. King

Readers of C.S. Lewis have wondered how it was that Lewis fell in love with Joy Davidman, while those who knew of his relationship with Ruth Pitter are puzzled that he chose to marry Davidman rather than Pitter. Based on the love poetry of both women, my contention is that Davidman "won" Lewis because of her passionate, aggressive, "winner-take-all" attitude toward romantic love, while Pitter "lost" Lewis because of her dispassionate, reserved, "you-must-win-me" attitude toward romantic love.

First some background. As I describe in *Plain to the Inward Eye* (Abilene Christian University Press, 2013) and *Hunting the Unicorn: A Critical Biography of Ruth Pitter* (Kent State University Press, 2008), Ruth Pitter developed a warm, friendly relationship with C.S. Lewis long before he met Joy Davidman. Due to efforts of mutual friends, Lewis and Pitter began corresponding in July 1946 and soon were writing regularly. Pitter was an established poet and winner of the Hawthornden Prize for poetry in 1937 for her volume *A Trophy of Arms: Poems 1926–1935* (published 1936). Later she won the William Heinemann Award and the Queen's Gold Medal for Poetry, the first time a woman won the latter award, for her finest volume, *The Ermine* (1953).

She impressed Lewis because she wrote the kind of verse he admired and wished to emulate. In many letters he lavished praise on Pitter's poetry. Pitter was pleased by Lewis' praise and friendship. She had long admired him, and was even in spiritual debt to him since she directly connected her move out of depression and her conversion to Christianity to having heard Lewis' BBC radio broadcasts during World War II. In many letters she writes about her excitement over her friendship with Lewis – such as to her friend Nettie Palmer:

> *My most exciting adventure of late has been making the*
> *acquaintance of C.S. Lewis. I think more of his work than*
> *anybody else's now… what a privilege to know anyone so*
> *learned and so humane. He is a poet too – has sent me*
> *some pieces in MSS. Almost appallingly clever in form,*
> *and fits the profoundest thoughts into it entirely without*
> *distortion… I do glory in knowing this man, and to think*
> *that he admires my work (5 August 1946;* Hunting the
> Unicorn, *145; hereafter* HU*).*

Pitter as Lewis' poetry mentor

Soon Lewis is inviting Pitter to luncheons. About one invitation Pitter writes:

> *The thing that looms largest on my present horizon*
> *is the prospect of a luncheon at Magdalen College on*
> *the 9th [October 1946]. C.S. Lewis has very friendly &*
> *unexpectedly invited me… I've always had a curious*
> *hankering after University society, due no doubt to*
> *ignorance: and the idea of entering those venerable courts*
> *as a guest instead of a mere sightseer seems to cure a certain*
> *ache (2 October, 1946;* HU, *146).*

About another luncheon Pitter writes:

I'm going to Oxford on Friday, to assist at a 2-day debate
on whether women ought to be parsons. I think not, though
it's not easy to say why. It's going to be held in C.S. Lewis'
rooms at Magdalen, & some of us are going to lunch with
him afterwards. This interests me a good deal more than the
debate (28 December, 1949; HU, 153).

Pitter's delight in getting to know Lewis better through meetings was keen, perhaps leading her to harbor hopes for an even closer relationship. Lewis, at least in letters, never encouraged a relationship beyond friendship, but he was clearly comfortable with Pitter and enjoyed spending time with her.

Over the years Pitter received copious notes from Lewis about her poetry, and, in turn, he often asked Pitter's advice about his own verse, admiring her native ability and appreciating her critical insights. She became a sounding board for Lewis' verse. In effect, Pitter became Lewis' mentor as a poet.

It's not hard to imagine Pitter's satisfaction in being called upon for her opinion, since she admired him as a writer, scholar, and sage. While it's impossible to document how often Lewis and Pitter met before Davidman came on the scene, the historical record suggests meetings ranged in the neighborhood of several dozen, one reason Lewis' friends believed he was attracted to Pitter. In his biography of Lewis, George Sayers recalls:

Ruth Pitter was one of the very few modern poets
whose work [Lewis] admired. His writing to her of
his appreciation developed into a witty and profound
correspondence and occasional meetings between them...
I [drove him to see Pitter]... It was obvious that he liked
her very much. He felt at ease in her presence – and he did
not feel relaxed with many people – and, in fact, seemed
to be on intimate terms with her. The conversation was a
mixture of the literary and the domestic... It was clear that

he enjoyed both the idea and the reality of domesticity...
After one visit in 1955, he remarked that, if he were not a
confirmed bachelor, Ruth Pitter would be the woman he
would like to marry... [When I said it was not too late, he
said] "Oh yes it is... I've burnt my boats." (Jack: C.S. Lewis
and His Times, *211–12*)

Colin Hardie was insistent that Pitter would have been a better match for Lewis than Davidman. Other friends found his marriage to Davidman odd. J.R.R. Tolkien referred to Davidman as "that woman," and Owen Barfield may also have been puzzled at Lewis' decision to marry Davidman.

Enter Joy Davidman

Whatever Lewis' feelings for Pitter, they were not powerful enough to cause him to pursue her. Instead, once Davidman came on the scene, Lewis was drawn to Joy. Perhaps naively, Lewis hoped the two women might become friends and arranged for the three of them to dine together at Oxford's Eastgate Hotel. In her most terse journal entry, Pitter writes: "It was at this luncheon that I met Mrs Gresham for the first and last time" (*HU*, 197). In spite of Lewis' best intentions, there is no evidence that the two women he most cared about at that time ever warmed to each other. The icy relationship between Davidman and Pitter is not surprising.

His friendship with Pitter notwithstanding, Lewis later fell in love with Davidman and married her – twice. Why? I believe part of the answer is revealed in the love poetry written by each woman. Pitter, born in 1897, came to sexual maturity during World War I. The devastating effect of the war on an entire generation of young men, decimating the pool of marriageable men, caused Pitter, like many British women of this era, to give up thoughts of marriage.

It would be misleading to suggest that love poetry dominates Pitter's work. More often her poetry concerns her deep, almost mystical love of the natural world, her musings upon the human condition, and her search for transcendent truth. Yet at times she did write about romantic love, albeit with some skepticism. Pitter, while neither frigid nor a prude, grew to have a circumspect view of the possibility of passionate love.

Consequently, while Pitter did have friendly relationships with several men throughout her life (including Eric Blair, a.k.a. George Orwell), and was probably sexually involved with several, she also had a powerful sense of self-protection – both against a broken heart and for her fiercely held Muse. No poem better expresses this sentiment than "If You Came In" from *The Spirit Watches*:

> *If you came to my secret glade,*
> *Weary with heat,*
> *I would set you down in the shade,*
> *I would wash your feet.*
>
> *If you came in the winter sad,*
> *Wanting for bread,*
> *I would give you the last that I had,*
> *I would give you my bed.*
>
> *But the place is hidden apart*
> *Like a nest by a brook,*
> *And I will not show you my heart*
> *By a word, by a look.*
>
> *The place is hidden apart*
> *Like a nest of a bird:*
> *And I will not show you my heart*
> *By a look, by a word.*

Pitter's initial invitation to the visitor is genuine and winsome, suggesting she is open to romantic pursuit, but it has to be initiated by the man. The discovery of her heart is possible, yet the poem ends abruptly, leaving the sense that no pursuit, no discovery, was attempted. In commenting on this poem, Pitter says:

> There is a deep instinct, a biologically sound one, I think, in women's hearts – that in love they must be sought out. They have a right of veto, but they mustn't make advances, even if they are deeply in love… (HU, 280–81).

"Love is a mighty Lord"

If Pitter was both personally and culturally prone to holding back with regard to matters of romantic love – waiting, indeed, to be pursued – Davidman was both personally and culturally prone to reaching out with regards to matters of romantic love. Even before her marriage to William Gresham, she had been sexually active, and no doubt had been pursued on many occasions. However, she was also used to being the pursuer; after her marriage fell apart and once she fell in love with Lewis, she pursued him with single-minded devotion. In saying this I am not criticizing Davidman. As Chaucer says, "Love is a mighty Lord," and a strong-willed person such as Davidman would have been even more given than other women to winning the love of the man she most admired. Accordingly, after her rejection of Communism and her conversion to Christianity, in which the writings of Lewis played no small part, she decided to seek out a relationship with him.

Davidman's volume of verse, *Letter to a Comrade* (1938), won the Russell Loines Memorial Award for poetry given by the (US) National Institute of Arts and Letters, and was published twelve years before she began corresponding with Lewis. What can this volume tell us about her? Quite a lot, I would argue. There is a definite, clear voice: focussed, hard, insisting to be heard, serious, determined, confrontational, zealot-like, and penetrating, yet at times vulnerable, tender, and desperately longing for romantic love. This voice suggests someone who, once knowing what she wants, will move heaven and earth to obtain it.

One romantic poem, "Yet One More Spring," ostensibly about the spring time, actually focusses upon death:

> *What will come of me / After the fern has feathered from my brain / And the rosetree out of my blood; what will come of me / In the end, under the rainy locustblossom / Shaking its honey out on springtime air / Under the wind, under the stooping sky? (*Letter to a Comrade, 65–66).

Davidman wonders rhetorically if she will be "voiceless" and "unremembered." She goes on to say she will be best remembered in the heart of her lover:

> *But I would be more than a cold voice of flowers*
> *And more than water, more than sprouting earth*
> *Under the quiet passion of the spring;*
> *I would leave you the trouble of my heart*
> *To trouble you at evening; I would perplex you*
> *With lightning coming and going about my head,*
> *Outrageous signs, and wonders; I would leave you*
> *The shape of my body filled with images,*
> *The shape of my mind filled with imaginations,*
> *The shape of myself. I would create myself*
> *In a little fume of words and leave my words*
> *After my death to kiss you forever and ever.*

She promises to live on in the mind of her lover. Anyone who has read Lewis' *A Grief Observed* will be struck by how these lines presage much of what he says about Davidman there. If ever a poet foresaw how her memory would affect her lover, it was Davidman in this poem. She could not have known, of course, when she wrote it that this lover would be Lewis, nor could he have had any inclination that he was being "pre-loved" by Davidman with such intensity. But later events suggest the inevitability of their coming together as friends, companions, and ultimately lovers.

Only Lewis knows what drew him to Davidman rather than Pitter. If Joy "swept him off his feet," he was a willing participant. While he enjoyed Ruth's company, poetry, and cooking (she was a marvelous cook), her reticence to push herself forward militated against Lewis being the pursuer. Nothing in Lewis' life before Joy demonstrated that he was capable of pursuing a woman; it would have to come from the other side. He had to be made to fall in love or he would have remained a bachelor. Of the two women, only Davidman knew how to do this, as her love poetry so convincingly illustrates. Pitter, on the other hand, wanted to be pursued.

Fire and ice, Joy Davidman and Ruth Pitter. Lewis chose heat and light.

• •

Dr Don W. King *is Professor of English at Montreat College, North Carolina; editor of* Christian Scholar's Review; *author of* C.S. Lewis, Poet: The Legacy of His Poetic Impulse; Hunting the Unicorn: A Critical Biography of Ruth Pitter; Out of My Bone: The Letters of Joy Davidman; Plain to the Inward Eye: Selected Essays on C.S. Lewis *(Abilene Christian University Press, 2013);* The Letters of Ruth Pitter: Silent Music *(University of Delaware Press, 2014);* The Collected Poems of C.S. Lewis: A Critical Edition *(Kent State University Press, 2014);* Yet One More Spring: A Critical Study of Joy Davidman *(Eerdmans, 2015); and* A Naked Tree: Joy Davidman's Love Sonnets to C.S. Lewis and Other Poems *(Eerdmans, 2015). He is married to his wife of forty years, Jeanine.*

CHAPTER FIVE

The Divine Comedy of C.S. Lewis and Dorothy L. Sayers

Dr Crystal L. Downing

When Dorothy L. Sayers died in 1957, C.S. Lewis was grief-stricken, Douglas Gresham reporting that it was one of the "rare times" he saw his stepfather "deeply upset."[1] Lewis' sorrow reflects the profound impact Sayers had on his life and thought. Sayers functioned for Lewis like the character of Beatrice in Dante's fourteenth-century epic *The Divine Comedy*. In its first two sections, Dante is led through Hell and Purgatory by the pagan poet Virgil. Beatrice, however, takes over for the third section, helping Dante ascend the various levels of Paradise until he finally enters the light.

My analogy is not arbitrary. Sayers became a Dante scholar thanks to Lewis and his friend Charles Williams, a poet, novelist and editor with Oxford University Press. As she explained to Williams in a 1944 letter, his 1943 book on Dante, *The Figure of Beatrice*, along with Lewis' 1942 book on Milton, *A Preface to 'Paradise Lost,'* got her thinking about Christian epics: "I cheerfully remarked to a friend that Milton was a thunderingly great writer of religious epic, provided it did not occur to you to compare him with Dante."[2] To verify her assessment, Sayers proceeded to teach herself medieval Italian so that she could read *The Divine Comedy* in Dante's original language. Her ensuing letters to Williams were so brilliant that he couldn't help sharing them with Lewis. Hence, when Williams died in 1945, Lewis asked Sayers to contribute to a collection of essays in honor of Williams. Choosing Dante as her subject, Sayers wrote her first piece on *The Divine Comedy* for publication: a preamble to her succeeding translations of Dante's *Inferno* (1949) and *Purgatorio* (1955), published by Penguin and praised by Lewis. In fact, Lewis hosted a party for Sayers after she gave a lecture on Dante in 1949 in Oxford, one of the few times they met face to face.

Lewis' attitude about Sayers is evident in a letter to the editor he wrote for the January 1963 issue of a journal called *Encounter*. Stating that Sayers, famous for her Lord Peter Wimsey detective novels (1923–37), "was the first person of importance who ever wrote me a fan-letter." Lewis continued, "I liked her, originally, because she liked me; later, for the extraordinary zest and edge of her conversation – as I like a high wind. She was a friend, not an ally."[3] Indeed, Sayers generated intellectual tempests that blew away Lewis' assumptions about women.

Unfortunately, Sayers' initial "fan-letter" has not survived. The earliest evidence of correspondence between the two is an April 1942 missive written by Lewis, its breezy content and casual style suggesting that other letters to Sayers had preceded it. In contrast, the first surviving letter from Sayers to Lewis, written May 1943, illustrates why Lewis later told Sayers, "You are one of the great English letter-writers."[4] Cleverly parodying *The Screwtape Letters*, Sayers ends her witty composition lamenting that "there aren't any up-to-date books about Miracles." Four days later Lewis wrote to her, "I'm starting a book on Miracles." As multiple scholars have suggested, Sayers was the Beatrice guiding Lewis to the light of *Miracles*.[5]

The creativity manifest in Sayers' letters, along with the creativity she encouraged in Lewis, is a natural extension of her 1941 book, *The Mind of the Maker*, where she argues that because Genesis presents God as Creator, humans fulfill the *imago Dei* – "the image of God" (Genesis 1:27) – when they create. Furthermore, human creativity reflects a Trinitarian view of

God. Just as God is comprised of Father, Son, and Holy Ghost, so human creativity is comprised of Idea, Energy, and Power: work as conceived, work as produced, and work as received. This is not a sequential process, however. As with the three persons of the Trinity, Idea, Energy, and Power are simultaneously active and mutually interdependent. People engaged in creative endeavors, whether making furniture or writing books, recognize that idea is enriched and strengthened by its actualization, the power of which affects themselves as creators. For Sayers, then, experiences of creativity reinforce that we have been made in the image of a Triune God, who calls us to creatively exercise our gifts.

Sayers stands up to Lewis

Though Lewis read *The Mind of the Maker*, he seems to have overlooked its implications for Sayers. In July 1946, he asked her to contribute something for "a sort of library of Christian knowledge for young people." When Sayers declined, saying that she could not with good conscience write merely to "edify readers," Lewis suggested that her "artistic conscience" might be interfering with her Christian duty. Incensed, Sayers blustered that she was called by God to engage in a certain kind of work, and to force her to drop it in order to "tell people what they want to hear, or even what they need to hear," would be an insult to the *imago Dei*. As she whimsically put it in her reply to Lewis, she didn't want to someday face her Creator and have to confess about her creations, "Well, I admit that the wood was green and the joints untrue and the glue bad, but it was all church furniture."

In July 1948, Lewis made another request, asking Sayers to write an article protesting the ordination of women in the Anglican church. Again Sayers declined, once again appealing to the *imago Dei*. Though sharing Lewis' concern that "female priestesses" would drive a wedge between Christians, and agreeing with him that priests represent Jesus, she argued that "Christ Himself is the representative... of all humanity," and that "woman is also made in the image of God." She then challenged Lewis' idea that "the Priest at the Altar must represent the [male] Bridegroom to whom we are all, in a sense, feminine." The metaphor, Sayers asserted, "is so very apt to land one in Male and Female Principles," reinforcing that males take action, like Christ, while the female position, as the recipient of salvation, is essentially passive. Such gender constructions do not "appeal to well-balanced women… who are apt either to burst out laughing or sniff a faint smell of drains." Writing Sayers back, "I see your point," Lewis published his own protest against female ordination, hoping that it was not "too drainy."

This may explain why, as late as December 1955, Sayers told her friend and fellow Dante scholar Barbara Reynolds that Lewis, unlike Dante, had "a complete blank in his mind where women are concerned." However, perhaps because she was in the midst of translating Beatrice's active part in guiding Dante through Paradise, Sayers proceeded to praise the Narnia Chronicles, because Lewis allows girls "to take active part in the adventures." Sayers knew that Lewis valued her own "active part in the adventures" in which they were both engaged: the integration of Christianity with scholarly inquiry and imaginative creation. Indeed, continuing to recommend each other's books to Christian seekers, they corresponded until weeks before Sayers died, Lewis writing her not only about Joy Davidman but also concerning literary criticism, medieval versus renaissance astrology, and, of course, Dante. In fact, Lewis' final mention of Dante in his collected letters appears in his last note to Sayers, dated 29 September 1957, six weeks before she unexpectedly died. Lewis' intellectual Beatrice, preparing him for Paradise with Joy, had entered what Dante called "that abyss of light."

Sayers' impact on Lewis' views about women

As Mary Stewart Van Leeuwen adeptly argues, "with regard to gender, it is likely that Lewis' slowly changing views owed much to the intellectual and Christian ties he forged with Dorothy L. Sayers."[6] But there was also something else. Sayers not only exposed Lewis to the power of a woman's mind (and personality), she also, like Beatrice, presented "the light of the world" in a new light. Along with her 1943 letter parodying *The Screwtape Letters*, Sayers sent Lewis a freshly printed version of her BBC radio plays about Jesus, *The Man Born to Be King*. This gift, I contend, helped change Lewis' attitude about women.

Three days before Sayers sent Lewis her newly published play-cycle, she had written to an angry skeptic about Jesus:

There is nothing whatever in any act or word of His that suggests any peculiar mystery, danger, excitement, or oddity about women or sex; and in His dealings with women He was completely unselfconscious, treating them quite straightforwardly as human beings with minds and souls of their own.

This, then, is the Jesus that Sayers presented in *The Man Born to Be King*. After poring through the plays, Lewis wrote to Sayers in May 1943, "I shed real tears (hot ones) in places," adding, "I expect to read it times without number again" – and indeed he did. Reading the plays for his Lenten devotions every year until he died, Lewis encountered a Jesus who, in the words of Sayers, "never patronised, or condescended, or scolded, or nagged at women for being women, or turned shy or silly or self-conscious or superior on them."[7] As late as 1961, Lewis was recommending *The Man Born to Be King* as "mouthwash for the imagination," having described it, years before, as a "great light in our own time."[8]

Like Beatrice directing Dante's eyes toward the light of Paradise, then, Sayers directed Lewis' eyes to the Light through whom both male and female were created in the image of God. Nevertheless, as Barbara Reynolds notes of Dante's journey in

The Divine Comedy, it was "a gradual progression… in which [he] sheds error after error, intellectual and spiritual," until at last, "like a star in heaven the truth is seen."[9]

· ·

Dr Crystal L. Downing *wrote* Writing Performances: The Stages of Dorothy L. Sayers *(Palgrave, 2004), which was selected as the first recipient of the Barbara Reynolds Award for excellence in Sayers scholarship (2009) by The Dorothy L. Sayers Society. Downing has also published a dozen essays* and given twenty lectures on Sayers in four countries. Sayers and her friend C.S. Lewis have entered into Downing's other two books as well, How Postmodernism Serves (My) Faith *(IVP Academic, 2006) and* Changing Signs of Truth *(IVP Academic, 2012). With a PhD from the University of California at Santa Barbara, Crystal Downing is Distinguished Professor of English and Film Studies at Messiah College in Pennsylvania.*

CHAPTER SIX

On Tolkien, the Inklings – and Lewis' blindness to gender

Dr Alister McGrath

From his letters of the early 1910s, it is clear C.S. Lewis knew that he wanted to pursue an academic career at Oxford. There really was no Plan B. Lewis had decided to study classical languages and literature, referred to in Oxford as *Literae Humaniores*. This was the diamond in Victorian Oxford's academic crown, and was still seen as the intellectual flagship of Oxford's undergraduate academic degrees up to about 1920. As if this was not enough, Lewis followed through with Oxford degrees in Classical Honour Moderations ("Mods") in addition to English language and literature for a triple First. This rich intellectual and cultural heritage would become the bedrock of Lewis' career as a writer.

Yet Lewis knew that writing is at its best when informed by the criticism of others. It was at a meeting of Oxford's Faculty of English on 11 May 1926 that C.S. Lewis first met J.R.R. Tolkien – a "smooth, pale, fluent little chap," as he noted in his diary, who had joined the Faculty as Rawlinson and Bosworth Professor of Anglo-Saxon the previous year. The relationship between Lewis and Tolkien is one of the most important of his personal and professional life. They had much in common, in terms of both literary interests and shared experiences on the battlefields of the Great War. Tolkien was a senior Oxford academic with a public reputation in the field of philology, but with a personal and intensely private passion for mythology. Tolkien had drawn the curtains aside from his private inner self and invited Lewis into his sanctum.

Lewis could not have known it, but at this point Tolkien needed a "critical friend," a mentor who would encourage and criticize, affirm and improve, his writing – above all, someone who would force him to bring it to completion. It is no exaggeration to say that Lewis would become the chief midwife to one of the great works of twentieth-century literature – Tolkien's *Lord of the Rings*. Yet in a sense, Tolkien would also be a midwife for Lewis. It is arguable that Tolkien removed the final obstacle that stood in Lewis' path to his rediscovery of the Christian faith.

Bonding with Tolkien

Lewis' regular meetings with Tolkien, which began in 1929, reflected an increasingly close professional and personal bond between them. Tolkien developed a habit (not discouraged by Lewis) of dropping in on his friend on Monday mornings for a drink, some gossip (usually about faculty politics), and a swapping of news about each other's literary works. It was, Lewis noted, "one of the pleasantest spots in the week."

As their personal friendship deepened, they even began to dream about occupying the two Merton Chairs of English and redirecting the course of Oxford's Faculty of English together. At this stage, Tolkien was Professor of Anglo-Saxon and a fellow of Pembroke College; Lewis was simply a fellow of Magdalen College. But both dreamed of a better and brighter future. And already there were hints of blossoming literary projects. In February 1933, Lewis told Arthur Greeves that he had just had a "delightful time reading a children's story" by Tolkien. This, of course, was *The Hobbit*, which would eventually be published in 1937.

This personal friendship between Lewis and Tolkien was supplemented by the many literary clubs, societies, and circles in Oxford around this time. Some focused on literary or linguistic themes (such as "Kolbitar", founded by Tolkien to enhance appreciation of the Old Norse language and its literature). Yet while Lewis and Tolkien were active members of various literary networks within Oxford, their own friendship transcended these, deepening when Lewis converted to Christianity. Tolkien read parts of *The Hobbit* to Lewis; Lewis read parts of *The Pilgrim's Regress* to Tolkien.

Enter the Inklings

Their small nucleus would expand into a group which has since acquired almost legendary status – the Inklings. There was never any intention that this would become an elite discussion group for matters of faith and literature. Like Topsy, it just "growed" – largely by accident and happenstance. Yet the invention of the Inklings in 1933 was as inevitable as the rising of the sun. It was how Lewis and Tolkien expanded their horizons: through books, through friends, and through friends discussing books.

The first addition to the Lewis-Tolkien axis was Lewis' brother, Warnie, who was then developing a passion for the history of seventeenth-century France. Like both Lewis and Tolkien, Warnie had served in the British army during the Great War. Tolkien seems to have acquiesced with gradually diminishing reluctance to the inclusion of Warnie in their discussions. Over time, others were drawn in. Most early members were already part of Lewis and Tolkien's circle – such as Owen Barfield, Hugo Dyson, and Nevill Coghill. Others gradually attached themselves by invitation and mutual consent. "Gate crashers" who came unbidden were not encouraged to return. The group's collective identity was slow to emerge, and shifted over time. The Inklings had no formal membership, no oaths, no agreed-upon means of electing new members, and no solemn initiation, as in Tolkien's legendary founding of the "Fellowship of the Ring." It was, as Tolkien put it, an "undetermined and unelected circle of friends." The Inklings consisted of a group of friends with shared interests. Its identity, to the extent that this can be pinpointed, lay in its focus on Christianity and literature – both terms being interpreted generously.

In fact, there was no name for the group until well after it had been formed. It is not clear at what point (or by whom) the group came to be called the Inklings. For Tolkien, it was always a "literary club." Charles Williams, a member of the group from 1939 to 1945, does not use the term Inklings to refer to this group in his correspondence with his wife: it is simply the "Tolkien-Lewis group." The title Inklings – which Tolkien attributes to Lewis – suggested "people with vague or half-formed intimation and ideas plus those who dabble in ink." This name was not original. It seems that Lewis borrowed the name of an earlier literary discussion group with which he had been associated, once it ceased to meet.

There was never any doubt throughout the 1930s about the identity of the central figures of the group. The Inklings were a system of male planets orbiting its two suns, Lewis and Tolkien (the latter regularly nicknamed "Tollers"). Neither can be said to have dominated or directed the group, as if they had some proprietorial rights over its functions and fortunes. There was a tacit and unchallenged assumption, which was reinforced as their literary reputations grew, that these two were the natural focus of the group.

In effect, the group that gathered around Lewis and Tolkien acted as "critical friends" for the discussion and development of works in progress. The Inklings were not strictly a "collaborative group." Their function was to hear works in progress read aloud and to offer criticism – not to *plan* such work. The only apparent exception here lies in the collection of essays gathered to honour Charles Williams. This, however, was clearly a project initiated and driven by Lewis himself. It is important to note that only four other Inklings were involved, and that it included one author from outside the group: Dorothy L. Sayers (1893–1957). (The high profile of this collection of essays may have fostered the belief that Sayers was herself a member of the Inklings, but she was not.)

Beyond the Inklings

We must remember that Lewis was part of an extended writing community far beyond the Inklings, and expanded further after 1947, during which time the group continued to meet but shed its more explicit literary functions. The importance of this wider community made up for an obvious shortcoming of the Inklings: there were no female members. In its historical context, this is not surprising; during the 1930s, Oxford University was still a firmly male institution, with its emerging women scholars restricted to a small group of all-women colleges, such as St. Hilda's College, Somerville College, and Lady Margaret Hall. (Dorothy L. Sayers' 1935 novel *Gaudy Night* is set in a fictional all-women college, and brings out well the prevailing university attitudes towards women of that time.)

Lewis was condemned by history to live and work in an all-male environment. He had no choice. His mother died shortly before his tenth birthday, leaving Lewis, his brother and his father to face the world without her. Lewis' father sent him to all-male schools (he had no say in the matter). Lewis later served as a junior officer in an all-male combat regiment in the British Army during the First World War. The two Oxford colleges with which Lewis was associated – University and Magdalen – were all-male institutions throughout Lewis' lifetime. Lewis had hardly any female academic friends throughout his Oxford period – not because he shunned them, or devalued them – but simply because the social realities of that age in British cultural history made it very difficult to do this.

Yet we must remember that Lewis' literary friendships included significant women authors such as Katharine Farrer, Ruth Pitter, Sister Penelope, and Dorothy L. Sayers. His letter to Janet Spens – tutor in English at Lady Margaret Hall (then an all-women college) – offering detailed appreciation of her *Spenser's Faerie Queene* (1934), punctuated with a few fine scholarly quibbles, is one of many indications that, in matters of scholarship, Lewis was alert to erudition and blind to gender.

There is no doubt that some of Lewis' views about women now seem problematic to his twenty-first century readers. Some will criticize Lewis for those views. Yet there is a more compassionate and more realistic way of understanding Lewis – as someone trapped within the social norms and conventions of a bygone age in British culture.

We are all condemned to live in a specific historical context, which we struggle to transcend. What is remarkable is that Lewis speaks so well, and so powerfully, to both men and women in later generations – despite his being embedded in a long-gone culture dominated by thoroughly masculine agendas.

Dr Alister McGrath *is Andreas Idreos Professor of Science and Religion at Oxford University. Dr McGrath is a bestselling author of more than fifty books and a popular speaker, travelling the world every year to speak at various conferences. His most recent book is If I Had Lunch with C.S. Lewis: Exploring the Ideas of C.S. Lewis on the Meaning of Life, published by Tyndale, 2014. His books C.S. Lewis, A Life (Tyndale) and The Intellectual Life of C.S. Lewis (Wiley-Blackwell) were published in 2013.*

C.S. Lewis and the friends who apparently couldn't really have been his friends, but actually were

Colin Duriez

A misleading idea about C.S. Lewis is that he believed friendship in any full sense was only possible between men and men. From this idea comes the even more misleading idea that Lewis thought women's minds are inferior to those of men.

Such misunderstandings have been taken even further, views some still hold – claims that Lewis was incapable of relating to women, and was in fact misogynous. Such views come from the pens of the Narnia-dismissive children's author Philip Pullman, and from a contributor to a dictionary of English literature: "Lewis was... a misogynist, of the opinion that women's minds are intrinsically inferior to men's. Not surprisingly his relationships with women were mostly fraught."

I've called these beliefs misleading. In fact, they are all untrue to various extents, though rarely I think deliberately untrue. Let's take the serious charge of misogyny.

Lewis, in fact, was so far from being unable to relate to women adequately that he had many friendships with diverse representatives of the half of the human race that was supposedly a dark mystery to him. These friendships were not contrary to his ideas of friendship, because he did, in fact, believe friendship was possible between men and women, as he made quite clear in his book, *The Four Loves*. He pointed out that what often stood against friendship between the sexes was the matrix of social conditions, making such friendships possible or impossible, which in Lewis' time had changed to where, for instance, men and women enjoyed the equality of companionship in shared professions, as he did as an Oxford don and as a writer. Friendship, according to Lewis, characteristically arises out of the matrix of companionship.

Lewis was far from perfect, and a product of his time, as we all are. However, if we look at his range of female friends and important acquaintances, it's clear that in many ways he was (or became) free of the gender limitations and prejudices of his period. These examples pinpoint the scope and growing maturity of Lewis' friendships and relations with women, demonstrating the richness and dimensions Lewis sought in relationships. Examining their existence and especially their importance to Lewis also confounds the sort of misleading beliefs about him I've mentioned.

Mrs Janie Moore, married but separated; single parent of one daughter and one son (later deceased)

Was Mrs Janie Moore really like a wicked stepmother? Much of the consensus view derives from negative comments that Lewis' brother, Warnie, put in his diary, in particular after Mrs Moore's death, following her long period of decline. I think it's worth questioning Warnie's later assessment – very different from his early impressions of her, which included his gratitude that she and his brother had warmly invited him to live with them after retirement from the British Army, in a household that included Mrs Moore's daughter, Maureen. His earlier, positive views correlate with the appreciative opinions of others, such as Owen and Maud Barfield and Lady Freud (June Flewett). Lewis' perceptions of Mrs Moore over the years also need to be taken into account.

In a fuller picture of Janie Moore, she emerges, I think, as someone who had an enormous impact on Lewis, both in the development of his character and in his increasing ability to write for a popular readership. (Much of a diary he kept for years was written very much for her benefit, it appears.) Lewis considered her a friend who, like Arthur Greeves (one of his greatest friends), was given the accolade of having a keen sense of homeliness. By this, Lewis meant a sense and appreciation of the ordinary, which, in her case, included hospitality to friends and those in need. (Tolkien captures this joyful homeliness in the opening section and first chapters of *The Lord of the Rings*, concerning The Shire and Hobbitry.) Lewis associated homeliness, in this sense, with the quality created by a group of true friends; within the friendship, friends were "snug and safe", not anxious about whether they were inside the circle. Lewis also appreciated Mrs Moore as a mother substitute. In both regards – for her homeliness, and as adoptive mother – she was important to Lewis.

Like the idea of the wicked stepmother, the idea of Janie Moore as Lewis' sexual partner fails more and more to fit the picture as their relationship is considered over the thirty years or so they were together. To my knowledge, the widespread belief that there was a sexual relationship (which, of course, is possible) seems to lie with particular firmness with some biographers of Lewis like A.N. Wilson and Michael White. Wilson characteristically insists: "While nothing will ever be proved on either side, the burden of proof is on those who believe that Lewis and Mrs Moore were *not* lovers..." The theologian Professor Ann Loades, who has considerable knowledge of Lewis, clearly would not agree with Wilson here. In reviewing one of my books on Lewis, she wrote that she had little patience with those who considered Lewis and Mrs Moore to be lovers. Wilson has no patience with those he regards as the naysayers. There is no consensus over what happened in private between the two friends, or even over its significance; only opinion, however judicious.

Jane McNeill, Belfast friend of strong literary interests; long-term carer of her mother

Lewis' circle of friends in Belfast has not yet been fully explored, with the exception of Arthur Greeves (though often not adequately viewed in his north of Ireland context). A long-standing and fascinating friendship existed between Lewis and Jane McNeill (to whom his *That Hideous Strength* was dedicated – a choice of book which annoyed her).

The duration, strength and deeply affectionate nature of this friendship (on both sides) reveals much about Lewis and his capacity for male–female friendship. Jane's life was severely limited by her mother's need for care and her own later disability, but she was nevertheless a distinctive and memorable person who made a deep impression not only on Lewis, but also on Warnie. One of her close Belfast friends was also known to Lewis at Oxford: medieval scholar Helen Waddell, who wrote the bestselling novel, *Peter Abelard.*

June "Jill" Flewett, later Lady Freud; actress and theatre director

Lewis had an uncle-like and deeply caring relationship with June "Jill" Flewett (later Lady Freud), which was to shape her life. Though too old at sixteen to be the usual child evacuee from bomb-blasted London in World War II, she was employed by the hospitable Mrs Moore in Lewis' wartime Oxford home, The Kilns.

By his financial generosity Lewis enabled June's training, and consequently long career, in the theatre. He was also very much a mentor for her, helping her develop a confidence in her considerable abilities. June eventually married Sir Clement Freud, grandson of Sigmund, later famous as an MP (member of the UK parliament) and broadcaster.

Stella Aldwinckle, poet, thinker, student pastoral worker; founder, Oxford University Socratic Club

Stella Aldwinckle made a deep impression upon generations of women students at Oxford with all shades of belief and ideology, as a parish worker associated with the Anglican church of St Aldate's. She enlisted the help of Lewis when, with great determination, she set up the Oxford University Socratic Club. With her as the Chair, and Lewis as President, they collaborated for a dozen years, until Lewis left for Cambridge University, together creating one of Oxford's most successful and well-known student societies. She had the inspired idea of inviting notable atheists and agnostics to present their cases, with responses by Christians (often Lewis himself).

Both the Socratic Club and the remarkable Stella Aldwinckle, who was a profound thinker and poet as well as pastoral worker, have been under-represented in Lewis studies. Yet she represents another example demonstrating his high view of women. Lewis himself devoted enormous time and care to her imaginative project of having an intellectual forum that included discussions on faith at one of the world's great universities, working with her closely on the programme and helping her as she led the club. Lewis' involvement coincided with his high-profile period as a Christian apologist and lay theologian.

Elizabeth Anscombe, leading British philosopher, studied under Ludwig Wittgenstein and translated his work; member, Oxford University Socratic Club

When she met C.S. Lewis, Elizabeth Anscombe was a young, married research fellow at Somerville College, previously having studied under Ludwig Wittgenstein while a research student in Cambridge (she was a favourite student of the eminent philosopher).

A Roman Catholic, she became a member of the Oxford University Socratic Club, and challenged some errors and a lack of clarity in Lewis' argument against naturalism, or materialism, in his book, *Miracles*. Naturalism is the view that, in Lewis' words, "nature is the whole show", excluding the supernatural element of Creator. Dr Anscombe thought the main point of Lewis' argument was robust, but in her public debate with Lewis, some of his friends considered that he had been humbled as a flagship Christian apologist.

Lewis had nothing but respect for the cheroot-smoking young thinker, and accordingly later revised his argument for a new edition of *Miracles*. Indeed, Elizabeth Anscombe became one of Britain's leading philosophers.

Sister Penelope CSMV, Anglican nun and scholar

Eight years Lewis' senior, Sister Penelope (Penelope Lawson) belonged to the Anglican (Episcopal) order of the Community of St Mary the Virgin, in Wantage near Oxford. The scholarly nun corresponded with Lewis before they met when he visited the convent to give a talk in 1942. They had many interests in common.

Sister Penelope wrote numerous books of theology and translated many volumes of the Church Fathers (all under the name "A Religious of CSMV"). Lewis wrote an important introduction to her famous translation of Athanasius' treatise on the incarnation.

Dorothy L. Sayers, mystery writer, advertising copywriter, dramatist, poet, translator of Dante, lay theologian; one-time unmarried mother

Dorothy L. Sayers, one of the greatest writers in the Golden Age of detective-story writing, and very much else, was the first person of importance, according to Lewis, to write him a fan letter. He liked the "extraordinary zest and edge of her conversation" as he liked "a high wind". Unravelling the code of this comment, it's clear he considered her to be of a high order of friend. (Most of his best friends had a distinctive quality about them, which Lewis treasured.)

At her funeral, he delivered a eulogy that was a remarkable attempt to capture her essence. In one letter to him, she described herself as a "fellow dinosaur".

Ruth Pitter, CBE, poet, painter

While working in a wartime factory, Ruth Pitter heard Lewis' broadcasts on Christian belief and turned to Christianity. Almost exactly Lewis' contemporary, she wrote to him after the war, asking to meet him. They became friends and corresponded frequently, as well as visiting each other before Joy Davidman became active in his life. Lewis liked her very much, and they were relaxed and at home with each other. After the death of Joy, they resumed visiting.

In 1955, Ruth Pitter was the first woman to be awarded the Queen's Gold Medal for Poetry, and she was made a Commander of the British Empire in 1979.

Joy Davidman, poet, novelist; divorced, single parent of two sons

Much has been written on the friendship between Lewis and Joy Davidman which eventually led to romance. What has only partly been explored (but notably by Lyle W. Dorsett, Diana Glyer and Don W. King) is the extent and significance of literary collaboration between Joy, the gifted poet and novelist, and C.S. Lewis. Perhaps this has been because the relationship has not generally been seen as friendship in the way that Lewis viewed it – as a shared way of seeing. Joy's literary impact is apparent in Lewis' *Till We Have Faces*, also *Screwtape Proposes a Toast, The Four Loves, Reflections on the Psalms,* and maybe *Letters to Malcolm*. Then, of course, the huge impact of Joy on Lewis is evident in *A Grief Observed*.

Before Joy, any collaboration that existed between Lewis in his writing and friends almost exclusively involved male friends – such as members of the Inklings, or Roger Lancelyn Green, a young writer who commented extensively upon the manuscripts of the Narnian Chronicles. In the light of her close collaboration with Lewis in his writings, Joy may have been partly responsible for his changing views about friendship itself, where he places less emphasis on friendship between man and man, and ultimately becomes more comfortable with friendships between the sexes.

Colin Duriez *has authored many books on C.S. Lewis, including* The A–Z of C.S. Lewis; C.S. Lewis: A biography of friendship; The C.S. Lewis Chronicles; J.R.R. Tolkien and C.S. Lewis: The Gift of Friendship. *His placing of Lewis in the context of his friends is reflected in two new books:* The Oxford Inklings: Lewis, Tolkien and Their Circle *(Lion Hudson) and* Bedeviled: Lewis, Tolkien and the Shadow of Evil *(IVP Books). Colin lectures on Lewis, Tolkien, and the Inklings. He has been a commentator on documentaries, Sony's* Ringers; *Walden/Disney's special edition,* The Lion, the Witch and the Wardrobe; *and the extended version of Peter Jackson's* The Lord of the Rings.

SECTION TWO

Lewis, the fiction author – how girls and women are portrayed in his novels

Paul McCusker writes about life at The Kilns with girls evacuated from London during World War II in *C.S. Lewis & Mere Christianity, The Crisis that Created a Classic*. Mrs Moore established rules, relegating the girls to the kitchen table for meals rather than the dining room with the family, insisting they were not to bother Lewis in his study. Jack avoided quarrels with Mrs Moore, but secretly he broke the rules himself by buying books for the girls to read and inviting them to his study for discussions, to listen to classical music or simply to chat. Some nights, after Mrs Moore was asleep, the girls would slip out and navigate their way to Jack's study to spend time with him.

The girls enjoyed The Kilns' pond for swimming, but it had to be done in shifts due to an insufficient number of bathing suits for all three. With much amusement, Jack told Warnie about their stalling tactics when he stood at the pond's edge calling to them to come out and into the house. The girls would dive under the water, their heads eventually bobbing up far away, calling back to him, "I can't hear you." Lewis' friend and biographer George Sayer thought the presence of the wartime evacuees in Jack's life provided him with sufficient understanding of childlike insight plus the creative inspiration to write The Chronicles of Narnia, a series which has sold more than 100 million copies in forty-seven languages.

* * *

Appropriately, we open Section Two by examining Lewis' fictional portrayal of girls and women with a chapter that asks: "Are The

Chronicles of Narnia sexist?" Dr Devin Brown lays out the claims of numerous Lewis accusers, including their names and complaints. Then he systematically refutes them in a ten-point discussion with excerpts from all seven Narnia books to back up his arguments.

Next, Steven Elmore discusses gender and hierarchy in The Space Trilogy, reviewing women characters and their relationships to men. His chapter is entitled "The Abolition of Woman," a play on the title of one of Lewis' most provocative books, *The Abolition of Man,* ranked by *National Review* as number seven in its list of 100 Best Non-Fiction Books of the twentieth century. Lewis wrote the fantasy/science fiction trilogy as a page-turning, fictionalized commentary on what he saw as de-humanizing trends in contemporary sci fi.

As an apologist – or one who explains the Christian faith – Lewis used fiction to introduce readers to the possibilities of the afterlife. *The Screwtape Letters* is Lewis' wickedly funny portrayal of spiritual warfare from the point of view of a demon writing to his nephew. Another Lewis novel focussing on Heaven versus Hell is *The Great Divorce*, a fantasy we explore in chapter three, "She is one of the great ones," by novelist Dr Joy Jordan-Lake, who examines the book for evidence of sexism.

Dr David C. Downing's fourth chapter ventures into *The Pilgrim's Regress*, comparing Lewis' treatment of women in his personal (and rather politically incorrect) early letters and diary to Lewis' portrayal of women in this first book after his conversion to Christianity, a quickly written allegorical tale modeled on John Bunyan's book, *The Pilgrim's Progress*.

Andrew Lazo explores Lewis' layers of meaning (and the possibility of joint authorship with his wife Joy) in *Till We Have Faces* as clues to the author's changing comfort levels with women as equals, his evolving feelings about friendship plus other gender issues in Lewis' fiction. He examines additional works by Lewis in chapter five, which wraps up our section on Lewis' fiction.

CHAPTER ONE

Are The Chronicles of Narnia sexist?

Dr Devin Brown

The headline in *The Guardian* on 3 June 2002 boldly announced, "Narnia books attacked as racist and sexist." The article included a number of scathing pronouncements about C.S. Lewis' Narnia series made by fantasy author Philip Pullman. "It is monumentally disparaging of girls and women," Pullman alleged. "One girl was sent to hell because she was getting interested in clothes and boys."

Pullman's account of what happens in the stories follows a pattern seen in many attacks on Lewis' position on gender in The Chronicles of Narnia. My claim is that rather than being monumentally disparaging of girls and women, the Narnia stories are quite progressive when it comes to gender. In this essay, I will examine a number of accusations, and then will make ten points in support of my position. Much of the ground I cover will be familiar to Lewis fans, but I hope to provide some new ways of thinking about this topic.

Representative accusations

Those who are unaware of the charges of sexism in the Narnia books might question the need to defend Lewis. After all, to many readers his female protagonists seem just as bright, capable, adventurous, and interesting as their male counterparts – often more so. But if readers assumed these positive female characters would be just the kind of heroine that Lewis' accusers would applaud, they would be greatly mistaken.

In A.N. Wilson's 1990 biography of Lewis, we find one of the first allegations that Lewis has perpetrated a crime of some sort against one of his female protagonists. Wilson asserts, "Only one of the children from the original quartet is excluded from heaven. This is Susan. She has committed the unforgivable sin of growing up."

In her book *The Fiction of C.S. Lewis*, Kath Filmer includes a chapter with a title – "Masking the Misogynist in Narnia and Glome" – that clearly indicates her position on the topic of Lewis and women. In it she states: "What is disturbing in the Narnian Chronicles, as well as in the whole range of Lewis' literary *corpus*, is the way in which ultimate good is depicted as ultimate masculinity, while evil, the corruption of good, is depicted as femininity."

In *The Natural History of Make-Believe*, published by Oxford University Press, John Goldthwaite sums up what he sees as Lewis' gender problem this way: "Lewis had no difficulty mating beavers happily, but whenever we find him placing a man in proximity to a woman, or in situations that might suggest a muse relationship it is to expose the pairing as unnatural and wicked... Lewis feared women and disliked them categorically. Femininity he saw as an imperfection."

The Lewis Centennial in 1998 was the occasion for more gender criticism. In "The Dark Side of Narnia," a piece which appeared in *The Guardian* on 1 October 1998, Philip Pullman alleges that in Narnia, "Boys are better than girls; light-coloured people are better than dark-coloured people and so on... Susan, like Cinderella, is undergoing a transition from one phase of her life to another. Lewis didn't approve of that. He didn't like women in general, or sexuality at all, at least at the stage in life when he wrote the Narnia books. He was frightened and appalled at the notion of wanting to grow up."

Philip Hensher published an article in *The Independent* on 4 December 1998, under the headline "Don't Let Your Children

Go to Narnia." There Hensher asks, "What on earth is *The Last Battle* going on about… with the poor girl who gets sent to hell for wearing nylons and lipstick?"

The release of the first Narnia film in 2005 prompted similar claims. In "No Longer a Friend: Gender in Narnia," found in *The Chronicles of Narnia and Philosophy*, Karin Fry asserts, "While many of the heroic characters have flaws, Susan is the only one who is not forgiven or given the opportunity to work out her problems."

A *TIME* article by Lev Grossman dated 17 July 2005, quotes J.K. Rowling as saying: "There comes a point where Susan, who was the older girl, is lost to Narnia because she becomes interested in lipstick. She's become irreligious basically because she found sex. I have a big problem with that."

Susan – no longer a friend of Narnia

Since Lewis' depiction of what happens to Susan seems to deeply offend his detractors, it seems a good place for us to begin. In chapter twelve of *The Last Battle*, the seven kings and queens of Narnia have joined Tirian on the other side of the stable door. When Tirian asks where Queen Susan is, we read:

> *"My sister Susan," answered Peter shortly and gravely, "is no longer a friend of Narnia."*
>
> *"Yes," said Eustace, "and whenever you've tried to get her to come and talk about Narnia or do anything about Narnia, she says, 'What wonderful memories you have! Fancy your still thinking about all those funny games we used to play when we were children.'"*
>
> *"Oh Susan!" said Jill. "She's interested in nothing nowadays except nylons and lipstick and invitations. She always was a jolly sight too keen on being grown-up."*
>
> *"Grown-up, indeed," said the Lady Polly. "I wish she would grow up. She wasted all her school time wanting to be the age she is now, and she'll waste all the rest of her life*

trying to stay that age. Her whole idea is to race on to the silliest time of one's life as quick as she can and then stop there as long as she can."

Looking closely at this section, we find that several observations can be made. While Philip Hensher claims that Susan is sent to hell for wearing nylons and lipstick and J.K. Rowling maintains that Susan is lost for merely being interested in these things, this is *not* what the text says. Jill does not say that Susan is interested in nylons and lipstick and invitations, but that Susan is interested in *nothing except* these superficial means and markers of being popular. Lady Polly, an older and wiser female character, correctly points out that rather than being a sign of being grown up, Susan's inordinate interests are an indication of the opposite.

My first five points relate to this passage about Susan and the claims that Lewis' critics have made about it.

Point number one: Lewis makes it clear that Susan's transgression is vanity – not growing up, and not being interested in parties, lipstick, or boys. Susan has made something that Lewis argues should be a second thing into a first thing. In The Chronicles Lewis does not condemn anyone's interests in nylons and lipstick and invitations *per se*. Here he is critical of the fact that, as Jill reports, these have become Susan's *only* interests. Ironically, one might expect feminist critics to applaud an author who casts a female character interested only in nylons, lipstick, and invitations in a negative light.

A careful reading of The Chronicles shows that simply talking about or being interested in clothes or parties is not enough to classify someone as being vain or no longer a friend of Narnia. For example, in chapter five of *The Voyage of the Dawn Treader* the narrator tells us: "Lucy thought she was the most fortunate girl in the world, as she woke each morning to see the reflection of the sunlit water dancing on the ceiling of her cabin and looked round on all the nice new things she had got in the Lone Islands – seaboots and buskins and cloaks and jerkins and scarves."

After returning to England in *The Silver Chair*, Jill does not get rid of her fine Narnian clothes, but instead we are told that she "smuggled hers home and wore them at a fancy-dress ball next holidays." And Lewis does not suggest that there was anything wrong with this.

We find a similar indication that it's not a crime to be interested in clothes at the end of *The Horse and His Boy*. There readers are told that Lucy and Aravis go off together "to talk about Aravis' bedroom and Aravis' boudoir and about getting clothes for her, and all the sort of things girls do talk about on such an occasion."

If Lewis were suggesting that only females, such as Susan, can be vain, then he would be guilty of sexism – which brings us to my second point.

Point number two: Lewis makes clear that in Narnia – as in life itself – males can be just as guilty of vanity as females.

In *The Magician's Nephew*, Uncle Andrew is described as being "as vain as a peacock." In chapter six, we find him admiring himself in the mirror, thinking his appearance is something that Jadis, who has just arrived from Charn, will find hard to resist. Lewis writes:

> *He put on a very high, shiny, stiff collar of the sort that made you hold your chin up all the time. He put on a white waistcoat with a pattern on it and arranged his gold watch chain across the front. He put on his best frock coat... He got out his best tall hat and polished it up. There was a case of flowers... on his dressing table; he took one and put it in his button-hole. He took a clean handkerchief (a lovely one such as you couldn't buy today) out of the little left-hand drawer and put a few drops of scent on it. He took his eye-glass, with the thick black ribbon, and screwed it into his eye; then he looked at himself in the mirror.*
>
> *..."Andrew, my boy," he said to himself as he looked in the glass, "you're a devilish well preserved fellow for your age. A distinguished-looking man, sir."*

Although a more positive character than Uncle Andrew, Bree is nearly as vain in *The Horse and His Boy*, and this is a besetting problem which almost keeps Bree from entering Narnia. When Hwin asks why, after all the hardship they have faced, he's reluctant to leave the Hermit's, Bree replies in words reminiscent of Uncle Andrew's: "Well, don't you see Ma'am – it's an important occasion – returning to one's own country – entering society – the best society – it is essential to make a good impression – not perhaps looking quite ourselves yet, eh?"

Hwin sees through Bree's excuses and with a laugh observes, "It's your tail, Bree! I see it all now. You want to wait till your tail's grown again... Really, Bree, you're as vain as that Tarkheena in Tashbaan!" The Tarkheena Hwin refers to here is Lasaraleen who, like Susan, is also excessively preoccupied with the trappings of popularity – "dresses and parties, weddings and engagements and scandals."

Through his depictions of Uncle Andrew and Bree, Lewis shows that excessive vanity can afflict males as easily and as completely as it does females.

Point number three: Despite claims to the contrary, a careful look at the seven books shows that Lewis is not against growing up and getting married. While most of the protagonists in Lewis' stories for young people are, understandably, young people, The Chronicles of Narnia also include a number of positive portraits of marriage and getting older.

The list of great married couples in Narnia includes Frank and Helen, Mr and Mrs Beaver, and Caspian and the Daughter of Ramandu. Bree and Hwin also get married, though not to each other. In *The Magician's Nephew* when Aslan asks Frank if he would like to stay in Narnia permanently, it is significant that Lewis has the former cabbie reply, "Well, you see sir, I'm a married man. If my wife was here neither of us would ever want to go back to London."

The story of what happens to Aravis and Shasta – now called by his rightful name, Cor – is perhaps The Chronicles' best-known story of growing up, getting married, and having children. In the final paragraph of *A Horse and His Boy*, readers are told that after their wedding, Cor and Aravis "made a good King and Queen of Archenland and Ram the Great, the most famous of all the kings of Archenland, was their Son."

Point number four: The reason Susan does not make it to Narnia in *The Last Battle* is because she is no longer interested in Narnia. Her interest in nylons, lipstick, and invitations has not barred her from the great reunion in Aslan's Country. She has barred herself.

In the passage from *The Last Battle* quoted earlier, Eustace makes it clear that Susan has frequently been invited by the others "to come and talk about Narnia or do anything about Narnia," but she's always refused, putting Aslan and Narnia behind her in order to pursue her interest in making herself appear more desirable through clothes, cosmetics, and invitations. Because of her choices, Susan is not present at the gathering convened by the Professor and Polly. Because Susan is not present, she's not on the train and thus not in the railway accident that leads to the arrival of the seven friends into Aslan's Country.

Point number five: Susan is not permanently locked out of Narnia. Just because she doesn't travel to Aslan's Country in *The Last Battle* doesn't mean Susan will never get there. Lewis makes this point in a letter dated 22 January 1957, where he writes: "The books don't tell us what happened to Susan. She is left alive in this world at the end, having by then turned into a rather silly, conceited young woman. But there is plenty of time for her to mend, and perhaps she will get to Aslan's country in the end – in her own way."

While time has ended in Narnia, it continues in our world. Other characters besides Susan are left alive in England. Presumably any of them desiring to go to Aslan's Country after experiencing death on Earth will be allowed to do so. This includes not only Susan but also Mrs Macready, the Telmarines who returned to Earth, the former bullies from Experiment House, and even Harold and Alberta Scrubb.

At the end of *The Voyage of the Dawn Treader* Lucy asks Aslan, "Will you tell us how to get into your country from our world?" He promises, "I shall be telling you all the time." From this we may infer that after the last chapter of *The Last Battle*, Aslan also will continue to tell Susan and others still in England the way they can reach his country. The question, of course, is whether they will be interested in hearing him.

Sexist remarks from imperfect characters

The protagonists Lewis gives us in The Chronicles of Narnia are not perfect. They all have flaws, but are all on their way to becoming better. In addition to faults that include impatience, laziness, cowardice, greed, selfishness, pride, and anger, Lewis occasionally adds sexism, or if not real sexism, at least occasional sexist comments. My next two points focus on this issue.

Point number six: Sexist remarks by his less-than-perfect male and female protagonists don't make Lewis or The Chronicles of Narnia sexist. Sexist remarks made by Lucy, Edmund, or any of the realistically portrayed protagonists in Narnia should not be taken as Lewis' approval or endorsement of sexism, but as accurate depictions of the kinds of things that these characters would say.

In *The Lion, the Witch and the Wardrobe*, Mrs Beaver complains to her husband and Peter, who are admiring Peter's sword, "Don't stand there talking till the tea's got cold. Just like men."

We find similar examples in *Prince Caspian*, where Edmund says to Peter and Trumpkin, "That's the worst of girls. They never carry a map in their heads." Lucy then snaps back. "That's because our heads have something inside them."

Lucy makes another sexist comment in *The Voyage of the Dawn Treader*, where she complains, "That's the worst of doing anything with boys. You're all such swaggering, bullying idiots."

Eustace tells Jill in *The Silver Chair*, "It's an extraordinary thing about girls that they never know the points of the compass."

In *The Horse and His Boy*, Corin thinks he is paying a compliment when he tells Shasta that Lucy is "as good as a man, or at any rate as good as a boy."

In a final example, this time from *The Magician's Nephew*, Digory tells Polly, "Girls never want to know anything but gossip and rot about people getting engaged." And Polly responds, "How exactly like a man!"

If there is sexism here, rather than merely careless comments said without thinking, it is Mrs Beaver's, Edmund's, Lucy's, Eustace's, Corin's, Digory's, and Polly's sexism rather than Lewis'. It is also accurate characterization – these are the kinds of remarks imperfect characters might realistically be expected to make from time to time.

Whether readers see mutual gender-bashing or ordinary bickering in these scenes, Lewis makes it clear that uncharitable comments like these are wrong and should be avoided. Lewis no more endorses or promotes such behavior than he does his protagonists' other offenses. When Jill and Eustace are reunited with Aslan in the final chapter of *The Silver Chair*, Jill immediately recalls "all the snappings and quarrellings" and wants to apologize. These sexist remarks in The Chronicles are part of Lewis' realistic depictions of his immature protagonists and are not part of their later development.

My next point completes the picture. *Point number seven:* Lewis *does* have sexist characters, and they are all villains. Lewis portrays habitual sexism as wrong by making it a persistent character trait of some of his most negative characters.

In *Prince Caspian*, the usurper Miraz ridicules Glozelle for believing "old wives' fables." Then he mocks Glozelle for talking "like an old woman." Finally he derides his senior advisors for their "womanish" counsels. With comments like these, it's not hard to imagine what Miraz's relationship with his wife, Queen Prunaprismia, must have been like.

In *The Magician's Nephew*, Digory's wicked Uncle Andrew exhibits similar persistent sexism. He explains to Digory, "You must understand that rules of that sort, however excellent they may be for little boys – and servants – and women – and even people in general, can't possibly be expected to apply to profound students and great thinkers and sages. No, Digory. Men like me, who possess hidden wisdom, are freed from common rules."

Later when Digory claims that his uncle is sure to be punished one day, Uncle Andrew replies: "Well, well, I suppose that is a natural thing for a child to think – brought up among women, as you have been."

In *The Silver Chair*, Rilian makes belittling, sexist remarks to Jill, such as calling her "our little maid," *only* when he is under the chair's evil spell. In fact, Lewis uses Rilian's sexism as one indicator of his evil enchantment. The moment Rilian is freed from the wicked spell, his disparaging sexist comments about Jill vanish.

The Calormenes living to the south are portrayed as antagonists to the good in Narnia, and among them are some of Lewis' most sexist characters. In Calormen, women are seen as the property of their fathers and husbands and, when necessary, are forced into marriage. Their proper role is to be passive and obedient. In Narnia we find the opposite, as Hwin points out to Aravis: "If you were in Narnia you would be happy, for in that land no maiden is forced to marry against her will."

What Father Christmas says

In chapter ten of *The Lion, the Witch and the Wardrobe*, Father Christmas' comments about women and warfare do not seem to fit under the heading of flawed remarks from flawed characters. Father Christmas, like Aslan, seems to be the kind of wise character who could be thought to be speaking for Lewis himself. Although he gives Susan a bow and arrows and Lucy a dagger, Father Christmas says he does not intend for either girl to fight in the battle – a position some see as sexist. My next point comes from this scene with Father Christmas and the claims Lewis' critics have made about it.

Point number eight: What critics call sexism in this passage is better viewed as individualism. Peter does not receive a bow nor is he given a healing cordial. Is Lewis saying that males cannot be archers or that boys cannot be healers? Not at all – in Narnia all are called upon to put their unique abilities to use and to follow their individual inclinations. If Peter is better suited to use a sword and shield in the service of Narnia, Lucy is better suited to serve as a healer, and, as we see in *Prince Caspian*, Susan is better suited to serve as an archer.

In *The Horse and His Boy*, Lewis returns to this point when Shasta explains that in times of war, "Everyone must do what he can do best." Readers find a similar incident in *The Last Battle*, when Tirian, Eustace, and Jill must travel through dense thickets making it hard to get a bearing. Jill is clearly the best pathfinder, and Tirian puts her in front to lead.

In *The Lion, the Witch and the Wardrobe*, Lucy wants to know why Father Christmas does not want her in battle, and her response shows both humility and self-awareness. She tells him, "I think – I don't know – but I think I could be brave enough." Father Christmas does not question Lucy's bravery, and readers find Lucy to be as courageous as either of her brothers. In chapter seventeen Lewis makes it clear that Lucy is definitely brave enough by calling her "Lucy the Valiant," a title demonstrating that courage is not limited to the battlefield.

Father Christmas reasons that "battles are ugly when women fight," a claim which could be said to tell only half the truth. Lewis, a veteran of World War I, knew that battles, whether in Narnia or in our world, are ugly no matter who is doing the fighting. In this instance Father Christmas could be said to be more guilty of overlooking the brutal nature of warfare than being sexist.

If Father Christmas romanticizes men's role in warfare, this is soon remedied. In chapter twelve Lewis realistically describes the climax of Peter's first battle as "a horrible, confused moment like something in a nightmare." The final combat in *The Last Battle* – where both males and females fight – is as ugly as anything we find in The Chronicles.

If not sexist, what makes The Chronicles of Narnia progressive on gender?

Point number nine: Over and over in the seven Chronicles, Lewis gives us female characters who are exemplary. From Lucy to Polly, from Jill to Aravis – confident, capable, and independent heroines are a distinguishing element of the Narnia stories. Let's examine three representative incidents that show Lewis' progressive stance on gender.

In chapter three of *Prince Caspian*, the four Pevensies come to the channel separating Cair Paravel from the mainland. Suddenly a boat rounds the point with two soldiers in battle gear. One stands up to throw a mysterious bundle overboard. By the time Peter figures out that the bundle is a dwarf the soldiers are planning to drown, an arrow has already whizzed past his ear and struck one soldier on the helmet. Peter turns to find Susan already deftly fitting a second shaft to her bow.

In *The Voyage of the Dawn Treader*, Lucy declares: "All right, then, I'll do it." What has Lucy agreed to do? To save the Narnian boarding party from imminent death, Lucy volunteers to go upstairs alone in the Magician's house, to find his mysterious book, and to say the spell that will make the invisible people visible again. Reepicheep declares that Lucy's willingness to do this is not only noble but heroic.

Finally, on their mission to Stable Hill to rescue Jewel, a scene from *The Last Battle* previously mentioned, Tirian, Jill, and Eustace lose their bearings in the dense thicket. Lewis points out, "It was Jill who set them right again." Later during the daring raid, Jill seizes the opportunity and without waiting for help or permission from anyone rescues Puzzle the donkey.

While his female characters prove just as competent as their male counterparts, Lewis does not simply make his girls into tomboys who reject everything stereotypically feminine and embrace everything stereotypically masculine, which in itself could be sexist. For example, at the end of *The Magician's Nephew*, we learn that during visits with Digory's family Polly learns "to ride and swim and milk and bake and climb" – a gender-neutral variety of skills.

Lewis also allows his female protagonists to carve out their own futures. Some like Helen, Aravis, and the Daughter of Ramandu will choose to marry and have little Narnians. Others will not. When we meet Lady Polly in *The Last Battle*, she has not married, and Lewis never suggests that we should feel sorry for her or feel that if only she had married, she might have found happiness.

And finally, **point number ten:** Lewis makes clear that males and females are equally capable of evil and equally capable of good.

Critics, such as Kath Filmer mentioned earlier, who argue that Lewis is sexist because the White Witch and the Green Lady – two of his most notorious villains – are both female seem to overlook all of Lewis' male malefactors. These male villains include the early versions of Edmund and Eustace, King Miraz, Sopespian and Glozelle, Pug, Governor Gumpas, Rabadash, Ginger, and Shift. Lewis gives Digory a wicked uncle, not a wicked aunt.

In the positive examples already listed, we find that Lewis' female characters are also equally capable of good. Lewis does not intend for us to admire Peter any more than Lucy, Eustace more than Jill, or Shasta more than Aravis – or the reverse.

Conclusion

In *The Taste for the Other: The Social and Ethical Thought of C.S. Lewis*, Gilbert Meilaender notes that for Lewis moral education "does not look much like teaching" but instead consists of students seeing examples of virtuous people for whom right responses have become natural. According to Meilaender, The Chronicles of Narnia are not just good stories but serve to enhance moral education and to build character.

To the dismay of those who find the books sexist, young people all over the world will continue to read, love, and be influenced by The Chronicles of Narnia. As they read, they will be encouraged to follow the positive examples Lewis sets before them and not the negative ones. And in doing so, they will be encouraged to treat all people with respect regardless of their gender.

. . . .

Devin Brown *is a Lilly Scholar and Professor of English at Asbury University, where, among other duties, he teaches a class on C.S. Lewis. He has an MA from the University of Florida and a PhD from the University of South Carolina. He served as consultant and Advisory Board member for* The C.S. Lewis Bible *and as an assistant editor for* The Annotated Screwtape Letters. *He is the author of eight books, most recently a new biography of C.S. Lewis,* A Life Observed, *featuring a Foreword by Douglas Gresham, Lewis' stepson. In summer 2009 Devin was Scholar-in-Residence at The Kilns, C.S. Lewis' home outside Oxford. He and his wife, Sharon, live in Lexington, Kentucky, with their fifteen-pound cat, Mr Fluff.*

CHAPTER TWO

"The Abolition of Woman": gender and hierarchy in Lewis' Space Trilogy

Steven Elmore

In the late 1930s and early 40s, C.S. Lewis ventured into science fiction with three published novels – *Out of the Silent Planet, Perelandra,* and *That Hideous Strength,* known together as The Space Trilogy (or Cosmic Trilogy). The Space Trilogy incorporates elements of science fiction (space travel, technological advancements, plotlines showing heroism and the battle between good and evil), and also has much in common with the fantasy genre (such as magic, secret orders, and spiritual involvement). Here are some quick plot details (spoiler alert for those who haven't read the books).

Each book takes place primarily on a different planet Mars (called Malacandra), Venus (Perelandra), and Earth (Thulcandra). The universe of the novels is a Christian one.

In the first book, Elwin Ransom, a scholar living in the contemporary world of the author as he wrote the series (1930s–40s), is kidnapped by two men – Weston and Devine – and taken to Mars. There, he discovers three races and the Oyarsa, a being who is akin to a higher level angel, and learns of the spiritual battle being fought over Earth (Thulcandra – "the Silent Planet"), which is under the interference of an evil Oyarsa, whom we can take as Satan, and his band of evil eldila, or demons.

In book two, Ransom is transported by the eldila to Perelandra (Venus), discovers a paradise-like world which hasn't yet fallen to sin, and meets an Eve-like figure, Tinidril. The chief villain is the returning Weston, but he is now possessed by an evil eldil/demon who tries to tempt Tinidril.

In book three, a married couple, Jane and Mark Studdock, encounter two factions – the good Fellowship of St Anne's and the evil National Institute for Coordinated Experiments (N.I.C.E.). To play their part in fighting the growing darkness of the N.I.C.E., the Studdocks must overcome their own weaknesses and sins. Ransom in this novel leads the Fellowship, comprised of faithful men and women, with spiritual backing from the good Oyarsa under orders from Maleldil (Jesus).

Lewis' Christian version of science fiction
The trilogy has inspired and intrigued readers for years, in part because it accomplishes something rare in science fiction writing – it presents a story of other planets and supernatural characters with a Christian underpinning.

Many who imagine life on other planets rule out the existence of one Creator. In most science fiction and fantasy – in books, films, comic books/graphic novels, video games – the created worlds are most often atheistic, pagan, or pantheistic. Religion, when presented, is often portrayed as superstition (generally of a tribal, pagan sort), anachronistic and oppressive (generally organized religion), or as a magical power that one can control through discipline (generally through membership in a secret society).

Lewis instead poses a universe in which God created life on planets other than Earth. Lewis also disputes ideas prevalent in science fiction novels he read, such as human colonization and enslavement of other inhabited worlds, science as always being a source of cultural progress, and "perfection" of the human race through scientific intervention.

This is not to say Lewis wrote allegorical Christian works. Lewis distinguishes stories with Christian themes from "allegory," and uses the term in its literary sense – a one-to-one, this-exactly-equals-that relationship between characters/settings in literature and real life ideas. (In the classic allegory, *The Pilgrim's Progress*, by John Bunyan, characters named "Faithful" or "Hopeful" exactly represent what the author says about what it means to have faith or hope.)

In The Space Trilogy, Lewis wrote novels of the kind he liked, with themes he enjoyed and readers have enjoyed his tales for generations.

Female characterizations, first and second novels

Out of the Silent Planet has few female characters; what's apparent is that it's a male world. Lewis characterizes Malacandra (Mars) and its Oyarsa (ruling spirit/angel) with attributes of the Greco-Roman god Ares/Mars. It's a dry, arid world, with a history of a destructive war that scarred the planet. Ransom engages in a hunt for a fearsome beast and must go through a physical journey that taxes his endurance. Both the planet and Oyarsa represent symbolic and mythic masculinity, particularly as contrasted in the next book with the femininity of the planet Perelandra (or Venus) and its Oyarsa.

In *Perelandra*, we're presented with a lush, fertile world filled with oceans, vegetation, and animal life, as opposed to the spartan Malacandra. These attributes of the Greco-Roman goddess Aphrodite/Venus contribute to a sense of mythic femininity.

Of particular interest to this discussion is Tinidril, Queen of Perelandra. As an Eve-type character in the clear tradition of Milton's Eve in *Paradise Lost*, she is tempted by Earth's Satan (or at least his agent). She is representative of a created woman in an unfallen world and is the queen and future mother of her race – tall, intelligent, and beautiful. One seeming contradiction as a result of her unfallen state is that she is incredibly innocent but also very intelligent. And as much as both Ransom and Weston underestimate her, she proves herself capable of resisting the temptor's logical arguments.

A problem in analyzing Tinidril from a literary perspective is what language/tools of analysis to use. If we use the language and ideas of traditional feminist literary theory, we must discuss Tinidril in terms of power and "agency." We'd ask whether she is the ruler of her destiny, whether she has true choice in what she does, whether she has power in the relationships with men around her. We'd have no choice but to say that while she avoids temptation, ultimately she lives in a world ruled by her husband Tor; that she must choose to believe one of two dueling male figures (Ransom or the possessed Weston); and that she is inevitably caught up in a patriarchal universe in which God is the head.

Given this, we'd likely take the next step and demonize Lewis by saying he is sexist (by comparing him to current prevailing views of gender) or minimize him by saying he's "just a product of his time." We also could take what some would call a more sophisticated, but equally problematic view, saying he is "progressive" in some areas as compared to other writers in his day, yet just as "old fashioned" in other areas. Or we could look at his body of work and the publication dates and say that he "progressed" in his views of women over time and that this makes it all "okay."

But there's a problem with this sort of inquiry. Not only does it partake in what Lewis called "chronological snobbery" (judging people in the past by the prevailing views of the present) and the "personal heresy" (seeing all writing as an autobiographical reflection of the author), but ultimately, the novel itself resists this sort of inquiry. In *Perelandra,* and later *That Hideous Strength*, Lewis specifically critiques the "fallen" way of seeing the world – seeing the world mainly in terms of power relationships – by contrasting it with obedience to God's design and hierarchy.

Perelandra is set in an unfallen world in which seeking power over others for self-gain is the sin of pride. To discuss such a world in terms of who has power in relationships is in some ways fitting (in that Lewis demonstrates a hierarchical structure), but it's also a problem, for Lewis shows us a world in which nobody seeks power over others. So a critic looking for power relationships in *Perelandra* finds Lewis declaring that, in itself, such a preoccupation with power is inherently fallen and sinful. As an alternative, we can analyze and describe *Perelandra* in terms of what the text bears out – a specific Christian ethos that Lewis imbues it with that challenges notions of power. Taking that view, we might conclude that each character is equal in power but different in characteristics. (This is a world in which Paul's discussions of gender in the New Testament meet the hierarchical and harmonious structure of the medieval worldview, as Lewis analyzes in his book *The Discarded Image: An Introduction to Medieval and Renaissance Literature*, a non-fiction work and the last book he wrote before his death in 1963.)

Equal in power but different in characteristics – we see this particularly in the characters of Malacandra and Perelandra, the two most "powerful" and authoritative beings in the novel. They are both Oyarsa, or ruling angels, who are equal rulers of planets, but Malacandra is more traditionally masculine and Perelandra is more traditionally feminine. Both have equal authority and power, are gendered without having sexual characteristics, and obey the higher authority of Maleldil. They live in harmony in a very complex hierarchy.

A further example of equality under God and yet different authority is that Tinidril is a monarch in her relationship with Ransom. When she first realizes that he is her inferior rather than on the same hierarchical level, she begins to treat him as such and Ransom defers. She treats him with extra authority but with an enhanced sense of true charity and hospitality towards him.

Lewis on gender roles

While Lewis sets up his ideal perspectives on gender, he also attacks some views of his day about gender roles. The most telling critique is that Weston, the tempter figure, uses a perversion of feminist concepts to tempt Tinidril. He makes out suffering itself is a virtue, no matter what might be the cause of the suffering – specifically, that women who are treated negatively by society, no matter how sinful they may be in their own actions, are virtuous and admirable and brave by the mere fact of their suffering alone. Weston tells Tinidril many such stories of women who were persecuted by society and plays up how they sacrificed their happiness because they knew better than the brutish men who kept them down. Ransom sees through this and realizes that the stories Weston uses are tales of pride and selfishness and vice rather than of virtuous bravery and sacrifice.

One charge some critics make is that it is Ransom who is the true savior of Perelandra rather than Tinidril, and that this illustrates Lewis as a misogynist. I disagree. Lewis wraps up the conflict with the possessed Weston with a physical battle between him and Ransom. While it's debatable whether this is a poor way to end the core conflict, this battle by violence doesn't truly minimize Tinidril's choices as the author takes pains to show that Tinidril has already passed her trials of temptation and has decided not to succumb.

Essentially, each reader has to make conclusions about the novel based on prior assumptions and a set of terminology, a lens if you will, through which he or she sees the meaning of the novel. If the reader uses traditionally feminist ideas regarding the language of power relations, then he or she will likely make a judgment that the female character is subservient to the male characters. However, if the reader uses traditionally Christian ideas and the language of a reversal of power relations (the strong will be made weak and the weak strong) and the concept that it is sinful to seek power over others, then he or she likely will make a judgment that the female character, with God's help and blessing, saves the planet from the possessed Weston and the evil eldila he serves.

Female characterizations, third novel

In *That Hideous Strength*, the theme of hierarchy reappears, both in relation to gender and otherwise. The main character is Jane Studdock, a human woman. She and her husband Mark are in danger of being tempted by the agents of the N.I.C.E. organization, a group led by "bent eldila" – the devil and demons.

In this novel, Lewis goes far in his critique of certain feminist views of his time. One wonders if Lewis intended this novel, along with the temptation passages in Perelandra, to be a companion to his book *The Abolition of Man*, in which he describes how our educational system and culture create men without values or virtue. In a similar vein, much of the latter two novels of the trilogy can be said to contain Lewis' views on what he might have characterized as "the abolition of woman."

Jane, a PhD student, is characterized as obsessed with not being anyone's inferior. In one sense, this results in feelings of superiority over her cleaning woman, Ivy Maggs. Mostly, though, Jane avoids anything that might make her seem too feminine, and thus "weak," especially in regards to her marriage. Throughout, she distances herself from characters in the story who try to help her, especially if they bring up her responsibilities toward Mark or any "old fashioned" notions of womanhood. She is her own individual, making her own decisions, not wanting to rely on anyone.

However, rather than being a positive portrayal of a strong, independent, self-made woman, Lewis sets this up as something taken too far. While we may have sympathy for Jane's critiques of the extreme of ultra-feminine, obsequious women, we also witness Jane over-avoiding being that type herself, and in doing so, cutting herself off from humanity and from God. On the other hand, the opposite extreme of ultra-masculine women is also negative, as evidenced in the portrayal of Fairy Hardcastle.

The women Jane meets in the Fellowship of St Anne's, in contrast to both extremes, range from stay-at-home wife to cleaning woman to professional woman. They evidence a broad set of gender characterizations but are equal members of the fellowship with the men.

One of the core problems in the novel is that both Jane and Mark see marriage in terms of power and ownership. Through the story's arc, both realize they're wrong. In encounters with Ransom and his fellowship, particularly with women, Jane begins to see the value of obedience and humility with respect to higher authorities and to her husband. However, by highlighting mutual deference as opposed to one-sided "submission," Lewis distinguishes Jane's obedience from a completely subjugated role. You see this in the growth of Mark also, who by the novel's end sees the problem of their marriage as his taking Jane for granted and having a sense of ownership over her rather than viewing it as a partnership. He also learns that he must have humility and submission in his love for her.

Overall, both women and men in The Space Trilogy are capable of and are required to make important decisions after undergoing various trials. While women in the novels possess traditionally feminine characteristics, like showing emotion, caring, and communicating with others, they are also written by Lewis as very intelligent. They are in a patriarchal system ultimately in the sense that God is masculine, and there is a sense that men are in authority over their families (Tinidril and Tor, Jane and Mark, other couples in the novels), or should be in an ideal, unfallen state. Yet while there's *authority*, Lewis shows that there should be little to no use of *power* of one over the other in their relationships.

A wider sense of Lewis' female characters

It is clear that Lewis respected his female characters as much as his male characters, despite critics who claim otherwise. One proof of his balanced view is that female protagonists so often appear in Lewis' stories in the first place, particularly when compared to those of his contemporaries. But more important, many central female characters in his novels are keys to the success of his stories. Lucy, in the Narnia books, is a character of strength and endurance and courage in *The Lion, the Witch and the Wardrobe*. She is the most faithful one throughout the novels, as illustrated in *Prince Caspian* when she sees Aslan before the other characters, who doubt Aslan is present. Other females central to Lewis' Narnia books are Jill, Polly, and Aravis. Even Susan, whose plotline in *The Last Battle* is often attacked, is central to the narratives.

The most prevalent issues critics have with Lewis' female characters have little to do with specific characterizations – their intelligence, capabilities, actions, or growth – but more with two plot decisions in The Chronicles of Narnia: first, Susan's fate in *The Last Battle* and second, the idea that female characters as children are not allowed to be soldiers in battles.

Again, if we look at the books in terms of power, then Lewis comes across at best as a product of his times and at worst as a misogynist (particularly in the case of Susan's final fate). Using a traditional Christian lens and the context of the stories themselves, we can see that Lewis' female characters are equal in importance to the males, though written with different gender expectations.

As for Narnia girls participating in battle, women were in the military during Lewis' lifetime (1898–1963), facing horrors of war with bravery and strength, but primarily as noncombatants. In *The Lion, the Witch and the Wardrobe*, Lewis seems to be against females participating in battle, as critics point out. However, few critics also mention that in *The Horse and His Boy*, Lucy, who is an adult at this point in the series, fights as one of the archers in the war against the Calormenes. Corin even critiques Susan a bit for staying home and not being part of the fight. It can be argued that rather than being "punished" in the final book for being too feminine as critics say, instead it is Susan's becoming preoccupied with being too adult (and forgetting the deeper, more important values of life) that makes her no longer "a friend of Narnia."

Lewis treated his female characters respectfully in other ways. Based on elements of *That Hideous Strength*, it is probably fair to say that Lewis would be opposed to today's objectification of women in pornography and the rise of sexual slavery. You see this most directly in the contrast between the positive sexuality at the end of the novel among the Fellowship of St Anne's and the negatively portrayed sexual views of Filostrato, Hardcastle, and Jules of the N.I.C.E, who respectively advocate a transcending of sex and the body completely, torture/extreme S&M, and a complete cultural openness regarding sex, which leads to both women and men becoming degraded and less than human.

Female characters in leadership
Lucy and Jill in The Chronicles of Narnia, Tinidril in *Perelandra*, Orual in *Till We Have Faces*, and other female characters are leaders in their interactions with others. Several are rulers or serve in other positions of authority (and Lewis did live in a country with a tradition of powerful female monarchs). Other contributors in *Women and C.S. Lewis* address characters from novels other than Lewis' Space Trilogy in more detail.

However, there are the two witches in Narnia and Fairy Hardcastle in *That Hideous Strength* who provide counter-examples of women leaders, mostly because they possess traits we generally associate with evil in men, such as power seeking, domination, and luring people into slavery. Some critics might say these examples make the case that female leadership is always negative because these are prominent leaders among Lewis' female characters. They also might add it's unfair that, when women are too masculine in Lewis' stories in aggressiveness and physical strength, they are depicted negatively. Yet Lewis' positive female characters aren't shown as overly feminine in contrast, but rather as balanced.

In summary, throughout Lewis' works, we see that whether we agree with his views on gender or not, Lewis is far more nuanced and complex as a writer than his worst critics – those who cry "misogynist" or "sexist" with little examination – give him credit for being.

 **Steven Elmore** *is Vice President of Events and Communications for the C.S. Lewis Foundation. Elmore has a BA in English from Pepperdine University and an MA in Literature and Film from Claremont Graduate University, both in California. Prior to joining the Foundation, he was a community college instructor in English composition, a software instructor in basic to advanced MS Office, a GED instructor in science and history, and he worked in technical and clerical support in the nonprofit, education, and small business sectors.*

CHAPTER THREE

"She is one of the great ones." The radical world of *The Great Divorce*

Dr Joy Jordan-Lake

Before turning to the intriguing question of C.S. Lewis' view of women as portrayed in his shortest novel, *The Great Divorce*, I have a confession. As an academic and a novelist, I'm typically a fair judge of when a literary work reveals signs of misogyny. And by fair, I mean brutal: a female scholar without mercy – giving no quarter for lurking shadows of flimsy stereotypes, narrow-minded assumptions and one-dimensional giggling types, no matter the author's firmly cemented place in the pantheon of English or American literature.

But in the interest of full disclosure, I'll admit Lewis poses more of a neutrality problem for me. I discovered him, you see, when the world of my reclusive nine-year-old self didn't extend much beyond my family and Twinkles the cat, who received my pronouncements with rather more disdain than was necessary. I'd stumbled upon Lewis' works in my private haunt as a child, my church's library, close enough to home that I could race barefoot – always barefoot – in summer across blistering asphalt and onto the cool of linoleum tile. I was always, *always* the only one there on a sizzling summer's day in mid-week, wondering who this C.S. Lewis might be, and why the fellow was hiding the name his mother gave him behind two initials.

Whether that tiny library offered major systematic theologians of the faith, I have no idea. But I also found my first Jane Austen there, and the Brontë sisters, authors I could imagine church deacons arguing against, including in our little church library. So I remain grateful for that heroine of a church librarian's broad selection of classics, forging as it did my assumptions that faith and fiction not only could but *should* be thought of together and revered in the way of a child, barefoot and blissfully unaware of time, burrowed into the corner of a deserted library with a book she'd just opened for the first time. There, in this haven of the literary arts, I fell in love with Clive Staples Lewis, believing in that knuckleheaded flush of nine-year-old wonder that I was the only one to see themes of grace, forgiveness, and crucifixion in The Chronicles of Narnia.

So with that most ferocious of loyalties (anything we've loved as a child), I'd be deluding myself and you if I claimed to read *The Great Divorce* with the kind of unsheathed approach with which I might attack (meaning impartial scholarly critique) Ernest Hemingway's depiction of women. But, for the sake of an early love, and for an actual literary discussion (and not mere propaganda on my part), I've re-read *The Great Divorce* with adult, professorial eyes – perhaps not more genuinely wise than a child's, but surely more impartial, more jaded. (And more seriously near-sighted.)

I'm happy to report that Lewis strongly attacks gender stereotypes in *The Great Divorce*. In fact, his most heroic character is a woman, the person through which he teaches readers the Truth.

Let's begin with his title

Lewis' title, *The Great Divorce,* has surely put off more than one reader. It's the Oxford don's generous assumption that we, his gentle readers, are as well read and erudite as he, which is not likely to be true. Ever. Still, Lewis assumes (in his choice of title and approach to writing this book) that we're familiar with

William Blake's *The Marriage of Heaven and Hell*, in which the poet, writing in the late eighteenth century, envisions a divine order encompassing materiality, sensuality... all that exists. As Blake's title suggests, he bucks any polarized idea of heaven and hell – or good and evil – as distinct from one another.

Lewis takes this on, holding up images of women and of men that commence with scathing gender stereotypes – but end with stereotypes utterly turned on their heads.

In college, the English Romantic poets drew me in: glades and cataracts painted by William Wordsworth and social justice inequities hammered by William Blake. Blake's rage at orthodox Christianity startled me – perhaps because it was far from my sweet, small town social order – and fascinated the revolutionary-wannabe in me. Blake rails against church hypocrisies, chafing at what he views as endless, razor-wire rules, seen in the final lines of his poem "Garden of Love": "And Priests in black gowns, were walking their rounds / And binding with briars, my joys & desires."

It's in *The Great Divorce*'s response to this understanding of Christianity that Lewis' brilliance shines, where he suggests a far more radical freedom for women *and* men than anything Blake penned or engraved.

Lewis' parade of characters

Before women appear in the narrative, a host of male characters representing distinctive types all have been castigated: the self-pitying Tousle-Headed Poet demanding attention for his work; the Decent Man, who believes his small, mean efforts at rule-following should win him a place in heaven; the Bishop whose intellectual bombast blocks his ability to experience grace. By the time any offensive female types arrive, Lewis has cast men in general as petty, self-focussed, small-minded and perpetually quarrelsome – when they're not murderous megalomaniacs.

Women characters appearing in heaven find themselves annoyed with or frightened by the shift of priorities. One is appalled that she's not properly dressed in heaven. Another cannot give up the habit of flirtation, appearing freakish and pathetic as she contorts herself in a vain attempt to appear seductive. One garrulous old woman only thinks of how ill-used and unnoticed she was on earth.

Writing in the mid-twentieth century, Lewis doesn't include, as he would if he were writing today, women from the workplace: writers or artists or academics or chief executive officers. But we can assume from Lewis' lacerating portrayals of male writers in hell – obsessing about their sales records (how uncomfortably true), or male painters, more concerned about their fame than the chance to live in the very Light that first inspired their work – what Lewis would do with female versions of these professionals.

Michael's Mother may be the most distressing of the female stereotypes, embodying both the good and the lethal of maternal instinct – mighty heart-ties making it difficult for a mother to leave her child are now strangling this woman. Her love for a son who died went stagnant, turned in on itself, and has become a monstrous, monomaniacal focus. She's ceased to be anything *but* a sorrowful mother, and is no longer an attentive parent to her daughter or spouse to her husband. Whatever other artistic, administrative or leadership gifts God might have lavished on her, she's refused to acknowledge, much less invest, them in others. Her dead son is an idol, and in sacrificing herself to it, she's shut out all other human or divine love.

Here, even before the crescendo of his final female character, Lewis turns traditional roles for women on their head. Rather than adulate some narrow understanding of women's proper roles limited only to hearth and home, Lewis' depiction of Michael's Mother suggests the opposite: that for a woman to limit her engagement with the world *only* to motherhood, as beautiful as that gift might be, is to miss the whole, varied breadth of God's love that could be lived out in and through her.

Which brings us to Lewis' vision of what human life rightly lived on earth ought to look like – and his vision makes its appearance in the form of a woman.

Enter Sarah Smith

Finally we meet Sarah Smith, an Everywoman who on earth lived as a person of no particular fame in a London suburb of no particular prestige. In heaven, though, the protagonist's guide George MacDonald explains, "'She is one of the great ones.'"

Unlike other characters, Sarah Smith arrives with a procession of dancers and musicians, flowers strewn in her path. Her earthly accomplishments, we learn, consisted "solely" of unbridled love and compassion for everyone she knew. Rather than being defined by her relationship to a bullying, manipulative husband, who appears next in the story, or by whether or not she's the biological or adoptive mother to her many "children," Sarah Smith's worth and nobility reside solely in the no-boundaries joy of her spirit, her serving as a mother figure, mentor, and spiritual model for the scores who now surround her. She represents ultimate freedom – from material, sensual or intellectual obsessions, or from earthly concerns over fame or fortune.

Like Una, a female knight in Edmund Spenser's sixteenth-century *The Faerie Queene*, a figure also set free by Truth itself, Lewis' Sarah Smith is beyond the reach of traditional gender roles or expectations. Sarah Smith is a creature of nobility, beauty, strength and greatness not because she has conquered, seduced, performed or achieved her way into newspapers or history books, but simply because the love of Christ has cascaded from her into all she has done and onto all she has known.

And in that, Lewis turns the world we know – academic degrees and book sales and job titles and familial status – smack on its head.

Unlike Blake's vision, Lewis' heaven becomes drastically distinct from hell, not because of lines drawn by a capricious, sneering God but by human insistence – that many of us cannot bear shedding our titles, pride and neuroses, essentially sending ourselves to hell.

The point here is precisely *not* gender, and not titles or roles, but only the freedom that comes in focussing on the Love beyond all other love. Yet Lewis uses a female character to show us this Truth.

A most radical vision indeed.

. . . .

Dr Joy Jordan-Lake *has authored five books, including Christy-Award winner* Blue Hole Back Home, *chosen as Baylor University's Common Book for 2009, now required reading at other universities and high schools. Her others include short stories and reflections,* Grit and Grace: Portraits of a Woman's Life; *an academic text,* Whitewashing Uncle Tom's Cabin: Nineteenth-Century Women Novelists Respond to Stowe; *non-fiction books,* Working Families: Navigating the Demands and Delights of Marriage, Parenting and Career, *and* Why Jesus Makes Me Nervous: Ten Alarming Words of Faith. *Joy holds a PhD and an MA in English and American Literature, and an MA from a theological seminary. While in Cambridge, Massachusetts, she led initiatives targeting low-income and homeless families, and was a Baptist chaplain at Harvard University. She lives near Nashville, Tennessee, where she writes, teaches as Adjunct Professor for the Honors College of Belmont University, blogs "Writing in the Midst of Real Life," and leads seminars, retreats, and workshops.*

CHAPTER FOUR

The Pilgrim's Paradox: female characters in *The Pilgrim's Regress*

Dr David C. Downing

In 1933 C.S. Lewis published his first Christian book: *The Pilgrim's Regress: An Allegorical Apology for Christianity, Reason, and Romanticism*. During his lifetime and ever since, Lewis has sometimes been called sexist, if not a misogynist (literally "woman hater"), so it is interesting to note that in his first book after becoming a Christian, Lewis chose to personify all three things he was defending – Christianity, Reason, and Romanticism – as female characters.

Though Lewis in his twenties was already showing signs of brilliance, earning three Firsts at Oxford, he was not immune to the prejudices of his generation and nationality. In a diary entry written in 1922, Lewis commented that there was "a certain amateurishness in the look and the talk of the people" at the school of English at Oxford, noting that "women, Indians, and Americans predominate" (*Diary*, 120). That same year Lewis wrote to his father that he was worried about teaching female students (whom he called "girls"), because he was afraid "the weakness of their sex (assuming they are the dunces)" would become apparent when they read for the same exams as the men (*Letters* I, 598). In 1927, Lewis wrote to his brother that he approved a new resolution limiting the number of women (which

Lewis spelled "wimmen") at Oxford, since the new statute warded off "the appalling danger of our degenerating into a women's university" (*Letters* I, 703).

Female characters in *The Pilgrim's Regress*

With comments like these appearing in Lewis' journals and letters in his twenties, it may come as a surprise for readers to discover that several of the most positive and dynamic characters in *The Pilgrim's Regress*, written in Lewis' early thirties and soon after his newfound faith in Christ, are female.

Modeled on John Bunyan's *The Pilgrim's Progress,* Lewis' first Christian book offers an allegorical tale of a young man's journey through the intellectual and spiritual landscape of the twentieth century. It is the tale of John, who escapes Puritania, a land of fear-haunted, legalistic faith, only to wander through the mazes of modernism, Freudianism, counter-romanticism, and philosophical idealism before discovering that he should return to the faith of his childhood.

When John and his walking companion, Vertue (whom Lewis calls "conscience" and "traditional morality"), reach an impassable gorge, *Peccatum Adae* ("Sin of Adam"), they first meet Mother Kirk, whom Lewis explained is intended to represent Christianity in general, not any particular denomination (Afterword, *PR,* 252). She offers to carry them over the chasm, but they refuse, having heard rumors that she might be a witch. It's only after many more misadventures that the two submit to Mother Kirk, receiving a symbolic baptism and undergoing a spiritual death and resurrection.

Lewis rightly observed that it would have been awkward to introduce a character named "Christianity" into the story. But one can imagine a wise old man, similar to the hermit "History," with a name such as Faith or Credo. So it is interesting that Lewis decided to portray Christianity as a wise and kindly old woman. This is biblically appropriate, since the church is called the Bride of Christ (Revelation 19:7), and Mother Kirk explains that the Landlord (God) is her father-in-law. But one usually imagines brides as younger and newly married, and Mother Kirk, as her name implies, is a gentle maternal figure.

Lewis' own mother died when he was only nine years old, and he had nothing but fond memories of her. Flora Hamilton Lewis (1862–1908) had a distinguished academic record, earning a college degree from Queen's University in Belfast, with honors in logic and mathematics, at a time when few colleges, including those at Oxford and Cambridge, offered degrees for women. Describing his parents in *Surprised by Joy*, Lewis reversed the usual gender stereotypes, remembering his father as emotional and easily upset, while recalling his mother as calm, rational, and even-tempered, descendant of a "cooler race… with a talent for happiness" (*SBJ*, 3–4).

Given Flora Lewis' academic accomplishments, including a talent for mathematics which her son Clive did not inherit (he flunked the math section of the entrance examinations for Oxford), it's a bit surprising that the young Lewis was not more open to seeing females as intellectual equals during his first decade at Oxford. But perhaps the memory of his mother had grown dim by then, and he'd begun to view women more through the lens of his "adoptive" mother, Mrs Janie Moore, who was not at all an intellectual.

However much the details had faded, Lewis always retained an almost sacred memory of his mother. In the highly polarized and politicized atmosphere of Belfast in the early twentieth century, she tended to downplay class and denominational differences. Though Lewis' father was a stout Ulsterman, his wife Flora made a habit of hiring Catholic workers for generous wages, even when threatening notes were pushed through the letterbox of their family home. Though she belonged to the Church of Ireland, part of the Anglican Communion, she couldn't help but make whimsical remarks occasionally about the zealousness of

Protestant booster clubs in the north of Ireland. In a very real sense, Flora Hamilton Lewis was an early model of the exemplary "mere Christian" for her son. So it should come as no surprise in *Surprised by Joy* when Lewis explains that his first encounter with George MacDonald's *Phantastes* showed him a quality of Holiness that combined his heart's deepest desires with his memories of childhood: "For the first time the song of the sirens sounded like the voice of my mother or my nurse" (chapter 11, 179).

Besides Christianity, the second thing Lewis proclaimed he would defend in *The Pilgrim's Regress* was Reason. Ever since the Enlightenment, many thinkers have found tensions, if not outright conflicts, between faith and reason. But Lewis maintained in all his books that clear thinking is always an ally of thoughtful belief. In *Pilgrim's Regress*, it is the characters being satirized who abuse reason. When John offers thoughtful criticisms of modernist art, no one attempts to refute him with rational arguments. Instead they engage in verbal and physical abuse and offer contradictory psychoanalytic arguments as to why John is so unenlightened. Later John is captured by the Spirit of the Age – Freudianism. He is rescued by Reason, a woman in armor, who slays the Giant by exposing how simplistic are psychoanalytic critiques of religion and Romanticism.

Lewis defies gender stereotypes

Once again, Lewis defies gender stereotypes by portraying Reason as a young woman, a maiden knight. When Lewis describes her as a "sun-bright virgin clad in complete steel" (Bk 3, ch. 9, p. 62), it is clear that her character is based on Britomart, the maiden warrior in Edmund Spenser's *The Faerie Queene*. Lewis portrays Reason as a virgin-warrior because she is not "wed" to any particular worldview, but strikes down errors of logic wherever they are found. Apart from liberating John from the "prison" of Freudianism, Reason becomes one of John's most valued guides in the story, someone who eventually leads him to Mother

Kirk. Given the usual gender stereotypes, it is amusing that the protagonist, John, in many ways a stand-in for Lewis himself, is so meek and ineffectual, allowing himself to be ridiculed and beaten by the effete intellectuals called the Clevers. By contrast, it is a young woman, Reason, who comes to the rescue, utterly clear about her mission and fearless in her battle with the mountainous Spirit of the Age.

The third thing that Lewis wanted to defend in *Regress* is "Romanticism," a term he clarified in the preface he added to the third edition of the book (1943). Realizing that the term "Romanticism" had come to mean so many things that it was almost useless, Lewis explained that he associated the term with an experience he'd been having ever since childhood, a sense of longing for the unattainable that was both painful and pleasurable. Calling this experience "Sweet Desire" or simply "Joy," Lewis noted that it could be evoked by "the sound of wild ducks flying overhead, the title of *The Well at the World's End,* the opening lines of *Kubla Khan,* the morning cobwebs in late summer, or the noise of falling waves." (Lewis added this to the third edition in 1943, as noted on page 237 in my new edition, *The Pilgrim's Regress: The Wade Center Annotated Edition.*) Eventually, Lewis would discover that "Joy" was a kind of homesickness for heaven, the soul's longing for God.

In *The Pilgrim's Regress,* this ache for the Infinite is portrayed in John's visions of an island paradise, similar to the Garden of the Hesperides in Greek mythology. At first John's longing for the visionary isle is confused with a more earthly kind of longing, the basic lusts embodied first by the "brown girls" and later by Media Halfways, the daughter of decadent Romanticism. Eventually, though, in John's clearest vision of the island, he "scarcely noticed the island because of a lady with a crown on her head who stood waiting for him on the shore. She was fair, divinely fair," reminding John of a queen (Bk 2, ch. 5, p. 40). For that one moment, John sees a perfect embodiment of the Feminine with no taint of lust.

These few sentences anticipate Lewis' second book in The Space Trilogy, *Perelandra*, where the Green Lady appears as a new unfallen Eve, whom Lewis described in a letter as "in some ways like a Pagan goddess and in other ways like the Blessed Virgin" (*Letters* 2, 496).

It is a pleasing paradox that the newly converted C.S. Lewis, whose early sexism can be seen in his diaries and letters from his twenties, chose female characters for the three things he thought most worth defending: Christianity, Reason, and Romanticism (or "Joy"). As Monika B. Hilder has shown in *The Gender Dance*, Lewis came to recognize that if the church is the Bride of Christ, then all Christians are feminine in relationship to the divine. Hilder argues convincingly that the more mature Lewis would come to view gender roles not in terms of strict hierarchy, a rigid chain of being, but rather as a Great Dance, as described in *Perelandra*. As Hilder aptly explains: "The city of God prevails because the players have understood the cosmic gender game. Hostility melts into receptivity. Egotism fails; receptivity prevails. Pride loses; humility wins. Humanity is a 'woman'; God is a 'man.' God becomes a 'woman'; humanity is raised to 'son-ship.' The gods bow down; humans ascend" (pp. 160–61).

. . . .

 **Dr David C. Downing** *is the R.W. Schlosser Professor of English at Elizabethtown College in Lancaster County, Pennsylvania. He is the author of four award-winning books on C.S. Lewis including* Planets in Peril *(1992),* The Most Reluctant Convert *(2002),* In the Region of Awe *(2005), and* Into the Wardrobe *(2005). Downing also published a historical novel,* Looking for the King *(2010), which features C.S. Lewis, J.R.R. Tolkien, and Charles Williams as characters. His most recent book is* The Pilgrim's

Regress: The Wade Center Annotated Edition *(Eerdmans, 2014). Downing graduated from Westmont College and received his MA and PhD from UCLA.*

Chapter Five

New perspectives: *Till We Have Faces*, *The Four Loves*, and other works

Andrew Lazo

L ewis' last novel was *Till We Have Faces*, which he called "far and away [his] best book." Written and published in 1956 after completing The Chronicles of Narnia, *Till We Have Faces* retells (and revises) the myth of Cupid and Psyche, a writing project Lewis had grappled with since his teenage years. Although he'd tried several times, he failed to complete it until after he became friends with his future wife, a brilliant and professional writer herself, Joy Davidman. Joy's help in inspiring and editing this novel proved so indispensable that, according to people close to him, Lewis called Joy the co-author of *Faces*.

By 1955, Lewis had left Oxford to take a professorship at Cambridge. This move provided more money and prestige, and allowed far more free time for writing, his lifelong passion. This freedom led to a kind of renaissance in his personal and creative life. These and other factors allowed Lewis to write his "best book." Many readers find themselves more deeply moved by this book than by any other Lewis ever wrote.

Yet *Faces* represents one of the great mysteries of C.S. Lewis' body of work. While it touches people deeply, it also give rise to difficulties and questions. Through my writing of articles and eventually a book, I hope to bring light to this compelling but often troubling novel.

Lewis helps us experience God's love

I began studying it in earnest while preparing to teach a course on *Faces* and Lewis' book, *The Four Loves*. I'd drawn inspiration from Dr Michael Ward's astounding work in *Planet Narnia*, wondering: if Lewis had a profound and deeply embedded system of meaning in the seven Chronicles, could we find a similar layer of systematic depth and symbol in *Till We Have Faces*?

I soon discovered layers and layers of masterful, intentionally constructed meaning. I began to understand why Lewis valued *Faces* so highly.

As I taught *Faces* around the country, a shocking experience began occurring. Once explained, this novel speaks to people so deeply that it often leaves them in tears – myself included! *Faces* reaches into the deepest places inside readers, opening them up to soul-shattering truths. On each of its many levels, Lewis writes the central fact of the universe: the love of God, and the lifelong, day-to-day struggle with believing and living into that love. I don't know a better description of that struggle since Jacob wrestled with Love himself at Bethel.

A central secret Lewis hid in *Faces* becomes clear once we unpack its many-layered symbolism, and a profound parable arises. His subtitle, "A Myth Retold," provides a clue. Lewis retells the myth of Psyche, whose beauty prompts comparisons with Aphrodite, which enrages the goddess of love and beauty. She orders her son Eros to punish Psyche cruelly, but he falls in love with her because of her beauty. Despite penalties, including banishment and a series of impossible tasks, Psyche is allowed to return and take her place as a goddess, the wife of Eros.

Lewis' brilliant retelling demonstrates the central message of the gospel, the key lesson of the universe: that God loves his creation, and redeems it through Christ.

For, of course, *Psyche* means "soul" in Greek. So in *Faces*, Lewis describes how Eros, the son of Aphrodite, the goddess of love, marries Psyche, the human princess. So, the son of the god of love, who is himself the god of love, marries the human soul. This is Lewis at his finest. From a pagan world predating the incarnation, Lewis uses mythology (which he always loved) to show how God sends his Son to become one with human souls. Aphrodite (both Love and parent of Love) sends Eros (Son of Love and Love himself) to marry Psyche (the human soul). At the book's end, this Son of Love tells Orual, "You are Psyche too." In so doing, Lewis makes his readers also Psyche, the human soul, who is joined eternally to God, the Son of Love. Amazing.

Lewis writes strong female characters

Lewis also makes *Faces* revolutionary by casting so many of the players of the parable as females. Ungit (the Aphrodite figure) is portrayed as a powerful goddess. In Psyche, the human soul literally takes on female form, echoing St Paul's words in 2 Corinthians 11:2 and Ephesians 5:25, calling all Christians the Bride of Christ, thus making us, in one sense, essentially female. Ungit is female, and incredibly powerful, a culmination of Lewis' increasing tendency to centralize and empower strong female characters in his fiction.

This astounded me, especially when I realized the breathtaking scope of the project. Lewis retells a classical myth in a medieval way to write a Modernist, perhaps even post-Modernist, work. *Faces* is at once a psychological novel and perhaps even a feminist novel. The recent movement of novelists such as Margaret Atwood and Ursula K. Le Guin writing about mythical women further points out Lewis' prescience in *Faces*.

Far and away his best book? Little doubt can remain.

Lewis helps us to see clearly

Faces also encapsulates many aspects of Lewis' deepest thinking. Owen Barfield claimed that what Lewis "thought about everything was secretly present in what he said about anything." One expects this to prove true – perhaps most true – in *Till We Have Faces*. And that's exactly what I've found.

Lewis produced no other work of fiction during the height of his creative powers, which occurred during that period when he experienced his greatest personal and professional ease. Simply put, we find Lewis writing *Faces* at a unique time of his life, with more resources, including Joy's help, than any other period in his career.

His new chair at Cambridge and his marriage later in life had set the stage for Lewis to achieve something extraordinary, which he accomplishes in this novel by presenting one of the overarching themes of his writing: how to see things clearly. Nearly all of Lewis' writings concern themselves with helping readers to see more clearly, but no book better embodies this theme than *Till We Have Faces*.

Lewis' consistent call to clarity of vision serves as a major theme in his writing. We find a useful example in his short essay "Meditation in a Toolshed" where he describes the distinction between "looking at" or "looking along" a beam of light. The reader can finish the essay in minutes but will spend a lifetime coming to understand Lewis' profound distinction.

Whether we sample Lewis' literary history and criticism, his popular theology and apologetics, his poetry, his several genres of fiction, his essays, or his voluminous correspondence, Lewis consistently *illuminates* our understanding and offers key insights. He waded through a century of writing to produce a volume that still *sheds light on* and clarifies scholars' thinking about a pivotal period of writing, *English Literature in the Sixteenth Century, Excluding Drama.* He wrote *Mere Christianity* in order to make the Christian faith not simple, but clear. In The Chronicles of Narnia, Lewis gave Lucy the privilege of seeing most clearly; she is the "lucid" one, who nearly always notices everything first. She *sees*, as Lewis repeatedly demonstrates. Lewis also offers perspective, good humor, and insight to hundreds of correspondents with his *illuminating* advice.

But where did he gain such insight?

Lewis encourages seeing oneself

Much of Lewis' wisdom and humility comes from how carefully he looks in his own mirror. He studied himself in order to live out his faith, and this rigorous self-examination allowed him to look into hundreds of lives with insight that continues to help and challenge readers.

In *The Voyage of the Dawn Treader*, Lewis writes the powerful scene of the un-dragoning of Eustace, a nasty cousin of the Pevensie children. He has embraced the selfishness and ugliness of heart and soul with the result that he has become a repellent dragon. Once he sees himself in the mirror of a pool of water and realizes his ugliness, he begins to try to remove his dragon skin. Three times he claws his way out, only to find that more dragon skin lies underneath the layers he tries to remove. When he allows Aslan to "undress" him, Eustace truly transforms.

In a similar scene at the end of *Faces*, Orual finds herself in a vision in the Pillar Room, before her father's mirror. They dig down three times into the floor, only to remain in the Pillar Room. On the third time, King Trom asks what she sees – and Orual realizes she is Ungit. She despairs, because she (wrongly) believes that Ungit, the goddess of love, means her harm.

In both novels, Lewis shows readers that only in seeing ourselves in all our ugly pride, and then allowing love to transform us, can we find our true selves. In essence, Lewis flips the old story of Narcissus, and in both cases his fiction demonstrates that when we abandon ourselves and our selfishness and pride, we discover, through the love of God who will not leave us as we are, that (as Lewis says in *Mere Christianity*) "our true selves are waiting for us in Him." In *Till We Have Faces*, Lewis repeats, flips, and presses home more effectively than ever his most important lessons for us.

In *Faces*, Lewis retells the myth through the mouth of Orual, Queen of Glome. In a kind of reversal that reminds readers of *The Screwtape Letters*, Lewis demonstrates the importance of clear-sightedness by showing Orual's blindness – her refusal to see. Christ told parables so that "seeing they would not see," and Lewis also sought to "catch the reader unawares, through fiction and symbol." Jesus claimed to speak in parables as a kind of test of whether hearers really paid attention and cared to find out his deeper truths. Lewis attempted to make things all the more clear by hiding them.

Lewis' attitudes about women

Till We Have Faces represents the crowning achievement, a culmination, of Lewis' thinking on gender. Yet, Lewis hadn't finished thinking about such matters.

Let's take the surface level. *Faces* offers a few firsts for Lewis. Diana Pavlac Glyer's discussion of collaboration among the Inklings in *The Company They Keep* helps much here. Yet *Faces* represents the first time Lewis worked directly with one woman, Joy. It proves telling that Lewis used the metaphor of pregnancy, of being "with book," when writing to friends about *Faces*. And the fact that Joy helped him "to conceive" the book, the writing of *Faces* had a great deal to do with gender and voice. In addition, Lewis seemed anxious about the reactions of other women friends, to whom he sent drafts – getting the feminine voice correct meant much to Lewis.

Another first comes from a statement Lewis made in a letter: "I believe I've done what no mere male author has done before," claimed Lewis, "talked thro' the mouth of, & lived in the mind of, an ugly woman for a whole book. All female readers so far have approved the feminine psychology of it: i.e. no masculine note intrudes."

Joy had become increasingly involved in Lewis' writing projects – she helped type part of the manuscript for *Surprised by Joy* and helped with proofs for *English Literature in the Sixteenth Century, Excluding Drama.*

In 2013 I spoke with Doug Gresham, Lewis' stepson, at The Kilns just after the memorial stone for Lewis was placed in Poets'

Corner at Westminster Abbey, fifty years after his death on 22 November 1963. Doug asserted that *Till We Have Faces* had "a double author," and that Lewis wanted to include Joy's name as co-author. In a letter to Bill Gresham, Joy herself reports that Lewis found her authorial and editorial assistance to be "indispensable." I agree with critics such as George Sayer, author of *Jack: A Life of C.S. Lewis*, who wrote about her work on *Faces* that "she can almost be called its joint author."

These points help our understanding of the impact women, and the most important woman in Lewis' last years, made upon Lewis. The extent to which Lewis' brilliant future wife helped him write a book full of strong women and narrated by Lewis' most complex female character shows the revolutionary significance of *Faces*. Lewis dedicated the book to Joy.

Jack sees through Joy's eyes

Note that Lewis had planned to write through the mouth of Psyche's sister ever since he began trying to retell the myth during his teens. Joy Davidman did not first bring this idea to him. In some ways, Lewis' views on gender were at once complex and in development. *Faces* offered Jack a literary opportunity to explore his ideas about the feminine even as his relationship with Joy continued to deepen.

For example, in *Faces*, Queen Orual becomes great friends with the captain of her guard, Bardia, but he pities that she isn't a man so they could be better friends, a statement that crushes Orual. Writing in a feminine voice, Lewis is aware of the insensitive comments his male character makes about his female protagonist. When Bardia speaks of Orual's excellence as a swordfighter, intending to praise her as a friend with whom he shares a deep interest, Bardia tells Orual, "it's a thousand pities [the gods] didn't make you a man." Orual's reaction: "He spoke it as kindly and heartily as could be; as if a man dashed a gallon of cold water in your broth and never doubted you'd like it all the better."

Orual here may echo Joy's sentiments; in other words, Jack may be seeing through Joy's eyes. Recently discovered sonnets by Joy Davidman appear to show her falling in love with a perhaps oblivious or unresponsive Lewis. Certainly Jack seems at this point to have thought of Joy as a trusted friend. But she clearly wanted more. Perhaps this passage in *Faces* demonstrates the increasing ambivalence of different loves (friendship, affection, and romantic love) that Jack and Joy began navigating about this time.

Perhaps he had Joy in mind when, a few months after writing *Till We Have Faces*, Lewis noted to a female friend that he didn't like "either the ultra feminine or the ultra masculine... I prefer *people*." Again, Lewis seems to be developing his attitudes about men and women. His changing relationship with Joy probably played a large part. And he likely had Joy in mind when, in *The Four Loves*, he refers to the ease with which a male–female friendship can develop into romantic love, which certainly happened for Jack and Joy.

We find more of Jack's thoughts about gender in *A Grief Observed*, which details his feelings of overwhelming loss after Joy's death. He describes a conversation with Joy wherein she had rebuked him for praising her masculine qualities, asking how he would like to be praised for his feminine qualities. Joy certainly made an excellent match for Jack.

While Lewis never explicitly states what it means to be female in the novel, he goes one better by making himself and all of his readers female – both for himself as an author and for us as readers – thus creating one of the most eloquent examples of an often-overlooked fact about being the "Bride of Christ": in God's eyes on some level we are all female. Lewis does this as deftly as any author I know.

In Orual, Queen of Glome, Lewis created his most complex character even as he appeared to identify with her. By any measure, *Faces* stands as one of Lewis' most profound literary explorations of the difficult and increasingly important questions in today's culture about gender.

. . . .

Andrew Lazo *is a speaker and writer on C.S. Lewis and fellow Inklings. He holds an MA in Modern British Literature from Rice University in Houston, where he was a Jacob K. Javits Fellow in the Humanities, and a BA in English (with Honors), with minors in Latin and Medieval Studies from the University of California, Davis. He is a frequent speaker at retreats, conferences, and seminars in the US and UK. Andrew has written articles and reviews on C.S. Lewis and J.R.R. Tolkien and a book,* Mere Christians: Inspiring Encounters with C.S. Lewis *(Baker Books, 2009). Andrew has also transcribed and edited a previously unknown book written by C.S. Lewis. The little-known "Early Prose Joy" was Lewis' first spiritual autobiography; in 2014 Andrew transcribed, edited, and published this revelatory work in* VII: An Anglo-American Literary Review, *a publication of The Marion E. Wade Center. Andrew teaches English and C.S. Lewis at Houston Christian High School, Houston, Texas.*

SECTION THREE

Lewis, the poet – surprises from his poetry

C.S. Lewis became a published poet when he was barely out of his teens. Throughout his life, he possessed the emotionalism and sensibilities of a poet. During a wartime sermon in 1944 at Oxford's Mansfield College, Lewis broke down. He was so overcome that he left the pulpit for a while. The college principal gave Lewis assistance and breathing room to collect himself. After a hymn was sung, Lewis finished the sermon, still with great emotion. His topic was "Transposition," based on his understanding of how God physically places a desire for himself into the hearts of men and women. The sermon was covered by journalists because of Lewis' prominence during World War II due to his BBC broadcasts explaining the life of Christian faith.

When Jack Lewis fell in love with Joy Davidman, an award-winning poet herself, he fell hard. And when he lost Joy to cancer, the loss was devastating. Lewis' book, *A Grief Observed*, is cherished for its depth of emotion. Lesser known is a poem he wrote after her death entitled "Joys that Sting," including this stanza: "To take the old walks alone, or not at all, / To order one pint where I ordered two, / To think of, and then not to make, the small / Time-honoured joke (senseless to all but you)…"

Jack's grief was profound; his discovery of Joy – in every sense of the way he used that word – even more so.

* * *

Section Three explores the poetry of C.S. Lewis, opening with some eye-winking fun in "Setting the man–woman thing to rights" by Brad Davis, a successful poet. He sets the stage for Lewis' ambition to be not just "a poet, but a great one."

Next, Kelly Belmonte's "Bridging the chasm between us" effectively shares her personal journey as a poet and what she finds about heroines in Lewis' poems. She pictures Lewis' wife, Joy, as he alludes to the person most responsible for helping him "grow man."

Revd Dr Malcolm Guite's chapter three is "Getting our goddesses together: Lewis and the feminine voice in poetry," an engaging examination by this prolific poet of how Lewis "boldly and unusually for his time, used a feminine voice, image, and presence to describe the complexity of his own inner life as a man."

Setting the man–woman thing to rights

Brad Davis

"From the age of sixteen onwards I had one single ambition..."
So wrote C.S. Lewis on 18 August 1930 to his lifelong friend
Arthur Greeves of his first and chief desire: not simply to be a
poet, but a great one. He even knew his subjects: "northernness"
(all things Icelandic, Norse, etc.) and the rational spirit's priority
over gross, even evil, matter. In practice, he wrote in the forms
and with the attitudes (what he called "stock responses") of the
classical and English poetry that he read, studied, loved, and later
taught. He was not much impressed with his contemporaries, the
modernists, who were abandoning the old forms and attitudes
for the new. The one contemporary poet whom Lewis thought a
great one, attracting little notice at that time, was fellow Irishman
William Butler Yeats, whom Lewis met twice in March 1921.

What most fans of Lewis' fiction and essays would not guess
is that his first two books (published under the pseudonym Clive
Hamilton) were volumes of poems: *Spirits in Bondage* (1919) and
the book-length narrative poem *Dymer* (1926). Indeed, Lewis
began his career with a grand vision for his poetic self, and though
he eventually gave up that dream, he never stopped writing
poems. Like an exclamation point on his lifelong love of poetry,
the brilliant person he married late in life was the Columbia-
educated, divorced, American mother of David and Douglas,
Joy Davidman. She herself was a poet and writer of distinction,

having won two major American poetry awards (1938, 1939), the Yale Series of Younger Poets Competition and the Russell Loines Award for Poetry, both for her book, *Letter to a Comrade* (1938). As well, shortly after two poems appeared in *Poetry*, America's leading poetry journal, Davidman was invited by founding editor Harriet Monroe to serve as a reader and editor for *Poetry*.

It is difficult to overstate the influence of poetry on Lewis' long, productive life as a scholar and writer. What I found a tad more difficult: finding poems of his that address women, especially contemporary women, as subjects. There are the occasional women from the Bible or from mythology and general history, but on the whole, Lewis wrote only infrequently of women – not because he wasn't interested; commentaries on women simply weren't among his literary priorities in the early days, when he was most eager to distinguish himself as a poet, which also coincided with his years as an atheist.

Women… and horses?

In two of his post-conversion poems (Lewis became a Christian in 1931), mention of women comes paired suspiciously with horses.

In "A Confession" (1954), a self-effacing send-up of modernist poetry that springboards humorously off T.S. Eliot's "The Love Song of J. Alfred Prufrock," Lewis mentions, tongue-in-cheek, "The shapes of horse and woman" in a list of "dull things" of which his writing makes "the poor best that I can" – a list that also includes "peacocks, honey, the Great Wall, Aldebaran, / Silver weirs, new-cut grass, wave on the beach, hard gem, / … Athens, Troy, Jerusalem." And in "The Prodigality of Firdausi" (1948), Lewis ends his re-creation of a legend about the revered tenth-century Persian poet, Hakim Abu 'I-Qasim Ferdowsi Tusi, with the poet in an Iranian bathhouse surrounded by his fellow male bathers and discoursing "On the beauty of women and horses and the brevity of the life of man." But notice, these references to women, though general and reductive, are apt in their respective contexts and carry with them no suggestion that Lewis regarded women as merely shapes for contemplation or a topic for bathhouse discourse.

Lewis was keenly aware of the debate underway in his own post-Edwardian England regarding the role of women in the home and workplace. Among his relatively small circle of good friends was the Oxford-educated novelist, essayist, poet, playwright, translator, and Christian humanist, Dorothy L. Sayers. She was a frequent speaker at meetings of the Socratic Club, an Oxford student group that Lewis, its first faculty advisor, helped found (1941–42) as "an open forum for the discussion of the intellectual difficulties connected with religion and with Christianity in particular." In 1947, Sayers published a book of faith-informed essays (*Unpopular Opinions*), two of which, later published as *Are Women Human?* (1971), dared propose such extraordinary, liberated ideas as "the person who does the job best is the person best fitted to it." That Lewis valued her friendship and participation in the Socratic Club suggests that he enjoyed the company of women with strong creative and critical minds – even such as would take public, sharp-witted aim at sexism in post-Edwardian English society.

Lewis' two-tiered evolution on women

Personally, I suspect Lewis of an evolving, two-tiered view of the place of women. On the one hand, because at Oxford Lewis was a victim of what today we call workplace discrimination (his strident Christian faith and outspokenness about it seemed to hold him back, although Cambridge eventually formed a chair for him), I doubt he ever objected to Sayers' argument that a job ought to go to the best possible person. On the other hand, there are moments in his Christian writings that express opinions for which he labeled himself a "dinosaur." For example, in marriage, it was the man, representing to Lewis the rational aspect of the divine image, who was destined to rule the wife and home: "I

149

believe the authority of parent over child, husband over wife, learned over simple, to have been as much a part of the original plan as the authority of man over beast" ("Membership," essay from *The Weight of Glory*, 1949).

This hierarchical view seems based in large measure upon his reading the Scriptures while still under the influence (albeit in the hangover stage) of his pre-Christian, gnostic worldview that saw matter and nature (female) as inferior, and reason (male) as superior. But after marrying Joy Davidman in 1956, it's significant that his friends said theirs was very much a marriage of equals in which no hierarchy was apparent. Of her as his spouse Lewis wrote in *A Grief Observed* (1961) that she was "my daughter and my mother, my pupil and my teacher, my subject and my sovereign; and always, holding all these in solution, my trusty comrade, friend, shipmate, fellow-soldier."

Thus, it appears that the pattern of his later-life marriage to Davidman trumps his earlier theoretical convictions. In fact, I suspect that his view of the matter evolved as, more and more, he submitted his imagination to the whole of what is revealed in the Scriptures – a decades-long evolution that prepared him for a rendezvous with, first, the mind (via letters) and then the person of Joy Davidman.

In the yellowed pages of my volume of Lewis' selected poetry entitled *Poems* (edited by Walter Hooper, 1964), there is one poem in the bunch, "The Adam at Night" (published in 1949, the year before he began corresponding with Davidman), which anticipates a fully developed, post-conversion view of the human being, of both man and woman. In it, Lewis explores what sleeping may have been like for Adam before sin gained a foothold in his existence, when "he was free from that dominion / Of the blind brother of death who occults the mind."

Here is a similar quality of speculation to that which Martin Luther demonstrated in his commentary on Genesis when he explored what would have happened had our primordial parents not eaten of the forbidden fruit; Luther supposed that, eating only of the tree of life, Adam and Eve would have developed from being earthy and mortal (as we are) to spiritual and eternal (as the risen Jesus is) without having to pass through death's dismal door. Likewise, Milton in *Paradise Lost*, which Lewis regarded as perhaps the highest achievement of English poetry, explored by way of imagination a more fully developed portrait of Satan's role in the Fall of Man than the Scriptures afford. Luther, Milton, and Lewis enjoyed a reverent freedom with the Bible, seen also in Jewish *midrash*, whereby their authorial imaginations played in and around the details of the biblical text in order, through their writings, to return readers to the Scriptures and their lives with new eyes.

In "The Adam at Night," the Human does not sleep "as men now sleep" since the Fall, but relaxing nightly after the good work of uncorrupted stewardship, the Human is portrayed as able, through the mind, to reunite with the fabulous stuff of the earth from which they came, and to soar through the heavens, "riding / At one with his planetary peers around the Sun." And within the fantastic description of this nightly cavorting, Lewis names the deep place in Adam's body where "bloom the gold and diamond" of his creative nature: "his dark womb." Here Lewis exercises delightfully his freedom to outfit Adam with a womb and, a few lines later, Eve with a humanity equal to Adam's – marvelously "gifted / With speech and motion."

Poetical, eye-winking fun?

So, Adam and Eve. Why portray them each as outfitted also with what the other has? For a bit of poetical, eye-winking fun? Or did Lewis' choice of imagery fit perfectly his evolving sense of what it means for human beings, male and female, to be made in the image of God? I believe the imagery fit perfectly; man and woman, though different, bear equally the stamp of divine nature, in creativity, intelligence, and gracefulness.

As well, the poem's final declaration affirms them as equal beneficiaries of terrestrial nature: "The Earth's strength was in each." No more gnostic blather about matter being evil.

"Yes, Bradley," you protest, "but Lewis was describing the situation before sin and death ruined everything." True enough. And yet, ruined as everything became, Scripture also teaches that what has been ruined will be set right – made new. And so I think that as Lewis redirected his life more fully toward the praise of no other's glory but God's, he stepped "further up and further in" to what the Scriptures call the new earth, an already-but-not-yet realm where, for starters, we begin here and now to know God, and where humanity's original, co-equal dignity and purpose is, beginning here and now, gloriously restored.

In the eight visionary stanzas of Lewis' "The Adam at Night," we glimpse a shimmer, as through a tiny window, of his best understanding of who we are as women and men, and how therefore we ought to begin, in the midst of our present muddle, to regard and treat one another. And with good reason: this original ideal will become the eternal, non-negotiable norm when we join the risen Jesus where he is (Luke 23:43) and God's kingdom arrives "on earth as it is in heaven." Thus, wisdom: that we begin practicing now what then will be normal.

Lewis the thinker and critic would admit that, over the millennia since the Fall, men and women have found innumerable ways, both systemic and singular, to mistreat, oppress, and otherwise abuse each other. And, at our worst, to do so in the name of God. But Lewis the believer and poet, though without a twelve-step program for setting the age-old, man–woman thing to rights, nonetheless treasured an ideal drawn from Scripture toward which he believed we should choose, creatively and critically, to direct our lives and relationships.

Brad Davis *is a poet and teacher from Pomfret, Connecticut, where he works at Pomfret School, a co-educational boarding school (grades 9–12). He also taught at the College of the Holy Cross in Massachusetts and Eastern Connecticut State University. His most recent books of poems are* Still Working It Out *(Poiema Poetry Series, Cascade Books, 2014),* Sunken Garden Poetry *(ed., anthology, Wesleyan University Press, 2012), and* Opening King David: Poems in conversation with the Psalms *(Emerald City Books, 2011). Individual poems have appeared widely in such US journals as* Poetry, The Paris Review, Image, Puerto del Sol, Michigan Quarterly Review, *and* The Connecticut Review. *He holds graduate degrees from Trinity School for Ministry (MDiv, 1980) and Vermont College of Fine Arts (MFA, 1995).*

CHAPTER TWO

Bridging the chasm between us

Kelly Belmonte

As a practicing poet, it's a risky business to assume you can know a person's complete view on any matter from reading their poetry – or reading anything they've written. Not the whole view. You can gather clues and make educated guesses. A good many poets tell the truth; they just "tell it slant" (thank you, Emily Dickinson).

That said, C.S. Lewis wrote poetry most of his life, publishing his first poem at the age of fourteen, so he left us more than a few slant breadcrumbs to follow the path of his potential thoughts about women. Taking the clue-gathering approach, I reviewed many of the poems collected so diligently after his death by Walter Hooper, which included more than a hundred ranging in date from the 1930s to well into the 1950s. The first two lines I happened on were from "A Cliché Came Out of its Cage":

Take as your model the tall women with yellow hair in plaits
Who walked back into burning houses to die with men,

And I laughed out loud! You see, my name (Kelly) in Gaelic means "warrior maiden," so I'm familiar with the myths about those tall blonde-plaited women. They are not shrinking violets.

Mythic heroines

Reading through other poems, it appears that mythic heroines captured Lewis' poetic imagination from an early stage. Does this mean Lewis had a high view of women? From taking in many of his poems written across a broad time span, I believe his poetry shows a high view of humanity in general. He hoped for – expected – great and glorious and terrible things from both men and women. They – men and women – were the stuff that myths were made of.

From Lewis' perspective, we are "…immortal horrors or everlasting splendors" as in "The Weight of Glory" (no, technically not a poem, but his consistent thinking on humanity is present throughout his writing). Returning to "Cliché," I read Lewis' disgust at the degree to which people shrink from the robust demands of being human:

> *Are these the Pagans you spoke of? Know your betters*
> *and crouch, dogs;*

I take away from this broad theme that Lewis was fine with the goddess ideal, even if from a somewhat academically removed perspective. I get a better idea of his view of "real women" (those who existed in his own time and with whom he mingled) from a few of his later, undated, poems. Thanks to Phil Keaggy, who put it to music, I am most familiar with "As the Ruin Falls."

This sonnet was with those found by Hooper among Lewis' later writings. A close reading reveals a man devastated by love – the kind of love that will tear down carefully built fortresses of intellectual safety. Here's a man who's had answers for the hard questions. He was used to employing "flashy rhetoric" as needed to "serve my turn," as indicated in this sonnet. He was in control, prescribed. He debated with geniuses. And then, only in the winter of his life, does he encounter someone to whom he can say:

> *Only that now you have taught me (but how late) my lack.*
> *I see the chasm. And everything you are was making*
> *My heart into a bridge by which I might get back*
> *From exile, and grow man. And now the bridge is breaking.*

To me it's obvious this poem is written to a woman he loved deeply, likely Joy Davidman Gresham, whom he married late in life and lost too soon to cancer. It expresses with eloquence the shock of love found late and a recognition that it – or more accurately, the object of the love – would soon be gone.

So the one person who *taught him,* who can help him "grow man" is, lo and behold, a woman.

Handling failure

Becoming a successful poet was Lewis' first literary pursuit, but some scholars and lovers of poetry claim he was not a standout in this area of literature. A disappointment to him? Perhaps.

But Lewis channeled his writing gift into areas in which he excelled. I appreciate this practicality as someone who has been writing poetry since my teens but only within the past few years has found some traction on the publishing side of things. I had written hundreds of pages of business proposals, grants, marketing and website copy, technical white papers, and blog posts before ever seeing a poem of mine in print. As a mentor of mine once shared with me, "You do what you have to do until you can do what you want to do."

We know from George Sayer, author of *Jack: A Life of C.S. Lewis*, that Lewis was able to put a philosophical, even devotional, spin on his thwarted poetic ambitions: "Although he was disappointed, he could also regard the cauterization of his literary ambitions as a blessing. He wrote to Arthur Greeves… that a man cannot enter the kingdom of heaven until he has reached the stage 'of not caring two straws about his own status'" (230). Having a view like this helps. Poetry is a tough business in the best of times. You have to be willing to slog it out, and then have a perspective that keeps you sane. That he was able to put it into perspective surely must have helped.

What's most obvious and significant about how Lewis handled this disappointment is that he kept writing poetry his whole life. No surprise. It's what poets do, no matter how they're received.

Writers write. Poets write poetry. No matter what. He kept at the writing of poetry as a practice and it paid off as evidenced in his later sonnets, including "Joys that Sting" and "As the Ruin Falls." They are, in my opinion, among his best. A lifetime of practice will make better, if not perfect.

Not flashy rhetoric

I've been a consistent reader of Lewis for the better part of four decades. That must have left a mark! I've absorbed much of what Lewis said about writing. Be direct, specific, choose the smaller word that fits rather than the big impressive word that rambles. Shun adjectives. Show, don't tell. Things like that.

My first experience of Lewis was The Chronicles of Narnia, which my mother got for me and my brother when I was around ten. We devoured the set – and so did Mom – and read the books over and over again. These were the most important books of fiction I read as a child, certainly the most memorable. As a young girl, they gave me a vision of a world where a daughter of Eve would be the pioneer, the explorer, the first to enter the wardrobe, the first to talk to animals; she would be part of the hunt, the fight. I also saw that not only can the female be a force for good, but also the evil power in the White Witch. Nothing about the women in these stories implied a prescribed or traditional view of male or female roles.

Maybe I have Lewis to blame for never fitting into the typical church "women's ministry groups" doing "feminine" things that women are supposed to enjoy (crafts, anyone?). No, I think the wiring and environment were there already, but the validation from this literary giant must have influenced my child's mind about what it meant to be a woman and a writer.

I happened upon Till We Have Faces in the college library. The feeling I had reading it was a revelation, like, "Oh, I didn't realize stories like this could be told." And about women.

Also in college, I won second place for my sonnet in a poetry contest sponsored by Zondervan. My prize was a gift certificate to acquire books from their catalog, among them *Letters to an American Lady*. It impressed me then – still does – that this busy English professor kept up such a long, consistent, and respectful correspondence with an American woman.

It's what he did – answered all his letters. I'm in awe of such commitment and courtesy. His practice of correspondence reinforces for me that writing is never just the writing of the thing itself; writing is never done in a vacuum. There are commitments to keep, community to build and maintain, people to care for.

My reading of Lewis impresses on me that he was a writer of deep commitments, that he kept those commitments, and that he cared for people – all people and specific people.

He reinforces my underlying belief that you cannot love the world generally without loving people specifically, real people with names and faces. Because ultimately the poetry and stories and essays are just "flashy rhetoric" if they're not a means to bridge the chasm between us.

· ·

 **Kelly Belmonte** *holds a BA in English Literature from Gordon College, Massachusetts, and an MSc in Business Management from New England College. Her poetry has been published in* Relief Journal: A Christian Literary Expression *and* Atlas Poetica. *Her books of poetry,* Spare Buttons *and* Three Ways of Searching, *are published by Finishing Line Press. She is a New England-based poet, blogger, and management consultant with expertise in non-profit organizational development and youth mentoring. She blogs from her site allninemuses.wordpress.com on poetry, writing, and creativity. She is a frequent contributor to www.12most.com and www.hieropraxis.com.*

Getting our goddesses together: Lewis and the feminine voice in poetry

Revd Dr Malcolm Guite

A simplistic caricature of C.S. Lewis sees him as a tweedy Oxford don at home in the male-dominated, patriarchal world of the university, a product of a boys' boarding school, of army life in the trenches of the First World War, a man who could only relax in the company of other men because that was essentially his only experience of life. The case for such a caricature can be further sustained by selective quotations from his writings, many of which celebrate his gregarious friendship with other men in famous groups such as the Inklings.

Purveyors of such a caricature tend also to assume that Lewis must therefore have shared with many men of his own time a dismissive or patronizing attitude toward women, rooted perhaps in a denial, ignorance or fear of the feminine side of his own nature. Though such simplification can be made outwardly plausible, anyone reading Lewis' works and so becoming aware of the range, variety and sheer depth of his inner life, will soon realize that this clichéd idea of Lewis bears no resemblance to the truth. Even brief attention to his biography will soon undermine any picture of Lewis as a donnish misogynist. His mother, the first and true source of his original happiness, was an intelligent woman with a college degree, and Lewis' life was patterned with genuine and respectful friendship and debate with women academics and creative writers, one of whom he eventually married.

But leaving his outward biography aside, I would like to examine ways in which Lewis, boldly and unusually for his time, used a feminine voice, image, and presence to describe the complexity of his own inner life as a man.

What it is to be a man

It is helpful to make a distinction – which Lewis certainly acknowledged – between sex and gender. In Lewis' view, our sex as either male or female is a "given" within which we work, a part of our identity. But while there are broad sets of attributes, regarded as "masculine" and "feminine" and associated generally with men or women, it's worth noting that Lewis, like medieval writers he followed, felt perfectly free to use language and imagery gendered as feminine to describe and explore aspects of a man's inner life. And this meant that his understanding of what it is to be a man was much more nuanced than we might think.

It also meant that, even before he began writing the novels in which his women are so well portrayed, he'd already imaginatively been able to write about himself in the first- and the third-person feminine without feeling that to do so in any way compromised his masculinity.

A good example of Lewis' awareness of the feminine powers within the masculine is an important poem called "Reason", written just before his conversion to Christianity. ("Reason" is found in *The Collected Poems of C.S. Lewis*, edited by Walter Hooper.)

Lewis' "Reason"

Lewis imagines his soul as ancient Athens, a city animated by the living power of two great goddesses, Athene and Demeter. In "Reason", Athene, goddess of wisdom, stands for Reason as a power of the human soul while Demeter, a mysterious goddess of fertility and fruitfulness, represents in Lewis the power of Imagination. The poem expresses allegorically Lewis' personal sense of dislocation as he longs to be true to both goddesses but finds them apparently contradicting one another. He opens the poem with a beautiful account of Athene/Reason:

> *Set on the soul's acropolis the reason stands*
> *A virgin, arm'd, commercing with celestial light,*
> *And he who sins against her has defiled his own*
> *Virginity: no cleansing makes his garment white;*
> *So clear is reason.*

Notice that the goddess here is praised for her clarity and direct insight into "celestial" or heavenly truth, and she's also given a commanding position on the heights and an unimpeachable authority. Lewis then goes on to evoke a contrasting but in its own way equally powerful image of Demeter/Imagination:

> *But how dark imagining,*
> *Warm, dark, obscure and infinite, daughter of Night:*
> *Dark is her brow, the beauty of her eyes with sleep*
> *Is loaded, and her pains are long, and her delight.*

Each goddess is allied with different physical and spiritual senses: Athene is linked with sight, daylight, waking; whereas Demeter is linked with night, dreaming, touch (later in the poem Lewis refers to "imagination's dim exploring touch"). The goddesses are contrasted but also in some sense complementary; each must be honoured and respected if Lewis the narrator is to be a whole person. As he goes on to say:

> *Tempt not Athene. Wound not in her fertile pains*
> *Demeter, nor rebel against her mother-right.*

Lewis is still struggling to become a whole person. He cannot by himself personally reconcile these two inner powers, inner goddesses: his reason and his imagination.

Lewis' state of mind

Years later in his autobiography *Surprised by Joy* Lewis was to describe his state of mind while writing this poem: "The two hemispheres of my mind were in the sharpest contrast. On the one side a many-islanded sea of poetry and myth; on the other a glib and shallow 'rationalism'. Nearly all that I loved I believed to be imaginary; nearly all that I believed to be real I thought grim and meaningless."

How might it be possible to harmonize the different insights of reason and imagination? Might there be a single reality to which both pointed? These are at the core of the poem as Lewis continues:

> *Oh who will reconcile in me both maid and mother,*
> *Who make in me a concord of the depth and height?*
> *Who make imagination's dim exploring touch*
> *Ever report the same as intellectual sight?*
> *Then could I truly say, and not deceive,*
> *Then wholly say that I BELIEVE.*

Before we look at how Lewis eventually answered his questions in this poem, it's worth reflecting a little further on his two inner goddesses, whom he here calls maid and mother. The first thing to notice is that Lewis avoids the masculine/feminine cliché of attributing one set of characteristics only and exclusively to the masculine and the other to the feminine. In the clichéd picture, the height, authority, command, clarity and "commerce with celestial powers," which characterize reason would all be seen as masculine, and Reason would therefore be configured as a god rather than a goddess. Such a god would then be seen to come down and marry or "fertilize" the contrasting feminine, receptive, passive, wombing Imagination.

Lewis does not fall into this trap

He recognizes there is in fact a feminine aspect in both powers (and indeed in his first Christian book, *The Pilgrim's Regress*, he goes on to develop the character of Reason as a heroic feminine power; she becomes the companion, guardian and rescuer of his pilgrim hero, John).

Having acknowledged the vital importance of these two feminine powers in his soul, which far from compromising his masculinity will actually go towards making him a whole person, Lewis calls for a third person who will reconcile Reason and Imagination within him. I argued in my essay, "Poet", in *The Cambridge Companion to C.S. Lewis* edited by Robert MacSwain and Michael Ward, how the answer to Lewis' question "Who will reconcile?" was in fact Jesus Christ in whom God was reconciling "the world to Himself". Indeed the very framing of the poem anticipates that answer for Mary, who brings Christ into the world as both "maid" and "mother". Paul in Ephesians 3:17–19, which Lewis surely knew, speaks of Christ allowing us to comprehend "both height and depth". Certainly the coming of Christ into Lewis' life did effect a reconciliation and integration of his powers of reason and imagination – bearing fruit in the works of scholarship, fiction and poetry which followed on from his conversion.

There is a further consequence of the coming of Christ as reconciler to Lewis for his understanding of the feminine: his belief that, imaginatively speaking, we are all, whether male or female, feminine *in relation to God*. This is not to say that he thought God was literally male – Lewis knew that all our language about God, including gender language, is the language of analogy. But Lewis felt the masculine/feminine analogy was the best expression of the difference between God as transcendent creator and ourselves as contingent creatures, as he put it in *The Problem of Pain*: "we are only creatures: our role must always be that of patient to agent, female to male, mirror to light, echo to voice. Our highest activity must be response, not initiative."

Of course, we might want to respond to such a passage by pointing out that this is only one analogy among many and that Jesus himself used a mother analogy (that of the mother hen) to describe his own love for Jerusalem. And we might also point out that the male part of Lewis' analogy, male as agent, light, voice, and initiative, is modeled not on a capricious and domineering tyranny of a Zeus or Wotan but on the self-emptying and self-sacrificing initiative taken by God in Christ.

Lewis' call to all Christian men

Lewis included himself and all Christian men in this call to a "feminine" receptivity towards God's initiative, and this profoundly and self-consciously "feminine" aspect of his spiritual life should be borne in mind by those who quote selectively from his other writings in order to portray him as either ultra-masculine or misogynist. Those who still subscribe to that caricature view of Lewis will certainly be surprised by what we learn of his real-life relationships with women, particularly the unexpected and life-changing intimacy of his late marriage to a strong American woman who was prepared to give as good as she got.

One of the things Joy Davidman did for Lewis was to show him how supposedly "masculine" characteristics can be deeply part of a woman's womanhood, just as supposedly "feminine" characteristics can be part of a man's manhood.

Indeed, Lewis came to see marriage as the healing and reconciling crucible in which these different characteristics are at once exchanged and fulfilled, so in *A Grief Observed*, written after Joy's death, he says of that marriage:

> [W]e did learn and achieve something. There is, hidden or
> flaunted, a sword between the sexes till an entire marriage
> reconciles them. It is arrogance in us to call frankness, fairness
> and chivalry "masculine" when we see them in a woman;
> it is arrogance in them, to describe a man's sensitiveness or

tact or tenderness as "feminine". But also what poor warped fragments of humanity most mere men and mere women must be to make the implications of that arrogance plausible. Marriage heals this. Jointly the two become fully human. "In the image of God created He them." Thus, by a paradox, this carnival of sexuality leads us out beyond our sexes.

So we see that Lewis was perhaps more at home with the "feminine" both within himself and in other people than most men of his generation. We can see that finding the right relationship between feminine and masculine both inwardly and outwardly was part of a deeper quest for truth, indeed part of his Christian vocation, and we can see the fruit of this quest and vocation in all his writing, but perhaps most especially in the character of Lucy in The Chronicles of Narnia. For all the leadership and authority given to Peter, for all the vivid and undoubted masculinity of Aslan, the figure in Narnia who represents the deepest spiritual insights and has the closest intimacy with the divine is not the oldest boy, but the youngest girl.

. . . .

Revd Dr Malcolm Guite *is a poet and singer-songwriter living in Cambridge, England, where he also works as a priest and academic at the University of Cambridge. He is the author of* What Do Christians Believe? *(Ashgate, 2010, paperback 2012) and* Sounding the Seasons: Seventy Sonnets for the Christian Year *(Canterbury Press, 2012). His next poetry book,* The Singing Bowl, *was published by Canterbury Press in 2013. He contributed the chapter on Lewis as a poet to the* Cambridge Companion to C.S. Lewis *(Cambridge University Press, 2010). He's also singer-songwriter and front man for Cambridge rockers, Mystery Train.*

His CDs, The Green Man *and* Dancing Through the Fire, *are out on Cambridge Riffs and iTunes. Dr Guite is a popular speaker at C.S. Lewis conferences and other events in the US and the UK.*

SECTION FOUR

Lewis, the influencer – how his life and literature impact the twenty-first century discussion about women

Gender issues and attitudes have changed over the years. How men with Lewis' personal and professional background thought about, spoke of, and treated women in his day might be considered quite unenlightened today. To extrapolate Lewis' attitudes and actions, we review comments from his correspondence and published works plus observations by Lewis authorities.

The chapters in Section Four provide detailed analyses – both scholarly and from the contributors' personal perspectives. Following are snapsnots of his views from 1926 to just before his death in 1963.

In *C.S. Lewis: A biography of friendship*, Colin Duriez tells of a philosophy class conducted by Lewis in 1926 at Lady Margaret Hall with only women students (before Oxford was fully co-educational). Duriez writes, "Contrary to some accusations of misogyny, Lewis seems to treat male and female students as equals." Lewis' diary entry for that date reveals his enthusiasm for the brightness of his women students, noting several by name, a progressive attitude by an Oxonian in the 1920s.

Lewis' view of women would develop more over the years. In *Plain to the Inward Eye*, Dr Don W. King notes: "Those who think that Lewis is misogynist are either wearing blinders or have not taken the time to do exactly as Van Leeuwen does in this chapter: investigate the facts about Lewis' relationships with women." King is referring to a work of deep scholarship by Dr Mary Stewart

Van Leeuwen, *The Sword between the Sexes*, and specifically to his critique of her fifth chapter, which he characterizes as one of her book's strongest and one that "has long needed to be written." In it, Van Leeuwen discusses Lewis' reaction to *TIME* magazine's story about him, published on 7 September 1947. Writing about it to one of his American correspondents, Lewis complained, "Who said I disliked women? I never liked or disliked any *generalization*." (Lewis emphasized the last word.) Van Leeuwen added that "…although Lewis sometimes wrote what Dorothy L. Sayers referred to as 'shocking nonsense' about women, his actual relationships with women students and colleagues were in the main quite laudable."

On 10 January 1952, C.S. Lewis wrote to Sister Penelope: "…there ought spiritually to be a man in every woman and a woman in every man," adding: "I can't bear a 'man's man' or a 'woman's woman.'" On 5 August 1955, he wrote to his friend Dorothy L. Sayers that he didn't care for the ultra-masculine or ultra-feminine – he just preferred *people*, emphasizing the word. These comments came long after his conversion to Christianity, but it's worth noting that for many years "in matters of scholarship, Lewis was alert to erudition and blind to gender," as Dr Alister McGrath wrote in *C.S. Lewis, A Life*.

One of Lewis' most quotable essays is also his last. According to Walter Hooper, "We Have No 'Right to Happiness'" was written as an article for *The Saturday Evening Post* shortly before his death on 22 November 1963. Addressing what someone asserts as their "right to sexual happiness," in this case meaning extra-marital relationships, Lewis warns, "A society in which conjugal infidelity is tolerated must always be in the long run a society adverse to women… Where promiscuity prevails, they will therefore always be more often the victims than the culprits." He adds, "… though the 'right to happiness' is chiefly claimed for the sexual impulse, it seems to me impossible that the matter should stay there. The fatal principle, once allowed in that department, must sooner or later seep through our whole lives... And then... our civilization will have died at heart, and will – one dare not even add 'unfortunately' – be swept away."

* * *

Section Four opens with Dr Monika Hilder's stunning chapter, "Jack, the 'old woman' of Oxford: sexist or seer?" She cites the names of individuals who have accused C.S. Lewis of being sexist and turns their arguments upside down by asserting: "It's not Lewis who's sexist: It's us." Her piece is built on questions she poses as she unpacks her theory that rather than being sexist, Lewis was a visionary who transformed Western gender paradigms as they relate to heroism in literature.

Chapter two is "A generation longing for C.S. Lewis" by Brett McCracken, who jumps right into the twenty-first century with commentary on why people of his (younger) generation need and seek Lewis' written truths and personal example. His explanation of how universities sometimes fall short is fascinating.

Dr Mary Poplin offers chapter three, "From feminist to mere Christian," in which she discusses, from personal experience, the issue of abortion. She tells of the journey many women have made from following the more radical feminist ideals to following Christ.

Women in the pulpit? In chapter four, "Lewis as teacher and servant... and my respectful disagreement on women as priests," the Revd Dr Jeanette Sears takes on Lewis and his still controversial essay on a subject she is uniquely qualified to discuss, as one of the first women priests ordained in England. She also examines ways in which Lewis' attitudes and conduct toward women inspire her.

Like Sears, Kathy Keller was inspired by Lewis from an early age. She sought his advice in her letters from America, becoming one of the British author's child pen pals. "On women's roles in the Church: Lewis' letters to me as a child lit my way" tells how she and her husband, Tim Keller, live out their complementary gender leadership model at Manhattan's Redeemer Presbyterian church. Chapter five is also based on Lewis' essay, "Priestesses in the Church?"

What could a man of Lewis' background and generation, who was a bachelor until his fifties, have to say about love and sex that's relevant today? A great deal, argues Dr Holly Ordway in her unflinching chapter six, "C.S. Lewis on love and sex."

Dr Michael Ward also unpacks Lewis' views on sexual matters in our seventh chapter, "Mistress for pleasure or wife for fruit?" He carefully analyzes shifts in cultural attitudes and church doctrine during Lewis' lifetime, including how he responded as a scholar and an author.

We close Section Four with a deep and delightful look at how C.S. Lewis and his feisty friend, Dorothy L. Sayers, were "Comrades against the zeitgeist" in chapter eight. Kasey Macsenti shows how Lewis and Sayers conspired against a new attitude of their time which still influences us today.

Jack, the "old woman" of Oxford: sexist or seer?

Dr Monika B. Hilder

The hottest question on C.S. Lewis today is whether or not he was sexist. Did he hate women? Did he soften over time? Or, was he not sexist but prophetic? And seriously, is this even an important discussion? In view of huge world crises – terrorism, ecological disaster, nihilistic greed – why under heaven should we spend time thinking about our answer? What possible relevance does Lewis' view(s) of gender have for personal and global challenges?

Lewis was sexist, right?

Jack, as he called himself, was sexist, right? Born in 1898, spending his life in the male-dominated British academic world, how could he *not* have been? Let's remember, this is a world that had only recently admitted females, as many have pointed out (Fredrick, McBride 4, 12). Lewis admitted to sado-masochistic fantasies as a young man (Sayer 55–56; Lindskoog 370). His close friend Owen Barfield said he hated women in a theoretical sense, although not in his everyday life (quoted in Green and Hooper 213–14). Sounds like Jack was a bit muddled, but who isn't?

Lewis had plenty of what Peter Bayley called "tough masculine clubbability" (176) and once said he enjoyed nothing so much as "male laughter" (W.H. Lewis 14). He believed in male headship in marriage (*Mere Christianity* 99–100; *Four Loves* 97–98); said wives were prone to "fidgetiness" (*Four Loves* 54);[1] thought mothers tended to unfairly defend their families (*Mere Christianity* 100); and worried that females might "banish male companionship" (*Four Loves* 71). Need we more proof? (There's a bit more.) Let's face it: Lewis was sexist! But so were most men and a lot of women too in earlier times, so why bother discussing this?

All right, the answer to the question might be more nuanced. Surely, Lewis might have changed. Mary Stewart Van Leeuwen maps this idea carefully. But Walter Hooper (50) thought it unlikely that it took Lewis fify-eight years to figure out what life was about.

With Lewis' conversion to Christianity, we would of course expect to see the increasing work of the Holy Spirit. Also, plain aging and his later marriage to Joy Davidman likely softened him.

Point: he wrote his last novel, *Till We Have Faces*, in the first person voice of a female character. That's big. Or maybe Lewis did it without changing his sexist views of women? But shall we forgive him in view of the much he did so well?

Who cares?

Scores of people. Philip Pullman (quoted in Ezard) and J.K. Rowling (quoted in Grossman 40) denounce his "sexism" in Narnia. Kath Filmer believes he was a misogynist throughout his life. Candice Fredrick and Sam McBride (xiv–xv) worry about his "Christian sexism" and "disturbing misogyny" for its likely impact on teaching Christians that we ought to perpetuate "restricted gender roles." So, if they are right, Lewis' sexism is not only relevant but poisonous.

What we think about one thing affects how we think about everything else. If this is true, then Lewis' supposed sexism is not an isolated problem. Take it from Pullman, who believes that Lewis was not only sexist but racist and a lover of violence (quoted in Ezard; Pullman, "Darkside"). It makes sense: if Lewis sinned as a sexist, why would he have stopped short of other forms of domination, even violence? Barfield says it this way:

"somehow what [Lewis] thought about everything was secretly present in what he said about anything." And Owen Barfield insisted that Lewis was always thinking about "the *moral* aspect of any question" (5, 122).

So whether or not Lewis hated or just thought females inferior, it matters: it affects everything he stood for.

How can we say Lewis was not, for the most part, sexist?

We have ample evidence that Lewis affirmed females, the "feminine," throughout his life, and disdained, if not males *per se*, the "masculine." For example, he called British schoolboys "coarse, brainless" (*Letters I* 59; age 15), and praised men who "blubbered like school-girls" (*Letters III* 432; age 55). From the old matriarch in *Dymer* (written years before he became a Christian), to Lucy in Narnia, and Psyche and Orual in his last novel, *Till We Have Faces*, Lewis portrays strong moral females. From the lustful youth Dymer, and treacherous Uncle Andrew in *The Magician's Nephew*, to the leaders of the scientist conspiracy in *That Hideous Strength*, Lewis portrays treacherous males.

Then, surprisingly, Lewis calls himself (*Letters III* 521) the "old woman" of Oxford! In *The Problem of Pain* (124), Lewis also said he didn't mind being thought of as an "old maid"! (Meaning?! I'll get back to this.)

And Lewis favorably compared pregnant women and women who worked both inside and outside the home to soldiers (*Letters III* 105, 310–11); cleaning women to poets ("Christianity and Culture" 24); authors to pregnant women (*Letters II* 555; *Letters III* 328); housewives to college professors (*Letters II* 855) – the last one, because the work is never-ending. And he should know; he did plenty of both.

Lewis' writings are one long testimony of his affinity with the "feminine."

If Lewis was *not* sexist, why is it so hard for us to understand this?

Is a hero self-reliant? Can a hero be passive? How we answer these questions has to do with which of the two Western heroic paradigms we see life by – classical or spiritual heroism.

The classical hero of ancient Greece and Rome prizes qualities such as activity, self-reliance, and pride. This is the brawny and sometimes brainy hero: Achilles, Odysseus, Hercules. He fights hard and conquers under his own steam. Passive? Never. Proud, self-reliant? Always. The classical hero is the Superman whom the Western world (and arguably, the rest of the globe) places on a pedestal and applauds. George Bernard Shaw predicted that the twentieth-century would worship him most (136–37). John Milton in *Paradise Lost* identified the classical hero as ultimately satanic: the fallen angel declares, "To reign is worth ambition though in Hell: / Better to reign in Hell, than serve in Heav'n" (1.262–63).

The spiritual hero of Judeo-Christianity prizes qualities such as passivity, dependence, and humility – such as these underdog heroes of the Bible: the poor widow who trusts God's prophet and is rewarded with food for life; the teenager David who slays Goliath by trusting the Lord; Mary who agrees to become pregnant with God. Passive, dependent? Yes, in the sense of waiting and relying on God. Humble? Yes, in the sense of giving up ego in obedience to God. Christ's submission to the incarnation and to death on the cross is the ultimate example of the spiritual hero. In *Paradise Regained* Milton described Christ's victory over classical heroism: "By Humiliation and strong Sufferance: / His weakness shall o'ercome Satanic strength" (1.161). The spiritual hero is the one who is, apparently, least understood. He illustrates the "foolish weakness" of God that Paul talked about (1 Corinthians 1:25).

And gender? We have gendered these heroic paradigms. We tend to think of classical qualities as masculine and the spiritual as feminine: the active male and the passive female. We see something of this in Scripture: God as the Initiator Husband; the church as the receiving Bride. But if we read life through classical (not biblical) lenses, then we call the active person heroic and the passive person unheroic. And when a writer like Lewis challenges classical convention with a biblical vision, we often miss it and so misread him. We're too busy thinking of self-reliance as heroic, and meekness as weakness.

It's not Lewis who's sexist: it's us.

Are the classical and spiritual heroic paradigms too rigid?

Yes, but only if we apply them rigidly. Classical heroes weren't completely "classical," for starters. As Lewis pointed out, the big brawny men wept, unlike the later idea which crept in with Shakespeare (*Letters III* 432; *English Literature* 52–53) that only weak people, usually women, weep. (Nietzsche's Superman outplays the Greco-Roman one.)

Yes, if we think of males as typically active and females as typically passive, we're too literal. It's also arrogant, Lewis said (*A Grief Observed* 58). And personally, as Lewis wrote to Sister Penelope, he couldn't stand the "man's man" or the "woman's woman" because he thought "there ought spiritually to be a man in every woman and a woman in every man" (*Letters III* 158).

I can't think that Lewis has ever been accused of androgyny; he was so committed to the idea of gender essentialism – masculinity and femininity. But he thought of biological sex as only an approximation of what gender meant in the cosmic sense (*Perelandra* 172). In our day we seem far less adept at thinking metaphorically. It's been said that we lost so much cultural knowledge during the past twentieth century, a hundred years of massive destruction through war. Perhaps that's why we're more literal-minded, having had less leisure to think metaphorically. Irony: we think we're progressive.

We must remember that the heroic qualities which we have gendered are human characteristics applying to both sexes. Men and women alike are candidates for either classical or spiritual heroism every day, with each waking moment. We strive, we fail, we succeed; sometimes we repent and ask to be changed. All of Lewis' spiritual heroes struggle with the temptations of classical heroism.

Also, the paradigms are a rough sketch of core truths. These binary opposites, such as active/passive, should be seen as somewhat fluid. For example, a spiritual hero is also "active," as the Christian knight is active, but it's passivity or waiting for God that's the motivating factor, not activity for his or her own glory. This is how Ransom fights the Un-man in *Perelandra*. (Note: Ransom's physical battle is an image of the spiritual one. Lewis warns against identifying a political enemy with pure evil [*Letters II* 391].) The classical hero is also "passive" and "dependent" in the sense that, in the end, as Lewis writes in *The Screwtape Letters*, either Heaven or Hell will declare of each soul, "Mine" (113–15).

All of Lewis' classical heroes are doomed; all of his spiritual heroes are redeemed.

Is Lewis original in how he saw gender?
No. Nor did he claim to be original, saying he quoted George MacDonald in everything he wrote ("Preface" 33) and overall praising conformity to the mind of Christ instead of "originality" ("Christianity and Literature" 3, 6–7). He did say in *Mere Christianity* that people will think of you as original if you try to tell the truth to the best of your ability (188).

Lewis said that MacDonald's *Phantastes* baptized his imagination ("Preface" 34). Yes, but he was also fed by a long tradition of "feminine" heroism in English literature. Lewis was an expert scholar on Medieval and Renaissance literature – one reason Cambridge established a chair for him – and his books on those subjects are still highly regarded in academia.

Let's consider examples. The ideal medieval chivalric knight: Malory's Launcelot, who combines, without giving up either, full fierceness in battle and humble meekness of heart.[2] Edmund

Spenser's Red Crosse Knight in *The Faerie Queene* where virtue (strength) means Christian holiness. (Such "masculinity" is a metaphor for human courage in the spiritual battle, and is founded on literary values which we metaphorically call "femininity." In other words, a spiritual hero, male or female, is like a "man" in courage because he is like a "woman" in humility toward God.) Milton in *Paradise Lost* who dramatized Eve's Christ-like heroism. William Wordsworth in *The Prelude* who championed those who are "wise as women are" (12.156) – underlined in Lewis' personal copy – described the moral person: "his heart / Be tender as a nursing mother's heart; / Of female softness shall his life be full…" (14.227–29).

People in earlier times understood gender-as-metaphor. Cultural chauvinism was clear to them: they either fought it or endorsed it. Friedrich Nietzsche, the German father of philosophical nihilism, hated "feminine" Christianity for its humility and applauded instead the "masculine" egotism of the Superman as humanity's salvation (44, 47, 56–57). Did our twentieth-century fascination with the Superman erase our cultural memory of the spiritual hero?

When Lewis whimsically called himself the "old woman" of Oxford (in the eyes of his atheistic colleagues), or considered the derogatory term "old maid" as complimentary, he knew full well that he had chosen to stand against the prevailing winds. He had cancelled his subscription to pagan and modernist paradigms – and for this he was and is either hated or loved.

To follow Christ is anathema to the classical hero, but life to the spiritual pilgrim.

What about Lewis' sexist comments?

It would be silly to say that Jack was sinless. But his comments on fidgety wives, unjust mothers, and females ruining male conversation deserve more thought.

When Lewis referred to wives' potential fidgetiness, he also spoke of husbands' natural laziness.[3] In other words, women tend to over-compensate for male sluggishness instead of relaxing somewhat so that their husbands have to "man-up." While this is gender specific, and surely intended as a generality, its correction sounds like a recipe for health to me.

What about Lewis' comments on mothers' tendencies to guard their own at the expense of others? We often refer to this indulgently as the "Mother Bear instinct." To whatever extent this is true of any mother, it is certainly something to guard against, don't you think?

And as for females ruining male conversation, in this context Lewis was talking about women who had far less education than those particular men. Moreover, he called this inequality "an impoverishment," and pointed out that in his own profession men and women worked alongside one another and friendship was common (*Four Loves* 68–69). He wished this could be so for all people.

As for male headship in marriage, Lewis did not see this as license for domination, but rather as sacrificial Christ-like servant leadership (*Four Loves* 97–98). He was sensitive to how a woman might lose or hurt her career through marriage (*Mere Christianity* 95). He also thought these were roles to be played, as in a game or dance, and to take them too seriously was to risk idolatry (*Four Loves* 95–96).

Then, Lewis argued for equality of the sexes in political and economic terms ("Equality"). He critiqued sexism, whether in his own country where he disapproved of men speaking to women as if they were children (*Letters III* 676), or in America, which he suspected had "a degree of male tyranny that is quite unknown [in Britain]" (*Letters III* 339) – "I wonder how you have the face to keep a statue of Liberty staring out over New York harbour. Or is the point that she looks seaward and turns her back on America? Or is there a subtle connection between public democracy and domestic despotism?" (*Letters III* 622).

What about all those crying girls in Narnia?

In *The Lion, the Witch and the Wardrobe,* Susan and Lucy weep when Aslan is tortured and killed, while the boys fight the witch and her army on the battlefield. In *The Silver Chair* and *The Last Battle* Jill cries easily. Evidence of female weakness? But many male characters in The Chronicles shed tears: Mr Tumnus and Caspian in penitence; Digory when bullied; and Aslan.

In fact, unlike the stoic Superman hero (the bullies don't typically cry), the hero's tears prove to be the superior strength. Although Peter and Edmund are valiant knights on the battlefield, the girls share in the central battle of Aslan's passion. Unlike the sleeping male disciples in Gethsemane, Susan and Lucy support the Lion in his grief. And it is Aslan's suffering and dying, not the military power of his subjects, that overcomes death and damnation – once he arrives on the battlefield where the boys have been faithful, the physical fight is all over within minutes.

Tears do not hinder military skill either, as shown with Jill's archery in *The Last Battle*; rather they have far greater power, as also shown in *The Magician's Nephew,* with Aslan's even more sorrowful tears over Digory's dying mother. Aslan's tears aid Digory in making the decisive moral choice, and strengthen him for the rest of his life.

Of tears, Lewis said that he had not shed enough (*Letters III* 32).

What about Jane Studdock in *That Hideous Strength*?

The young wife and PhD candidate Jane Studdock is a litmus test as to whether or not we think Lewis is sexist. Her portrait is criticized for two reasons: one, she is cured of independence in coming to believe that for wives "obedience – humility – is an erotic necessity" (146); two, she decides to give up PhD studies to take care of her wimpy (or not so wimpy) husband and have children instead. So Jane is seen as the domestic slave submitting to patriarchal bondage: as wife and mother, probably without a PhD and academic career, she is seen as passive, of lesser value.

Really? Are we serious?! Women who devote their lives to raising the next generation are inactive (who knew?!) and essentially of lesser worth? Whatever happened to "the hand that rocks the cradle rules the world"? Not the psychopathic nanny (1992 film) but the moral mother, as England's Mary Wollstonecraft applauded in what's been called the first feminist manifesto, which she wrote in 1792, *A Vindication of the Rights of Woman* (140–41, 152, 263–65, 292, 304–305).

Maybe what we're really saying is that personal power and prestige trumps the next generation. Lewis, however, like Wollstonecraft and others throughout the ages, believed that the home is the most important place in the world. It's for domestic work that all other forms of work exist – to support the home (*Letters III* 580). Some think Lewis is an either/or thinker who can't count beyond two[4]: either a woman is a stay-at-home mother or she is a childless career woman. But his applause for the woman who also works outside the home, as only one example, suggests otherwise.

The point is this: Jane Studdock in *That Hideous Strength* is a classical hero who becomes a spiritual hero. Instead of fierce independence and privileging of intellect over motherhood, Jane rejoins her husband and welcomes children, and therefore will endure pain and death (380). Her new humility as a moral agent allows love and life to flourish. Jane is an image of what every Christian needs to do and be: give up ego and take up one's cross. Nor is Mark Studdock's role any less obedient – and therefore liberating. I know of no better example in literature of repairing male chauvinism as in the transformation of Mark from selfish arrogance to loving meekness.

The right sort of humble submission that places God first and one's marriage partner second is a requirement for both sexes. It's a receptivity that results in moral agency – and re-entry into dancing creation.

Didn't Lewis think women were more practical, less philosophical than men?

Lewis did once say that the masculine mind was predominantly philosophical, the feminine mind practical, so that intellectual exchange between the two was weakened ("Modern Man and his Categories of Thought" 62–63). My fellow Canadian scholar, Adam Barkman (who seems to agree), underscores this point (432).

However, Lewis also felt bested by philosopher Elizabeth Anscombe in debate.[5] As a result, he revised and expanded a chapter in *Miracles* in a subsequent version published in 1960, based on Anscombe's comments. Lewis also recommended Anscombe to be his successor as leader of the Socratic Club.

Lewis cherished friendship in which both sexes shared the same intellectual training and work (*Four Loves* 68). He admired his wife's intellect (*A Grief Observed* 3, 56), and that of many other women throughout his life. His mother was educated in mathematics, and it was perhaps from her that he got much of his own logical disposition.

Moreover, when Lewis identified women as more practical than philosophical (a reflection of lesser or different educational opportunity?), we need not assume this was a slur. (Barkman, I believe, sees it more as fact than insult.)

While we might privilege intellect over practicality, Lewis did not. In many instances Lewis speaks of the inferiority of analytical reason and applauds intuitive reason and imagination.[6] Likewise, he criticized people who worshipped intellect at the expense of physical life, as we see with the organization called N.I.C.E. in *That Hideous Strength*. I do think Lewis is like Mother Dimble in that novel, gently reminding her college professor husband that his ideas ought not to be disembodied philosophical exercises, but are taking shape before their very noses in the marriage of Jane and Mark Studdock, and in the battle surrounding them all (281).

Mind is not over matter: to separate mind from body, to fail to make real-life connections, is a most dangerous thing.

What about his negative view of women's ordination?

Even Dorothy L. Sayers, an author and friend whom he highly regarded, disagreed with him here (quoted in *Letters II* 861).

But what exactly did he say in "Priestesses in the Church?"? He distinguished between a female preacher (pointing to biblical examples) and a male priest who also "represents us to God and God to us" (236). Lewis did not object to females who preach or, in priestly manner, speak for us to God; he objected to the idea of a priestess symbolizing God to humanity (236). Not because a woman is "less holy or less charitable or stupider than a man"; in many cases a woman might be more qualified (236). He objected for one reason: the scriptural image of God as masculine before whom humanity is feminine (237, 239). This mystical image surpasses common sense: it is "supra-rational" (238). Lewis refused to give up on the gender metaphor because he insisted we are not exchangeable neuters (238). To read equality as sameness is to reduce the human being to a political animal – the requirement of any totalitarian state, as George Bernard Shaw (232), Margaret Atwood (*The Handmaid's Tale*), and George Orwell (*1984*), for example, have also observed.

We are, Lewis insists, eternal beings engaged in a cosmic dance in which the grand ideas of gender are somehow intrinsic.

Did Lewis think he could speak for God?

C.S. Lewis did not assume that his own ideas were correct. He spoke of God as the great "Iconoclast" who shattered our ideas of him (*Letters to Malcolm* 84; *A Grief Observed* 76). He emphasized that the paradigms of each age are transient – teaching insights useful for correcting blindness ("On the Reading of Old Books" 202; *Discarded Image* 14–18, 220–23).

In *The Problem of Pain* (33), Lewis speaks of the biblical gender analogy as limited and even dangerous if worshipped, but he insists it's the best one we have to illustrate our relation to the divine.

So what? What do Lewis' views of gender have to do with us in the twenty-first century?

Everything. What Lewis thought about gender affects every area of life. Whether the challenge is personal or global, sexism destroys. For instance, our commitment to science and technology without reference to ethics – the religion of scientism – will ruin us. Scientism rapes the earth and seeks to erase our very identity as made in the image of God. On the political level, if we lose the sense of over-arching Good, barbarism wins. On the personal level, if the autonomous ego has free rein, then all others become targets to be manipulated and conquered – and relationships, even lives, end.

Jack was not a sexist but a seer. He is not only the "old woman" of Oxford but what he also once called himself, an *"enfant terrible"* (*Letters III* 521) – the "child" who protests against the teachings of his elders: in this case, the legacy of inherited cultural chauvinism. As seer, Lewis fought the "masculine" Superman where "might makes right," predicted Superman's ultimate downfall, and celebrated the "feminine" spiritual person whose so-called "weakness" of Christ-like humility and patient endurance overcomes satanic hatred.

Lewis is a prophet whose moral vision potentially transforms our world. As human beings who are "feminine" in relationship to the "masculine" God of the Bible, we are subjects called to reign with justice and mercy, regardless of our gender. In the present world and throughout eternity, receptivity is the proper response to God and to each other – then truth and peace and joy will flourish. For Lewis, truth – God's sovereign purpose – will triumph.

Meanwhile, Jack's question to us is this: whose side are we on?

Dr Monika B. Hilder *is Associate Professor of English at Trinity Western University in Langley, British Columbia, Canada, where she teaches children's and fantasy literature. She is the author of* The Feminine Ethos in C.S. Lewis' Chronicles of Narnia; The Gender Dance: Ironic Subversion in C.S. Lewis' Cosmic Trilogy; *and* Surprised by the Feminine: A Rereading of C.S. Lewis and Gender. *She is a 2011 recipient of the Clyde S. Kilby Research Grant, Marion E. Wade Center, Wheaton College, Illinois, and co-director of the Inklings Institute of Canada. Hilder received her PhD in literature education from the Faculty of Education at Simon Fraser University, for which she received the Dean of Graduate Studies Convocation Medal for Academic Excellence. Her BA and MA degrees in English are from the University of British Columbia.*

CHAPTER TWO

A generation longing
for C.S. Lewis

Brett McCracken

L ewis' humility in seeing how an intellectual woman like his wife
Joy could help him so profoundly "grow man" is instructive in
my own life, personally and professionally. His respect for women
and understanding of them as worthy academic interlocutors
continues to be instructive in a world that's made progress but
where full gender equality is not yet a reality.

What I love about Lewis – and I think my "Christian twenty-
something" peers love about him as well – is that he models the
sort of winsome Christian public intellectual we aspire to be.

He communicates deep, profound theological, philosophical
and personal truths in eminently readable, popular-level
writing in several genres – fantasy, fiction, apologetics, poetry,
philosophy, memoir, etc. He's modeled a rare combination of
intellectual fortitude and humility, left-brained logic and right-
brained poetics. His writing is eye-opening and convicting on
both head and heart levels, and that's a powerful combination.

There's so much in the actual content of Lewis' work that resonates
with my generation. The three novels of The Space Trilogy and *The
Abolition of Man* contain prescient commentaries on politics and
philosophy that have never been more relevant. *Mere Christianity*
and other writings explaining the Christian faith remain timeless
in clarity and helpfulness. Narnia will never stop charming readers
with its visionary worlds and profound spiritual resonances.

The blog I contribute to, Mere Orthodoxy, is inspired by the kind of thoughtful dialogue that characterized people like C.S. Lewis, G.K. Chesterton and the Inklings. You don't see many college students sitting around today discussing ideas or logically working through debates in a collegial, Inklings-esque manner. Similarly, you don't see many students getting excited about the "well-rounded" liberal arts education, valuing the broad spectrum of literature, art, science, music and so on. Everyone is specialized and pragmatic, and so concerned with internships and job prospects; they have neither the time nor the inclination to ask "extraneous" questions or pursue "superfluous" curiosities.

The "mere Christian"

Today's university has lost the "uni" part, lacking consensus on the Big Questions which have historically undergirded Western intellectual tradition. By insisting on subjectivism (which hyper-specialism has amplified), today's secular universities have rendered themselves incapable of having anything important to say about the *why* of education or the questions of morality. They churn out smart scientists, savvy lawyers, capable tradesmen and talented artists; what they don't do (because they can't) is train men and women in *character*, developing them on the soul level and making them better people.

The result is a real deprivation. If education is only a material but not a metaphysical pursuit, we're soon going to live in a world populated by mere materialists and "men without chests," as Lewis described in *The Abolition of Man*. "When all that says 'it is good' has been debunked, what says 'I want' remains." Lewis saw this already beginning in his day, and it has sadly become commonplace in today's world.

Lewis preferred logical, biblical thinking that would lead him to examine cultural issues through that lens and not through the popular consensus of the day. One of Lewis' contributions is his notion of the "mere Christian" – practical ecumenism that doesn't dismiss differences between Christian denominations or traditions but acknowledges that what we have in common (belief in the gospel of salvation offered through Jesus Christ) is what matters most.

I love his metaphor of the hall and its many rooms (Preface to *Mere Christianity*). All of Lewis' work seems geared toward getting people from outside the house to inside the house. New Christians will find their particular room at some point, an important step in their growth.

C.S. Lewis was no chauvinist

He had great respect, both intellectually and personally, for women. Whether debating Elizabeth Anscombe, discussing literature with Dorothy L. Sayers, or corresponding with female fans and fellow writers, Lewis was egalitarian in his views of women and the value of their unique perspectives. Unlike some men of his day who would have preferred that women keep their opinions in the private realm, Lewis encouraged and supported women in their ambitions to have a voice in the public square.

Lewis espoused a fundamental respect for the dignity of all human beings, calling all of us to treat each other with the respect we would treat a holy being, for that's what every human is. "There are no *ordinary* people. You have never talked to a mere mortal," wrote Lewis in his sermon, "The Weight of Glory," my favorite Lewis work. "Next to the Blessed Sacrament itself, your neighbor is the holiest object presented to your senses." This is a major thread in Lewis' work. In the wake of the dehumanizing forces of modernism, war and technocratic society, Lewis' writing captures the charged mystery and sacredness of human life, recognizing the inherent value in every human life, whatever one's background, ethnicity, gender or affiliation.

Lewis beckons us to not be satisfied with the status quo in our lives and in society broadly, but to go "further up and further in"

(*The Last Battle*), paying attention to the mysterious longings and desires filling every human heart, reminding us that we were made *for more than this*. "We are half-hearted creatures, fooling about with drink and sex and ambition when infinite joy is offered us, like an ignorant child who wants to go on making mud pies in a slum because he cannot imagine what is meant by the offer of a holiday at the sea," wrote Lewis in "The Weight of Glory." "We are far too easily pleased."

The fight for women presses on, and Lewis' charge is to shun complacency, despite our fears or challenges that may come. It's an encouragement we can all take to heart.

Brett McCracken *is the author of* Hipster Christianity: When Church and Cool Collide *(Baker, 2010) and* Gray Matters: Navigating the Space between Legalism & Liberty *(Baker, 2013). A Los Angeles-based writer and journalist with degrees from Wheaton College and UCLA, he works as managing editor for Biola University's* Biola *magazine and is pursuing an MA in Theology at Talbot School of Theology. A frequent contributor to publications such as* Christianity Today, Relevant *magazine and* The Wall Street Journal, *he comments on popular culture, movies, the media and other issues on his blog, The Search, and also Mere Orthodoxy.*

CHAPTER THREE

From feminist to mere Christian

Dr Mary Poplin

*There is no act, no sermon, no parable in the whole Gospel
that borrows its pungency from female perversity; nobody
could possibly guess from the words and deeds of Jesus that
there was anything "funny" about woman's nature.*
– Dorothy L. Sayers, *Are Women Human?*

In 1953, before they completed their marriage with an
ecclesiastical ceremony in 1957, C.S. Lewis wrote the foreword
to Joy Davidman's book, *Smoke on the Mountain*.[1] Lewis fans
will revel in her insights and similarities in their styles. Douglas
Gresham noted that his mother first sought out Lewis when she
was writing this book on the Ten Commandments, which she
began in America.[2] It's sprinkled with bits of her testimony, and
Lewis notes, "Every story of conversion is the story of a blessed
defeat."[3] Being an adult convert like Lewis and Joy, this is very
real to me. Like Joy, I was a Marxist (critical theorist) and radical
feminist – or so I thought.

Lewis was unique as a highly educated man who took women
scholars seriously. In *A Grief Observed* about grieving Joy's death,
Lewis refers to her mind as

*...quick and muscular as a leopard. Passion, tenderness and
pain were all equally unable to disarm it. It scented the first*

whiff of cant or slush; then sprang, and knocked you over
before you knew what was happening. How many bubbles
of mine she pricked! I soon learned not to talk rot to her
unless I did it for the sheer pleasure – and there's another
red-hot jab – of being exposed and laughed at. I was never
less silly than as [her] lover.[4]

He'd noted her "Jewish fierceness, being there also modern and feminine, can be very quiet; the paw looked as if it were velveted, till we felt the scratch."[5]

He described her as

...so many persons in herself. What was she not to me?
She was my daughter and my mother, my pupil and my
teacher, my subject and my sovereign; and always, holding
all these in solution, my trusty comrade, friend, shipmate,
fellow-soldier. My mistress; but at the same time all that
any man friend (and I have good ones) has ever been
to me. Perhaps more. If we had never fallen in love we
should have nonetheless been always together and created
a scandal. That's what I meant when I once praised her for
her "masculine virtues." But she soon put a stop to that by
asking how I'd like to be praised for my feminine ones. It
was a good riposte, dear. Yet there was something of the
Amazon, something of Penthesileia and Camilla. And you,
as well as I, were glad it should be there. You were glad I
should recognize it.[6]

And I'm certain she did.

Lewis admired another woman who was a late convert, apologist, and writer – Dorothy L. Sayers.[7] He called her one of the great British letter writers, reading her play *The Man Born to Be King* every Holy Week, and writing in her elegy, "She aspired to be, and was, at once a popular entertainer and a conscientious craftsman: like (in her degree) Chaucer, Cervantes, Shakespeare or Moliere… it is only such writers who matter much in the long run." Sayers told Lewis the difference between them was that his passion was for saving souls; hers was for righting minds.[8]

These friendships reveal the magnitude of the man. Lewis was a giant, so sure of himself and God that in the presence of these brilliant women (even if prickly) he was neither repelled nor timid.

Our contemporary fixation on differences

I sometimes muse about particular women in the Bible. I wonder how Deborah told her husband she was going to war with Barak. I imagine odd conversations, "Honey, I'll be back in a few weeks. Barak refuses to go into battle without me." I imagine Jael explaining she'd just killed the acquaintance of her husband, Heber the Kenite. "Heber, dear, I know there's always been peace between us Kenites and the King of Hazor, but I have some bad news." Esther was more subtle, but surely the king wondered why he was being invited to dinner two days in a row.

I appreciate the Bible for depicting people for their call and not for their gender. Not that I believe Jael, Esther and Deborah were radical feminists – I do not. They simply heard the voice of God. Our contemporary fixation on gender/culture/class/ race differences diminishes people's identities to essential but incomplete aspects; it draws even Christians away from their first identity as followers of Jesus, responders to the Holy Spirit, people in whom God has placed a holy desire and purpose. We unconsciously apply stereotypic assumptions to others, but Paul said there is no Jew or Greek, male or female, slave or free in Christ Jesus (1 Corinthians 12:13; Galatians 3:28, both ESV) and John prayed we would all be one (John 17:21, ESV).

After my conversion, God sent me any number of his people from widely different parts of his body – rich and poor, all races, educated and uneducated, Pentecostal, Catholic, Evangelical,

Charismatic, denominational and non-denominational – all faithful men and women. They shared three things – strong faith, profound love of God, and orthodox understanding of Christendom. They were "mere Christians." Few were so strongly attached to their denominational roots that they did not accommodate other true believers from Christ's "orthodox" body.

Lewis' writings are timeless and refreshing because of his close attention to biblical text and his avoidance of narrow theological doctrines and denominational strife. Yet he never hesitated to challenge secularism, nor did he compromise the Christian message. I'd come to see from reading the Bible and visiting every kind of church that each had its own strengths in terms of Christ's teachings and each its own weaknesses. I found that theological doctrines and narrow denominationalism threatened the simplicity of God's word with delimiting abstractions, yet they dealt too simply with paradoxes inherent in Christ's teachings. The more I understand, the more I love the mind of God and the intricacy and precision of his creation and laws, which are as sure and true as the oxygen we breathe.

Embracing "mere Christianity"

To be honest, for the first three years after my conversion I did not read books outside the Bible. Though people often referred me to Lewis and others, I was not the least bit interested in anything but the Bible. Eventually, I was led to hand copy the Psalms, Proverbs and New Testament; God used this time to heal my mind and draw my heart. I don't remember what year I began to read Lewis but I do remember that soon afterward I bought CDs of *Mere Christianity*, *The Abolition of Man* and others for cross-country drives.

One summer I almost wore out the section on Christian marriage in my *Mere Christianity* CD. Here, at last, lay the wisdom of the genders – the idea that marriage is to make one person out of two, and the difference between marriage in a church and in a state. Lewis explained how husbands and wives work to come to agreement and, in those rare occasions when they do not, there needs to be a head and why it should be the man. He described the wife as the "special trustee" of the family interest and the husband as its "foreign policy" adviser. At first I bristled, then gradually I began to settle in to study and think and pray – to turn the questions on myself. The more I read and reflected on my life (and lives of others), the more I found these concepts to be true.

It was like many battles fought and won by God in the adult convert – an initial resistance gives way first to a willingness to study and pray, then comes an ever-so-dim recognition of truth, until one relaxes into the process. The secret longing for truth that long ago we buried begins to resurrect. At last there's an awakening that refreshes one's soul and revives one's spirit until one's heart finally docks with the truth. If we keep going, the longing for more truth takes complete control of the fear and douses the fiery desire to conform to the social norms of our contemporary fellows.

After that I tiptoed into the so-called offensive passages by Paul and paid closer attention to Paul's statements on women and men. I began to see that the woman was to respect the man and the man to love the woman. The man the woman respected was the one to whom she was voluntarily to submit. And the woman the man loved was the woman for whom he was willing to die.

I analyzed my relationships, which had often been the reverse. I thought I loved the man and he respected me. Can I tell you how many competent women find themselves in this place? We love these men out of our loneliness and fear, and the men rest in our fierceness, become dependent on us and often never develop their own call. The woman then takes the head. For those of us who eagerly joined and promoted the reverie of radical feminism, this is exactly what we thought we wanted, until we got it. We were trying desperately to control everything, including our own bodies.

Remorse over my two abortions

As a result I had two abortions in my twenties. When I began to follow Christ, I was deeply remorseful. I know (and research reveals) there were problems in my body, soul, and spirit directly related to those decisions. For several years after my conversion, I repented over and over, unsure whether God could forgive me for what I now understood as grievous sin. One day when I was going through the process again, the Lord spoke into my spirit in an angry voice, "Who are *you* not to forgive someone I have forgiven?" I stopped, stunned and confused by the question. Not understanding, I continued walking along a river and the question came a second time and then a third. I finally stopped walking and asked, then the voice came into my spirit a final time, "I forgave you the first time you asked me. I do not want you to ask me again."

This had now become the sin of unbelief.

Christian counselors had told me I needed to forgive myself, a task that's frankly never done. But God was saying, *I am the one who forgives. I have forgiven you; it is over.* "…forgetting what lies behind and straining forward to what lies ahead, I press on toward the goal of the upward call of God in Christ Jesus" (Philippians 3:13–14, ESV).

There's no indication in the Bible that anyone forgives herself or is told to forgive herself. It's not a principle of human flourishing. I can forgive others, and I must, but only God (and others, if they will) can forgive me. I cannot forgive myself because that's not how God's universe is made. Trying to do something that's not true will never work.

Lewis notes wisely that until we grieve a loss for what is lost to the other (for me, the child) we are not grieving; we're only feeling sorry for ourselves. As a radical feminist, I was trying to live amidst massive contradictions. I was like the feminist who wrote an entire book on caring, then called the human embryo "an information speck." No one called the unborn Prince George a fetus or any such thing; he was always a "baby."

Although feminists frequently claim superiority in such things as love and care, it is often a thinly veiled love of self. Joy Davidman saw this and wrote,

> *The false gods of today are things of the spirit, and as hard to pluck forth as it is hard for a man to pluck out his right eye. The beast in the heart is always the self... We disguise the beast in the heart as a worthy cause... The ardent feminist, who smashes her own home in the name of equal rights for women... what started, perhaps, as a genuine move toward virtue has decayed into an excuse for self-righteousness and self-importance and personal power: a disguise for the beast in the heart.*[9]

One of secular humanism's victories is its persistent message that abortion is good for women and society; that it's safe; and that it's just one of many personal existential choices we should make to construct our own identity.

In *The Weight of Glory*, Lewis describes the other spirit behind abortion – material-naturalism. "The extreme of this self-binding is seen in those who, like the rest of us, have consciousness, yet go about to study the human organism as if they did not know it was conscious. As long as this deliberate refusal to understand things from above, even where such understanding is possible, continues, it is idle to talk of any final victory over materialism... There will always be evidence, and every month fresh evidence, to show that religion is only psychological, justice only self-protection, politics only economics, love only lust and thought itself only cerebral biochemistry."[10]

Lewis could interpret both the appearance of the sky and the signs of the times – he had an uncanny way of understanding what was coming into the culture from the storm he saw developing in the "modern" university where he lived his life. He knew "mere Christians" would need to stand united – men and women, rich and poor, Catholic, Protestant, Pentecostal, and Evangelical – to resist the coming cultural tsunami, to stand on the mountain and cry: Move, be ye thrown into the sea.

Lewis still lives with us as he did in life – a bit in the future and a bit in the past. That's the joy of eternity with our Lord and his great cloud of witnesses!

Dr Mary Poplin *is the author of* Is Reality Secular? Testing the Assumptions of Four Global Worldviews *(InterVarsity Press, 2014) and* Finding Calcutta: What Mother Teresa Taught Me About Meaningful Work and Service *(IVP, 2008). She earned her PhD from The University of Texas at Austin and is a professor in the School of Educational Studies at Claremont Graduate University in Claremont, California. Her work spans K–12 to higher education. Professor Poplin, whose career began as a public school teacher, conducts research on highly effective teachers in urban schools educating the poor. Her work in higher education has included administration, serving as a dean and as director of teacher education. In her latest work, she explores contemporary intellectual trends dominant in the larger culture and in university academic disciplines – the sciences, humanities, and social sciences. She speaks frequently at Veritas Forums throughout the United States.*

Lewis as teacher and servant… and my respectful disagreement on women as priests

Revd Dr Jeanette Sears

My first encounter with C.S. Lewis was seeing *The Lion, the Witch and the Wardrobe* on Sunday afternoon teatime TV in England in 1967, black-and-white weekly episodes. I remember scenes vividly – Lucy and Mr Tumnus in the snow; when Peter and Susan mentioned Narnia to Professor Kirke in his study. What amazed me was this clever elderly gentleman taking the children seriously and even taking the side of little Lucy! As a seven-year-old girl, this impressed me immensely. I went on to read all seven Narnia Chronicles (probably falling in love a bit with Mr Tumnus, then Prince Caspian) and formed a secret club based around Narnia with my friends, using passwords from Underland in *The Silver Chair*. I was hugely affected by the death and coming-to-life-again of Aslan, the great lion, but had no idea he represented Christ until becoming a Christian at age eleven on a youth camp. It seems Lewis had successfully "baptized" my imagination with Christian imagery, as was his intention.

As a teenager I branched out, reading Lewis' popular theology and devotional works – finding he challenged me to use my reason to understand and defend the Christian faith. He made theology far more interesting than anything I was studying at school and it gave me a thirst for more. What could be more fascinating and exciting than studying God?! So I did Theology at university, up to PhD level. Unfortunately few other writers were as interesting as Lewis, but I was delighted to discover I could go back to his thinking and find it as fresh and inspiring as ever. Even after years of teaching Theology myself, I'm glad each reading of his books still takes me deeper and wider in my thinking and, I hope, in knowledge of God.

However, that doesn't mean I always agree with him...

C.S. Lewis and women priests

Lewis' essay "Priestesses in the Church?" is one of his most controversial pieces of writing.[1] I felt disturbed when reading it as a teenager. Not only did I find his Catholic stance strange at the time, but Lewis just didn't sound like his usual self. He came across as blinkered and bombastic, not the rational enlightening Lewis I'd grown to love. It was shocking to suddenly have to disagree with my mentor.

The reason for his essay was an attempt, not in his own Church of England but elsewhere in the wider Anglican community, to appoint a woman as priest. Lewis at first wrote to novelist and Christian apologist Dorothy L. Sayers, asking her to write a polemic on this subject so he didn't have to, but she took him by surprise by stating the opposing view and contradicting his interpretation of Scripture and tradition.[2] Lewis' position was the classic Roman Catholic or Anglo-Catholic view that the priest has to represent Christ at the altar during communion and therefore needs to be male. Sayers pointed out that woman too is in the image of God and so can represent the divine (Genesis 1:27). One can also argue that, if Christ only represents the male and not the female, how can he save women? Plus there's the question: if the priest represents Christ (male) and his Bride the church (female), why is it the male representation that is the decisive one?

A full treatment of the Lewis–Sayers disagreement would involve delving into early church Christological heresies such as Apollinarianism and Nestorianism, wrangling over St Augustine's theological anthropology in *De Trinitate*, debating the meaning of *kephalē* in 1 Corinthians 11:3 and Ephesians 5:23 and whether a man is the "head" or "source" of a woman's spiritual authority, the depiction of gender relations in Milton's poetry, etc.[3] However, this short opinion piece is not the place for the deeper rigorous scholarly debate necessary on this biblical and theological minefield; from a personal perspective, I can only touch on a few things.

Even as a teenager, I knew from experience that the church and its leadership in practice were more complex than Lewis' 1948 essay implied. I'd been converted by Methodists (who first ordained women ministers in the UK in 1974) and by thirteen had already spoken from the front in church services: leading prayers, reading Scripture, giving my testimony. I was then part of a Plymouth Brethren assembly where there were no ordained ministers as such; women weren't allowed to speak and had to wear hats to show we were under male authority (though we were allowed to sing). This, of course, was hurtful at times, but I also had huge respect for those in the assembly and the strong emphasis on Scripture, the atonement and the priesthood of all believers.

Simultaneously with this I was part of an American charismatic house church that had come to my home town, where men and women spoke out in worship as led by the Holy Spirit, and again, there were no nationally ordained leaders. When I went to university, I joined the Church of England. By the time I went to America in the late 1980s for post-doctoral research at Harvard University, I joined a local Episcopal church that was Anglo-Catholic in its liturgy, use of symbolism, and church seasons; was evangelical in its preaching, evangelism and attitude to Scripture; had a "social gospel" of action on behalf of the poor and oppressed; and was charismatic in using the gifts of the Holy Spirit in healing and worship. It was at this church where I first encountered a woman priest as a visiting speaker, and I too was encouraged to preach and take as full a part as possible in ministry. At last I felt I was in a whole church that wasn't split along the usual lines but which expressed the fullness of our Christian tradition and openness to the Spirit.

This means that on re-reading Lewis' 1948 essay in later years, although I have a greater appreciation of the Catholic theology and experience, I've been struck again by how blinkered Lewis' vision is here and how conditioned by extra-biblical sources. Dorothy L. Sayers was right to warn Lewis against an over-appropriation of pagan mythology and philosophy. Platonist theories of ideal forms and hierarchy and essence, and adoption of a belief in Jungian archetypes – all of these made Lewis susceptible to sexual stereotyping in his theorizing on gender in church life.

But it has to be said that, although Lewis' imagination had been baptized by his classical education in pagan myths and philosophy, we do see a gradual baptism of his imagination by biblical material as he progressed in his Christian walk. This development can be seen particularly in his doctrine of God and his eschatology, for example, but it seems to apply to his writings on women as well. His gradual opening up emotionally to the influence of women in his life, especially in his marriage to Joy, mirrors this progress – from the "frightened bachelor" who was "unsafe on sex" and talked nonsense about women and marriage, in the words of Dorothy L. Sayers,[4] to the man who rejoiced in all aspects of his relationship with his wife and begged God not to let him retreat into his shell again after Joy's death.[5]

Meanwhile one could speculate and extrapolate from the trajectory of the development of Lewis' ideas on women (and denominationalism, for that matter), concluding that arguably his position today (had he lived another fifty years!) might be that of the post-conservative evangelical or liberal Catholic for whom there would be no problem with women as priests. Indeed for him now it might be the priesthood of all believers that would be the point of emphasis, and even lay celebration of communion might not be a problem. Many men from a similar background to Lewis have changed their views along these lines in the Church of England.

Also, it's encouraging that Lewis' female characters are often the most spiritually mature and discerning in his fiction and at times are the *de facto* spiritual leaders of men; for example, Lucy Pevensie in The Chronicles of Narnia and Jane Studdock in The Space Trilogy. Lewis died in 1963 just as a radical re-evaluation of much of the scholarship involving the role of women in the Bible, church order, and Christian doctrine was about to explode and develop over subsequent decades. He was already far from traditional in his view of Scripture, evolution, hell – who knows how his thoughts would have evolved? Of course he was not able to experience the ministry of women as priests, or to see them function in a ministry team of ordained men and women together, and so this practical experience could not inform his theological reflection.

Even in keeping the idea of male authority or "headship" over women, there are still plenty of examples of women being able to exercise the full range of their spiritual gifts in leadership – whether as apostles, prophets, evangelists, healers, preachers, pastors or teachers. I am grateful to have experience of this. The Church of England to which Lewis belonged has not only agreed to have women priests but also in 2014 made the decision to join other parts of the Anglican Communion in having women bishops.

As someone who was ordained one of the first women priests in England in 1994, I remain indebted to Lewis for helping me to become a theologian and church leader who could grow up to disagree with him, as indeed has his church. I think he would see that as the role of a good teacher.

It was a particular blessing for my journey to ordination and beyond to have so many resonances from the life of Lewis and the women he knew contained within it. As an ordinand in the Diocese of Oxford, I was sent on a pre-ordination retreat to the Convent of St Mary the Virgin in Wantage – the "ladies at Wantage" whom Lewis visited and where he gave talks, to whom Lewis dedicated *Perelandra* and where Sister Penelope was based, who was such a good friend and correspondent. I was curate and the first female priest to ever celebrate Holy Communion at St Aldate's Church, Oxford, where Lewis had also preached. And I later worked as a chaplain for the Oxford Pastorate, the same job as Stella Aldwinckle who had set up the Socratic Club with Lewis in 1941.

Also, I've been blessed to always be part of large leadership and ministry teams where, though we have been consciously or even unintentionally under male "headship" in each context, we have all been able to function to the fullest extent in the power of the Holy Spirit. I think, with Lewis' emphasis on being "mere Christians" together, he would have come to see the issue of women priests as one of the *adiaphora* ("things indifferent" to salvation) and would not have allowed it to destroy our unity in Christ in the church. He may well have come to agree with Rowan Williams, former Archbishop of the Church of England and now Master of Lewis' old Cambridge college, who stated that the traditional symbolism of the priesthood in the Anglican church had been used in the past to reinforce patterns of inequality and had wrongly become part of the systematic devaluing of the female.

Lewis and female self-image

Despite my disagreement with Lewis over women priests, he was my teacher in other ways. For example, growing up as a girl in our culture is not easy. There is the constant emphasis on appearance and attractiveness, and the view that girls shouldn't be too bright and funny and successful in case it intimidates boys. There is also an unprecedented level of pressure on the young to have sex as soon and as often as possible. The writings of Lewis are a fantastic antidote to this. He encourages everyone to find their true identity in their relationship with God rather than in human approval.

As a young girl I was inspired by Lucy and her devotion to Aslan. She was attractive as a character but also extremely sensitive spiritually and had gifts of healing, insight and leadership. She had to learn it was Aslan's opinion of her and her obedience to him that mattered rather than the opinions of others (as in her temptations in the Magician's house in *The Voyage of the Dawn Treader*). There was also the negative example of Susan, who seemed to allow her beauty and superficial vanities of this world to lead her away from the truth.

As a seventeen-year old I was hugely influenced by the experience of the Green Lady on *Perelandra* in the struggle with the Unman and his playing on her potential vanity and narcissism (the role of the mirror in the life of a woman is scarily portrayed!). And I was amazed at the insight Lewis seemed to have into what it was like to be a woman in his portrayal of Psyche and Orual in *Till We Have Faces*. Even though I now know that Joy Davidman had a large role in the writing of that book, I don't think it diminishes my view of Lewis' understanding.

Also, Lewis was clear that total sexual "liberation" in society would actually damage women much more than men, who would be able to abandon women at will and move from one sexual partner to another with much greater ease.

To summarize, Lewis presents a very positive view of girls and women who can think and be spiritually discerning leaders. But there are also his warnings that we are as fallen as men and can turn to evil in the same way (for example, misusing power like Jadis the Witch or Fairy Hardcastle). As already stated, engaging my imagination early meant that my mind was baptized with Christian imagery, just as Lewis intended for his readers. So I can say that Lewis had an extremely important role in my self-understanding as a woman and the potential of the feminine as an instrument of God's will on the earth.

Lewis as carer

Finally, I admire Lewis as a "man's man" who wasn't afraid to do "women's work". He was aware of how we tend to leave drudgery to other people in order to get on with our own work and lives (such as in his profound understanding of the role of Drudge in *The Pilgrim's Regress*). Domestic drudgery is so often left to women while men get on with the task of fulfilling themselves.

However, Lewis was a radical example in real life of a man who managed to combine immense status in his career along with humble caring for those in his life and society at large who were weaker or desperately needy, especially women. There are numerous examples – his taking Mrs Moore and her daughter into his care and visiting Mrs Moore every day when she was old and in a nursing home; accommodating evacuee children during World War II; looking after the cancer-stricken Joy; caring for his alcoholic brother; forming the Agape fund to help the poor, into which he poured profits from his writings; and even helping look after sick pets.

He assisted Mrs Moore in the kitchen with such humble chores as making jam, and it was his job to do the washing up after evening meals. He cared for the grounds around the house. Even though they had domestic help and a gardener at The Kilns, there were fewer electrical time-saving devices, and there were times when Lewis chose domestic drudgery himself instead of delegating to others.

Lewis considered the life of the home to be the ultimate point of civilization, for which all wars are fought, and so the work to keep it going was most important. Warren Lewis would become annoyed at how much his brother did to help Mrs Moore, but it's possible that the famous Oxford professor needed it to balance out the rest of his life, as well as showing honour and respect to Mrs Moore, an important mother figure for him. In his attitude here, Lewis was an example of the Christian chivalry he so much admired. He constantly tried to emulate the humility and servant heart of his Saviour. For Lewis it was part of his spiritual discipline, along the lines of Brother Lawrence's "practice of the presence of God" and echoing Jean-Pierre de Caussade's statement: "There is no one in all the world who cannot reach the very pinnacle of holiness by performing with love the most common and mundane tasks."[6]

The Lewis who wrote *The Screwtape Letters* and *The Four Loves* was obviously very familiar with the pain and frustration of those who sacrifice much to serve others in private, unnoticed ways, often going unthanked and at the mercy of the vagaries of others' dysfunctional personalities. But Lewis had taken on board his Saviour's message of love. As a man who didn't just have women serving him but was willing to serve them, Lewis remains a great role model and man of integrity for both women and men to admire and emulate. This is especially important when we are faced with an "ageing population" that will need care from us in future.

Though rich – in money, career, experience, relationships, opportunity – C.S. Lewis was willing to become poor and, like his Lord, take the form of a servant.

. . . .

Revd Dr Jeanette Sears *is a writer and speaker specializing in Lewis, Sayers, and Tolkien. She was a postdoctoral Fellow at Harvard on a Kennedy Scholarship and is a trained teacher. Formerly President of the Oxford C.S. Lewis Society and Curate at St Aldate's Church, Oxford, she has most recently lectured in Christian Doctrine and Church History at Trinity College, Bristol, for seven years. She was a contributor to* The C.S. Lewis Bible *and to the Symposium at Lewis' inclusion in Poets' Corner at Westminster Abbey. Her writing includes a tour guide to the Inklings' Oxford and two novels:* Pig's Progress *for children, and now the first in a series of murder mysteries,* A Murder in Michaelmas. *Her website is www.jeanettesears.com.*

CHAPTER FIVE

On women's roles in the church: Lewis' letters to me as a child lit my way

Kathy Keller

Once, in the north of Scotland, I chimed in during a Q and A session that my husband, Tim Keller, was conducting after a service. Since we ordinarily did Q and As together at our home church, Redeemer Presbyterian in New York City, I never gave a thought to voicing my opinion. However, every head turned to look at me with disbelief written on each face, male and female. It was as if the dog had suddenly spoken.

In some places I've been looked on with suspicion as a "raving feminist" because I encourage women to teach and lead, and I do so myself. In New York I've been called "self-hating" and worse because I continue to believe that God gave us a good gift when he created complementary gender roles in the church for men and women. As the wife of a pastor, a joint founder of Redeemer, and a woman in ministry, I have seen it as my role to talk women – and men – off the ledge once they realize Redeemer's complementarian position. It's not as if we hide it. Elders' names are printed in our bulletins every Sunday, and they regularly stand before the congregation – each one a man – for ordination of officers and other events. However, women are so visible on staff and in ministry at Redeemer that it sometimes takes a while for the penny to drop.

I've been influenced by many sources (including Gordon-Conwell Theological Seminary where I graduated with my MA in Theological Studies) and will name an important one here: C.S. Lewis' 1948 tract on "Priestesses in the Church?" (published in *God in the Dock: Essays on Theology and Ethics by C.S. Lewis*, edited by Walter Hooper). I used Lewis' essay and other sources in my book, *Jesus, Justice & Gender Roles, A Case for Gender Roles in Ministry* (Zondervan, 2012). Although Lewis' essay made no difference in the decision of the Anglican church regarding ordination of women when he wrote it, his tract makes a thoughtful point about the difference between the secular world and the church. Lewis points out that, in the secular world, men and women can and must be treated as unisex, interchangeable neuters – citizens and workers. However, that is a fiction we are allowed to shed when we return to the world of reality, God's world, where we may resume our real identities as men and women.

In Lewis' words:

> ...the kind of equality which implies that the equals are interchangeable (like counters or identical machines) is, among humans, a legal fiction. It may be a useful legal fiction. But in church we turn our back on fictions. One of the ends for which sex was created was to symbolize to us the hidden things of God. One of the functions of human marriage is to express the nature of the union between Christ and the Church. We have no authority to take the living and sensitive figures which God has painted on the canvas of our nature and shift them about as if they were mere geometrical figures... With the Church, we are farther in: for there we are dealing with male and female not merely as facts of nature but as the live and awful shadows of realities utterly beyond our control and largely beyond our direct knowledge.

Before proceeding with my commentary on women's roles in the church, I'll provide biographical information relevant to this book on Lewis' treatment of girls and women in his life and in his literature.

My letters from C.S. Lewis

I corresponded with Lewis as a child growing up in 1950s America, a time and place where Lewis was not as known as he was in Britain. (I'm the Kathy near the end of the delightful volume *C.S. Lewis: Letters to Children*, edited by Lyle W. Dorsett and Marjorie Lamp Mead.) So this British professor and author, whose hard-to-find books I sought in my hometown of Pittsburgh, Pennsylvania, and treasured when I found them, helped to fuel my intellectual growth.

One way was through his devotion to answering mail from me with thoughtful comments – like encouraging me when I wrote of problems important to me as a child. Lewis' answers showed that he considered me, an American child – and a girl at that – to have value, worth and dignity. When his letters to other children were published after I was well into my thirties, I was fascinated to notice that he answered the girls with the same depth of interest and attention that he paid to the boys.

In October and November of 1963, Lewis and I corresponded about my upcoming travel to England with family friends, including a chance to meet him in person. Lewis died a few months before my trip. But I visited The Kilns anyway, and his brother, Warnie, welcomed me, showing me their home – even allowing me to pick flowers from their garden.

Women's roles in the church

Now, to jump ahead into my adulthood and return to women's roles in the church, a subject on which I write and speak. I accept and embrace the Bible as the word of God, inspired and without error. This was not always the case.

God made his claim on my life while I was in high school, but I was slow in trusting the Bible as more than a collection of Aesop's fable-like stories and poetic sentiments useful on ceremonial occasions. I was dimly aware that there were people – vaguely referred to as "fanatics" – who held more robust views. Yet my perspective on Scripture did not detract from my intention to enter ordained ministry. I knew God was real, and I had encountered him in every way possible *except* through Scripture. I had no notion that I was missing anything.

It wasn't until college that I met intelligent believers who accepted the Bible as God's word, the only infallible rule of faith and practice. I wrestled with the authority and inspiration of the Bible for several years. Choosing to do an independent study course on the subject, I went through a reading list given to me by a professor, but I came to the conclusion that all the books were written from the same point of view. Several reading lists later, I found myself intimately acquainted with textual criticism, textual variants, oral tradition, the Q document, the Essenes, liberalism, neo-orthodoxy, demythologizing, fundamentalism, evangelicalism, and a lot more.

For me, exploring the fields of higher, biblical, and textual criticism revealed the fundamental accuracy of the canonical texts. Yet it was an answer to a very simple question that resolved the deeper issue of authority: Jesus trusted the inspiration of the Old Testament and promised the inspiration of the New Testament. He quoted Scripture at every point in his life, including his words on the cross from Psalm 22. Jesus *bled* Scripture. If I trusted Jesus to be who he said he was, why wouldn't I also trust his view of the authority and inerrancy of the Scriptures? An example is found in Matthew 5:17–19. This was a game-changing realization for me. And it changed a lot more. For example, now that I trusted God's word as truth, written to aid my flourishing and not to diminish it, my choices needed to be submitted to Scripture. When my choices and God's commands clashed, he won.

Hermeneutical imperatives

The subject of hermeneutics is vast, and not all of it is relevant to the topic of women in ministry, so I will only summarize the basics. In the past generation there have been many new works on the science of biblical interpretation, and they contain much of value. Yet these books, even while recognizing the complexity of the task, if written by evangelicals with a high view of Scripture, still hold to the same two touchstones. For me, the following two principles have made all the difference, particularly in the area of gender roles, ministry, and the collision between them.

First, *Scripture does not contradict Scripture*. What is clear in the Bible interprets what is cloudy.

I am always amused, and sometimes annoyed, that common sense doesn't figure into the discussion of the understandability of Scripture. If you can accept the existence of a being powerful enough to be called God – the creator and sustainer of the universe – why is it difficult to believe that he would be capable of communicating authentically and clearly to his creatures?

Second, *every text must be understood in its context – historical, cultural, and social*. What was the author's intent in each book, passage, and sentence, and what did it mean to the original hearers? The corollary to this principle is: we must find a way to obey faithfully whatever we discover to be God's revealed will, even if our cultural situation has changed since it was first revealed.

Again, common sense should be an aid. God inspired human beings to write his revelation. The Bible is therefore a human book, using human language. Yet if God is immutable and in his providence assembled a book to guide his people in all times and places, then what he revealed yesterday about his character and his design for his creatures will not be changed today. God is not capable of "new and improved" anything, because his perfection is such that any change would be a step away from complete holiness, complete love, complete justice, and complete mercy.

Sometimes I'm asked: do we have to obey – or even care about – something said so long ago and in a time and place so unlike the twenty-first century? And why did God arrange things the way he did with a gender-based division of labor in the church? The answers are "yes" and "I don't know." Yet, although I cannot know God's reasons for gender-based roles in the church, I am confident it is not a bad, injurious, unfair, oppressive thing.

In Lewis' "Priestesses in the Church?", he made the point that we monkey about with gender roles at our peril. What did God mean to accomplish by making us male and female? Why not some unisex being? Or hermaphrodites? Or why didn't God make us able to choose for ourselves whether to generate or incubate life? Why assign different roles? Deep mysteries of revelation hang on our gender and on playing our assigned roles. If God is teaching us something about himself and about our relationship to him (we are all female to God, says Lewis, echoing Ephesians 5:25–27 and Revelation 21:2), do we dare edit God's choice of analogy? Of metaphor? Of language itself?

Perhaps some inkling resides in the dance of the sexes, by which we reveal truth about the inner life of the triune God. The rest is clothed in mystery, to which we yield, with full confidence that it is meant for our good.

Kathy Keller *corresponded with C.S. Lewis as a child. She is co-founder of New York City's Redeemer Presbyterian with her husband, Tim Keller. She wrote* Jesus, Justice, & Gender Roles: A Case for Gender Roles in Ministry *(Zondervan, 2012). She and Tim collaborated on* The Meaning of Marriage: Facing the Complexities of Commitment with the Wisdom of God. *They married one semester before their graduations from Gordon-*

Conwell Theological Seminary. West Hopewell Presbyterian in Virginia extended a call for Tim as a three-month interim pastor while they searched for someone more experienced. Nine years and three sons later, they moved to Philadelphia, where Tim taught at Westminster Theological Seminary and Kathy edited for Great Commission Publications. In 1989 they moved to Manhattan to plant Redeemer Presbyterian. She writes and speaks with Tim, who is a New York Times *best-selling author, with awards from* World *and* Christianity Today. *Tim was described in* Newsweek *as a "C.S. Lewis for the twenty-first century," although he disavows comparisons. Media coverage has treated growing and influential Redeemer Church as an anomaly because it appeals to Manhattan yuppies and intellectuals.*

CHAPTER SIX

C.S. Lewis on love and sex

Dr Holly Ordway

"Christianity," C.S. Lewis pointed out, "is a statement which, if false, is of *no* importance, and if true, of infinite importance. The one thing it cannot be is moderately important."[1] The same holds true for Christian claims about sexuality, which are not merely recommendations, but statements about reality. Lewis did not live to see the consequences of the "sexual revolution," such as the rise of single motherhood, the hook-up culture, and legal abortion. Nonetheless, he diagnosed many of the underlying issues that would lead to our culture's confusion about sexual ethics – a state of affairs that is damaging to both men and women, but with a disproportionate effect on women.

For insight into Lewis' views on love and sex, it might seem natural to turn immediately to *The Four Loves*, but a key idea appears in *The Abolition of Man*. Lewis draws attention to the modern desire to have total control over ourselves on every level, including determining what moral values we accept. The necessary result, he warns, will be the rule not of a more enlightened morality but of raw power: "When all that says 'it is good' has been debunked, what says 'I want' remains."[2] If we reject objective morality, eventually the only foundation for action is pure impulse. Thus, for a culture that has "debunked" traditional sexual morality, there can be no consistent grounding for emotional or sexual restraint.

Paradoxically, the rejection of traditional sexual morality has resulted in sex itself becoming somewhat like a religion. In our secularized culture, sexual activity has become almost the only remaining avenue for an experience of the transcendent: as Lewis noted, "The longing for a union which only the flesh can mediate while the flesh, our mutually excluding bodies, renders it forever unattainable, can have the grandeur of a metaphysical pursuit."[3] Sexual activity is considered essential for both identity and personal fulfillment, but the body itself is seen as a physical "thing" without inherent meaning; thus, sexual activity becomes like a sport, with no particular significance attached to playing a game of sex with someone. This separation of body and soul, action and meaning, in the sexual act is completely contrary to the Christian understanding of sexual ethics.

Lewis on chastity

"Chastity," Lewis wrote, "is the most unpopular of the Christian virtues. There is no getting away from it; the Christian rule is, 'Either marriage, with total faithfulness to your partner, or else total abstinence.' Now this is so difficult and so contrary to our instincts, that obviously either Christianity is wrong or our sexual instinct, as it is now, has gone wrong."[4] The modern approach is to declare that our instincts are right and Christianity is wrong; a claim which requires justifying the gratification of all our impulses, sexual and otherwise.

Here we return to *The Abolition of Man*, where Lewis warns that "It is in Man's power to treat himself as a mere 'natural object' and his own judgements of value as raw material for scientific manipulation to alter at will... if man chooses to treat himself as raw material, raw material he will be."[5] The idea that the body is "raw material," a thing that is subject to our wills but not significant in itself, leads directly to the degrading objectification of women. In *The Four Loves*, Lewis points out that while Eros, at its best, desires the whole person, sexual desire by itself aims for mere gratification: "a sensory pleasure; that is, an event occurring within one's own body." He goes on to say:

We use a most unfortunate idiom when we say, of a lustful man prowling the streets, that he "wants a woman." Strictly speaking, a woman is just what he does not want. He wants a pleasure for which a woman happens to be the necessary piece of apparatus. How much he cares about the woman as such may be gauged by his attitude to her five minutes after fruition (one does not keep the carton after one has smoked the cigarettes).[6]

Lewis is prophetic here, if we consider the catastrophic rise in the hook-up culture and the use of pornography. "Hooking up" treats sexual release as something independent of any emotional connection whatsoever, let alone commitment, which is particularly devastating for women. Unfortunately, the trend in secular culture is to push promiscuity as a form of liberation, encouraging women to treat their own bodies as sexual objects and willingly to cooperate with using, and being used by, others for physical gratification. Pornography contributes heavily to this mindset: a man who uses porn does not need even the physical presence of a woman to gratify his sexual desire, and so the woman is fully objectified. Porn changes the way men perceive women in real life as well, creating wildly distorted expectations for women's appearance, behavior, and needs.

Additional consequences

Another terrible result of this shift in the view of the body is that abortion is more easily justified. An unborn child can be killed at the convenience of the mother, even if the child is recognized as a person, because the mother's own flesh is also a "thing" that the mother is free to modify physically, through drugs and surgery; or to use for any acts of physical pleasure she likes; or to kill, if she should decide to end her life.

We can also see the consequences of the distortion of sexual ethics in the media's glorification of the emotion of romantic love. Film, television, and magazines suggest that "falling in love" is the peak of human experience. Eros is idolized – and Lewis warns what happens when that is so. For two people in love,

> *[Eros] seems to sanction all sorts of actions they would*
> *not otherwise have dared. I do not mean solely, or chiefly,*
> *acts that violate chastity... The pair can say to one another*
> *in an almost sacrificial spirit, "It is for love's sake that I*
> *have neglected my parents – left my children – cheated my*
> *partner – failed my friend at his greatest need."*[7]

The desire for emotional gratification can be as strong as any other desire for power – and unchecked, it can have results that are just as ugly. For one thing, ironically, idolizing romantic passion makes marriage itself harder to sustain. To begin with, unchecked Eros can easily trump good sense in choosing a spouse: "Will he or she make a good husband or wife?" is an unwelcome question in the erotic mood. Christians may even inadvertently contribute to the cult of Eros by an over-romanticized view of marriage. Lewis notes: "Idolatry both of erotic love and of 'the domestic affections' was the great error of nineteenth-century literature... the novelists habitually oppose to 'the World' not the Kingdom of Heaven but the home."[8]

Such an idealization of marriage can foster unfulfillable expectations, leading Christians to forget that every marriage requires self-denial and the sustaining grace of God, for erotic passion will inevitably fade. As Lewis puts it, "all the time the grim joke is that this Eros whose voice seems to speak from the eternal realm is not necessarily even permanent. He is notoriously the most mortal of our loves."[9] When the feeling of "being in love" has passed, it is necessary to have the support of a mutual recognition of the objective moral value of fidelity and commitment – which is precisely what has been "debunked" in modern culture.

Abandoning Christian marriage

The abandonment of the Christian understanding of marriage as a permanent commitment has serious consequences. If marriage is defined primarily, or exclusively, as an emotional bond of love accompanied by sexual gratification, it becomes much more difficult to defend traditional, lifelong marriage. Cohabitation has become a widely accepted way to meet a couple's emotional and sexual needs without the seemingly restrictive imposition of lifelong fidelity, while contraception has allowed for the emotional and physical pleasures of the sexual act to be separated from children as the natural consequence of sexual union. The result has been to seriously undermine the role of men as husbands and fathers in our culture, with great harm to women and children.

Lewis helps us to see that the modern-day confusion about sexuality has its roots in a shift in our culture's view of reality itself. Apparent liberation from sexual ethics turns out to be no liberation at all. If there is no objective morality, and no supernatural dimension to reality, then the body is an object like any other, and can be treated as such. If we do not address these underlying ideas, our attempts to argue for Christian sexual ethics will be met by blank incomprehension at best, or virulent hostility at worst.

Although this is a depressing prospect, at least in the short run, Lewis' analysis does offer a glimmer of hope. At the end of *The Abolition of Man*, he calls for a "regenerate science":[10] a scientific outlook that is not reductive in its analysis, but rather sees each part in the light of the meaningful whole. In our culture, where sex and love are reduced to merely physical and emotional impulses, Christians are called to live out a "regenerate sexuality" and show what it means to be fully human.

Dr Holly Ordway *is Professor of English and Director of the MA in Cultural Apologetics at Houston Baptist University, and the author of* Not God's Type: An Atheist Academic Lays Down Her Arms *(Ignatius Press, 2014). She holds a PhD in English literature from the University of Massachusetts, Amherst;* her academic work focuses on imaginative apologetics and on the writings of C.S. Lewis, J.R.R. Tolkien, and Charles Williams.

CHAPTER SEVEN

Mistress for pleasure or wife for fruit?

Dr Michael Ward

Truth has ceased to be a mistress for pleasure and become a wife for fruit...
– **Letter of C.S. Lewis to Owen Barfield, 28 June 1936**

Lewis' lifetime (1898–1963) coincided with a period of unprecedented change in women's roles and expectations. That change had many and various causes. In this essay, I concentrate on one of those causes: contraception.

Contraception naturally impacts men as well as women, but I will direct my attention more to its effects upon women, given the subject of this volume of essays. To maintain a tight focus, I will avoid examining *The Abolition of Man*, where Lewis says a fair bit about contraception but in the context of an argument too wide and deep for consideration in this short chapter.[1]

Contraception has become much more effective and socially acceptable than it was at the time of Lewis' birth. Indeed, so acceptable is it now in many quarters, even among Christians, that contraceptive practice is considered an unquestionable good, whether it be within marriage (where couples can more easily plan the size and spacing of their family) or outside it (where the promiscuous can practise at least some semblance of responsibility).

These are the principal goods achieved, so the defenders of contraception argue; there are also evils avoided. Without contraception, many more unplanned or unwanted babies would be conceived. Women carrying these unplanned or unwanted babies would be faced with an unenviable choice: opt for an abortion or carry to term a pregnancy that may impair the health of the mother, curtail future opportunities, and reduce her standard of living. Since contraception helps avoid this unenviable choice, it is widely considered a moral advance. Women may continue to have sexual relations with men, unhindered by a significant risk of becoming pregnant or "falling pregnant", as is increasingly the preferred terminology. The negative connotations of "falling" indicate that pregnancy has come to be regarded as a health "problem" to be prevented; contraception prevents the problem and is to be welcomed accordingly, as we welcome inoculations against TB and measles and so forth.

A human right?
In the legal and political sphere (especially in the United States), access to contraception is considered so good a thing that, in many people's eyes, it amounts to a basic human right. From this perspective, to exclude contraception from a statutory health insurance package, for example, would be to infringe on the health prospects and civil liberties of women.

The pill became available on the National Health Service of the United Kingdom in 1961, two years before Lewis' death. He did not live to see the full revolution in sexual ethics that easy access to effective contraception has helped bring about. Public attitudes to sex, motherhood, and marriage have changed significantly since 1963, when – according to poet Philip Larkin's famous line – "sexual intercourse began". However, although Lewis did not live to witness these changes, he knew which way the wind was blowing and he knew that the direction was away from traditional Christian teaching. In a letter to a Mrs Baxter (19 August 1947),

Lewis writes: "I've never propounded a general position about contraception. As a bachelor I think I shd. be imprudent in attacking it: on the other hand I shd. not like the job of defending [contraception] against almost unbroken Xtian disapproval."

It may come as news to some that there was an "almost unbroken" disapproval of contraception in the history of Christian ethics, but Lewis is quite correct in what he says. The tradition of Christian opposition to contraception had indeed remained "almost unbroken" at the time of Lewis' letter to Mrs Baxter. The Catholic church, the Eastern churches and all major Protestant denominations were officially against it until a mere seventeen years before Lewis wrote his letter.

The first major Protestant denomination to break ranks was, ironically, Lewis' own Anglican church (most others followed soon afterwards), but it did so very tentatively. In 1930, the bishops of the Anglican Communion, at their ten-yearly meeting, the Lambeth Conference, issued a Resolution (number 15) which said:

> *Where there is clearly felt moral obligation to limit or avoid parenthood, the method must be decided on Christian principles. The primary and obvious method is complete abstinence from intercourse (as far as may be necessary) in a life of discipline and self-control lived in the power of the Holy Spirit. Nevertheless in those cases where there is such a clearly felt moral obligation to limit or avoid parenthood, and where there is a morally sound reason for avoiding complete abstinence, the Conference agrees that other methods may be used, provided that this is done in the light of the same Christian principles. The Conference records its strong condemnation of the use of any methods of conception control from motives of selfishness, luxury, or mere convenience.*

It's interesting to compare this resolution with others from the same Lambeth Conference, for the comparison shows how disinclined the Anglican bishops were to make any change whatsoever. For example, Resolution 9 says that "the functions of sex" are "essentially noble and creative". Resolution 13 says that "the primary purpose for which marriage exists is the procreation of children". Resolutions 14 and 17 make similar points.

As these other resolutions reveal, the tradition of Christian opposition to contraception continued to be "almost unbroken" even at this 1930 Lambeth Conference. It was only in Resolution 15 where there came a break, and that was evidently controversial. Whereas all the other resolutions I've mentioned were passed unanimously, number 15 had to be fought for and passed by 193 votes to 67. When one refers back to the previous Lambeth Conference, ten years earlier in 1920, and its Resolution 68, which gives "an emphatic warning against the use of unnatural means for the avoidance of conception, together with the grave danger – physical, moral and religious – thereby incurred", one can see why this topic remained vexed. There were still enough bishops of the old persuasion for the revised ethic to be resisted.

Lewis on contraception among unmarrieds

The resolutions mentioned above discuss contraception within marriage. Let's see what the bishops of Lewis' Anglican church said about the use of contraception by unmarried couples. Resolution 18 states:

> *Sexual intercourse between persons who are not legally married is a grievous sin. The use of contraceptives does not remove the sin. In view of the widespread and increasing use of contraceptives among the unmarried and the extension of irregular unions owing to the diminution of any fear of consequences, the Conference presses for legislation forbidding the exposure for sale and the unrestricted advertisement of contraceptives, and placing definite restrictions upon their purchase.*

Lewis shares his bishops' opinion on "the diminution of any fear of consequences". In *God in the Dock*, Lewis points out how contraceptives have made "a profound difference" in the way people think about fornication: "As long as this sin might socially ruin a girl by making her the mother of a bastard, most men recognised the sin against charity which it involved, and their consciences were often troubled by it. Now that it need have no such consequences, it is not, I think, generally felt to be a sin at all."

He makes a very similar comment in "Christian Apologetics", where he observes that most non-Christians "do not feel fornication to be wrong". He goes on: "Now that contraceptives have removed the obviously uncharitable element in fornication I do not myself think we can expect people to recognize it as sin until they have accepted Christianity as a whole."

And in *Mere Christianity* he remarks: "Contraceptives have made sexual indulgence far less costly within marriage and far safer outside it than ever before, and public opinion is less hostile to illicit unions and even to perversion than it has been since Pagan times."

We see that Lewis, although he never propounded a "general position" on the subject and never explicitly attacked the practice as invariably and intrinsically evil, nonetheless clearly believed contraception had a tendency to anaesthetize the conscience. Both women and men will have their consciences dulled by a contraceptive culture, but men will probably become more calloused than women. Men will feel free to exploit women for sexual purposes more than ever now that they don't have to seriously worry about causing them to become unmarried mothers. Women, on the other hand, will still be risking pregnancy. If the contraception fails, the woman can be blamed and left more completely holding the baby than if no contraception had been tried. Thus, the moral advance that supposedly liberates women contributes further to their oppression. They can be exploited more thoroughly and discarded more scornfully.

That Lewis should consider the social stigma of illegitimacy dates him to a generation that is largely without issue, for few people nowadays think a woman ought to suffer social disgrace for becoming an unwed mother. Indeed, it is now very generally held to be yet another constraint on a woman's sexual freedom if she has to put up with even mild social disapproval upon bearing a child while unmarried. But until the 1960s, it was still widely thought to be shameful for a woman to give birth out of wedlock. We see this in the case of Dorothy L. Sayers who, till her death in 1957, kept secret the fact that she had an illegitimate son, for fear of the social implications.

What is often forgotten, however, is that it was not just the "fallen woman" who might be socially ostracized; the man responsible could expect to be shunned by polite society too. We see it in fiction written before general acceptance of contraception: for instance, in E.M. Forster's *Howards End*, published in 1910, Leonard Bast is made to suffer for having impregnated Helen Schlegel while not married to her.

"...the evils of our present tameness"

But by 1958 things were beginning to be different. When, in that year, Lewis published *Reflections on the Psalms* he reflected on how society had changed. In the past, he noted, people had been all too ready to deal pharisaically with those who fell below certain "respectable" standards of morality. Now, however, the problem was the equal and opposite problem of "connivance", with society winking at sexual ethical failings, thereby perhaps allowing them to flourish and increase. Lewis was not actively recommending a return to the days when "certain important people were pariahs... liable to the print of the riding-crop or fingers across the face if they were ever bold enough to speak to a respectable woman". He acknowledges that this kind of social disapproval had many dangers which were "very great: so are the evils of our present tameness".

"Tameness", Lewis seems to be suggesting, is the natural consequence of the widespread use of contraception, for in such a culture the whole moral tone of society gradually weakens. A woman may no longer lose "respectability" by becoming pregnant outside marriage, nor a man be "blackballed" for "deflowering" her (how old-fashioned this language now sounds!), but society in general will lose the very notion of what is and is not "respectable" – literally "worth looking back at" – because hypocrisy will be so much easier to practise. People will take precautions to maintain the outward signs of moral behaviour while privately engaging in illicit intercourse that is carefully contracepted. They will live "life" to the full, but make sure not to get caught out. As Lewis puts it in *Studies in Words* with regard to D.H. Lawrence's 1913 novel: "Since the young people in *Sons and Lovers* never appear either to hope or fear fertility, we may assume that they have prudently taken measures to be 'carried by *life*' just so far as is convenient and no further."

Soon after his conversion to Christ, Lewis reflected on the "tameness" of a contraceptive culture in his 1933 semi-autobiographical work, *The Pilgrim's Regress*. There, the worldly Mr Sensible expatiates on the value of disciplining our appetites, "not, heaven help us, in the interest of any transcendental ethic, but in the interests of our own solid good". We are to lift the cup of sweetness to our lips, he says, missing no faintest ingredient in its flavour, "yet ourselves, in a sense, unmoved – this is the true art. This tames in the service of the reasonable life even those pleasures whose loss might seem to be the heaviest, yet necessary, price we paid for rationality." Mr Sensible continues:

> *To cut off pleasures from the consequences and conditions which they have by nature, detaching, as it were, the precious phrase from its irrelevant context, is what distinguishes the man from the brute and the citizen from the savage. I cannot join with those moralists who inveigh*

against the Roman emetics in their banquets: still less
with those who would forbid the even more beneficent
contraceptive devices of our later times. That man who can
eat as taste, not nature, prompts him and yet fear no aching
belly, or who can indulge in Venus and fear no impertinent
bastard, is a civilized man. In him I recognize Urbanity –
the note of the centre. (Book 5, chapter 4)

If this tame game, this bloodless surrender, is what is meant by "civilisation", then Lewis apparently wants none of it. The very mention of "Urbanity" should put us in mind of Lewis' hollow view of urbanization and the "contraceptive tarmac" laid over fertile countryside in his poem, "The Future of Forestry". To be "sensible" in the manner of Mr Sensible is to have fewer sensations and worse. It is the price "paid for rationality". But – to use terms from *The Abolition of Man* – the rational head only looks so impressively large because of the atrophy of the chest and belly underneath.

Of course, one cannot mention "tameness" in the vocabulary of C.S. Lewis without conjuring that famous line from the Narnia Chronicles: "He's not a tame lion." The Christ-like Aslan is a true beast, with a tail, whiskers, velvet paws, a mane, golden fur, sharp claws and teeth, and a roar that can bend the trees. It is when one begins to assess Lewis' view of Christ, the Lion of Judah, whose relationship with believers is very far from bloodlessly tame, that one reaches the final and fullest reason for his doubts about the justifiability of contraception. Christ is the bridegroom and the church is the bride. The relationship between divinity and humanity is a mystic marriage, in the language of the New Testament (Ephesians 5:31–33; Revelation 21:2ff.), which one cannot imagine as being contracepted in any way. The Holy Spirit overshadowed the Virgin and she conceived in her womb (Luke 1:35). And as with Mary, so with all believers: Christ "loved us and gave himself for us" (Ephesians 5:2, International Standard

Version) and in response we "humbly receive the implanted word, which is able to save" (James 1:21, Holman Christian Standard Bible).[2]

Matrimony – mother-making

Interestingly, in the final volume of Lewis' The Space Trilogy, *That Hideous Strength*, the married protagonists, Mark and Jane Studdock, practise contraception. The very first word of the novel is "matrimony" – literally, "mother making":

> *"Matrimony was ordained, thirdly," said Jane Studdock to herself, "for the mutual society, help, and comfort that the one ought to have of the other."*

It's significant that she jumps to the third purpose for which matrimony was ordained, according to the Anglican Book of Common Prayer, and skips the first two (procreation of children and avoidance of fornication). Part of the reason why the Studdocks' marriage has been so sterile at the emotional level is because it has been deliberately infertile at the physiological level. But as the story progresses, the Studdocks abandon partial actions. Mark gives himself completely when he risks his very life in order to reverence Christ (refusing to trample on a crucifix), and Jane encounters Christ (in a chapter entitled "Real Life is Meeting"[3]) "with no veil or protection between".

Mark and Jane thus become, respectively, a true man and a true woman, aligning themselves with the cosmic powers of masculinity and femininity as displayed by Mars and Venus in the first two books of the trilogy. Mark realizes that he has hitherto been regarding Jane with an offensively proprietorial eye. He repents and resolves no longer to behave like a Lothario who keeps a mistress for pleasure: "How had he dared? And who that understood could forgive him?" Jane, "descending the ladder of humility", thinks of Mark's sufferings and "of children, and of pain and death". She had always been justly proud of her Tudor ancestry, and now, at the last, unforced, she embraces the chance to perpetuate that lineage and be known as a wife for fruit.[4]

Thus The Space Trilogy ends with what Lewis in *The Allegory of Love* calls "the typical medieval theme" of the proud young man "tamed by Venus". But it is a good kind of tameness, bespeaking repletion and consummation, not reticence or avoidance. Venus tames Mars, love conquers all, by giving and receiving unreservedly.[5]

Lewis' beliefs about contraception, unfashionable as they were in the middle of the twentieth century, are now virtually incomprehensible to many in the twenty-first. But as the sexual revolution continues and people increasingly wonder how society ever came to this pass, they may well look back to the tradition of Christian ethical teaching on contraception and wish, perhaps, that it had remained unbroken. Lewis, it seems, would very probably be one such.

• •

 **Dr Michael Ward** *is Senior Research Fellow at Blackfriars Hall, University of Oxford, and Professor of Apologetics at Houston Baptist University, Texas. He is the author of* Planet Narnia: The Seven Heavens in the Imagination of C.S. Lewis *(Oxford University Press, 2008), co-editor of* The Cambridge Companion to C.S. Lewis *(Cambridge University Press, 2010), and presenter of the BBC television documentary,* The Narnia Code *(2009). He was the lead organizer of the project to commemorate Lewis in Westminster Abbey, and unveiled the memorial in Poets' Corner on the fiftieth anniversary of Lewis' death, 22 November 2013.*

Chapter Eight

Dorothy L. Sayers and C.S. Lewis: comrades against the zeitgeist

Kasey Macsenti

Few women in Lewis' life could match his intellect. I'm aware of two: Joy Davidman Gresham, an American author who eventually became his wife; and Dorothy Leigh Sayers, a British author I've admired for years.

The lives of Sayers (1893–1957) and Lewis (1898–1963) had many intersections, mostly through their fascinating, witty – and somewhat flirtatious – correspondence. The intellect displayed in Sayers' letters brought out the spirited side in Lewis. His replies were lively, carrying a tone that he had met his match. I think she could sense his admiration, but like a good comrade, she didn't hesitate to display her biting wit or unflinching opinions. On one occasion, she used the snarky sign-off, "Yours indignantly." But Lewis takes no offense. Instead his letters show high praise for the woman he claimed was the "better writer." At one point Lewis even asked her to contribute to a writing project, and – knowing that the request was a compliment – he declared, "there, I can't speak of you fairer!" Although their letters were frequent, they met only a handful of times. In fact, it would take twelve years of corresponding before they would address each other using first names.

When they weren't exchanging jabs, teasing one another or admiring their respective works, they were spurring one another to do what each did best – excel at writing. It's clear that Lewis loved their intellectual companionship. Sayers achieved a letter-writing voice that appealed to his mind in a way that only a few other women correspondents brought forth (until Joy, whose mind he described as "muscular").

Reading letters between Lewis and Sayers, I imagine what would have happened if they'd met at a pub and started a friendship during college years. They might have enjoyed each other's keen minds, but it's important to note that Lewis would have been in a very different place in life. During college he was an ardent atheist with a very unfortunate view of women. His pre-conversion diary, *All My Road Before Me*, notes many encounters with females, and he rarely misses an opportunity to hone in on the occasional silly and weak ones (as he describes them in cynical observations). After his conversion, he sees women differently – as people with value, worth, and dignity. It's as though his newfound faith opened his mind to God's view of women – thus freeing him not only to admire them but to enjoy them, as he did his close friend, Sayers.

So who was Dorothy Sayers?

She was a renowned crime writer, known for mysteries featuring amateur sleuth Lord Peter Wimsey. Set between the world wars, her novels have stood the test of time and – like Lewis' – remain popular today. Also like Lewis, Sayers was prolific in multiple genres – poetry, essays, criticism. They shared an interest in medieval literature and classical languages and were able to translate ancient texts. Sayers considered her translation of Dante's *The Divine Comedy* to be her best work. With her formidable mind and tremendous talent, she even became known as a popular playwright.

Sayers began corresponding with Lewis in 1942, remaining a faithful writing companion until her death on 17 December 1957. In a letter to an editor, Lewis tells the story of their initial encounter: "She was the first person of importance who ever wrote me a fan-letter. I liked her, originally, because she liked me; later for the extraordinary zest and edge of her conversation – as

I like high wind." They would go on to write dozens of letters to one another. Working through their correspondence, I found more than just a lively friendship. I found two kindred spirits with striking similarities.

Both were Christian believers, whose faith emanated from their entire being. Each loved the life of the mind, an underpinning for their kinship. Reading, writing, and studying were as natural to them as breathing. Each maintained schedules, friendships, and vocations which accommodated their intellectual pursuits. Both examined deeply the Christian faith and individually became satisfied that not only did it not interfere with their logic, their faith complemented their intellect by providing the full circle of reason their minds required.

Both graduated from Oxford with first-class honors, the university stimulating their pervasive intellects. After finishing, he stayed mostly in Oxford, while she spent much of her career in London. Lewis was a philosophy tutor for a year at University College and in 1925 was elected a Fellow and Tutor in English Literature at Oxford's Magdalen College. In 1954 he became Chair of Mediaeval and Renaissance Literature at Magdalene College Cambridge University, but continued to reside in Oxford.

Both became renowned medieval scholars – and proficient translators from ancient and medieval languages into English. Also, Lewis and Sayers were prolific writers in fiction and non-fiction. As such, each claimed to be reluctant theologians, yet the BBC called on both independently to broadcast their ideas via radio to their fearful fellow Britons during World War II. Lewis' broadcasts became a forerunner to his best-seller, *Mere Christianity*, which ran for over three years during the war. Sayers' landmark literary and dramatic portrayal of Jesus Christ, a series of twelve plays collectively entitled *The Man Born to Be King*, was broadcast over ten months.

Both endeavored to make Christianity accessible and relevant. However, as they observed the culture they were addressing, they also became compelling critics. They critiqued culture in many ways, but their most compelling critique was against the rising secularist thinking known as "scientism." Scientism is a philosophy of radical empiricism – its primary tenet is that all truth must be "proven" through the scientific method. It is a philosophy that scoffs at belief in God, particularly in the influential setting of higher education.

Their stand against the deification of science

Beginning early- to mid-twentieth century, accepting truths based on religious faith was becoming outdated, especially in academia – an ironic shift in culture since universities were first established as seminaries and were primary training grounds for the learned. Over time science rose as the primary authority in education, making religion less important. This trend, which disturbed Lewis and Sayers, grew to be more than just a passing fad. Biblical truth was no longer an acceptable foundation, and not just in education – it was becoming taboo in broader culture as well. What started inside the walls of academia had slipped out of the front door and begun dwelling with the common man – the idea that science "saves."

In short, science was becoming the new religion. Lewis and Sayers observed culture's rising trust in science to solve every problem known to man. Readers of *The Abolition of Man* or *That Hideous Strength* will recognize Lewis' stance. Scientism required of the humanities and social sciences the same standards of empirical proof available in natural sciences, such as biology, chemistry, and physics.

To be clear: C.S. Lewis and Dorothy L. Sayers were not against science. They were against science *deified* – against science being used as the ultimate authority for everything under the sun, particularly the increasing popularity for using science as the authority when it came to communicating "truth." This includes "truths" that are not empirically proven through science, such as statements of faith ("I believe God is real...") and statements of ethics ("This is wrong!"). Historically, people had expressed such statements through appeals to inner conviction, religious teaching, family expectations, and cultural tradition. Now there was becoming one standard: empirical verification. So the change seeping into academic life and spilling into culture was becoming a new standard, and such statements were beginning to require scientific proof. This trend became enormously popular in society. (We feel the longevity of this trend today when someone ends an argument with "Prove it!" – an irritating by-product.)

Sayers waged her literary war against scientism in *The Mind of the Maker* and *Christian Letters to a Post-Christian World*. Each author wrote specifically to redeem religion in the eyes of secular society, a controversy that took the world by storm – even capturing the headlines of *TIME* magazine, 8 September 1947: "With erudition, good humor and skill, Lewis is writing about religion for a generation of religion-hungry readers brought up on a diet of 'scientific' jargon and Freudian clichés. His readers are a part of the new surge of curiosity about Christianity." Later the article lauds Sayers' insight that people "have discovered by bitter experience that when man starts out on his own to build a society by his own power and knowledge he succeeds in building something uncommonly like Hell; and they have seriously begun to ask why."

On both sides of the pond, the two authors were viewed as comrades against the zeitgeist, the established philosophy of the day. The *TIME* article captures their intentions wonderfully – to provide a religion-deprived, science-saturated generation with alternatives, namely a fresh approach to Christianity. And it's in this battle, which they took on independently of each other, that I find the most profound similarity between them.

Taking on the West's new view

Their defense was simple: science could not provide people

with the purpose they craved, or the context for their existence. Humanity needs both meaning and a meta-narrative.

Science has always been an important voice throughout history. Lewis and Sayers recognized that many technical and medical achievements wrought by science had improved the quality of life in the Western world. But, as Christians, they believed scientific proof could not provide humanity with the meaning of life for which people were searching – thus, they argued, scientific proof was insufficient as an all-encompassing worldview. If people relied only on science, how could they navigate through life? How could they live virtuously when "virtue" was no longer a steadfast concept? Scientism placed parameters on "what can be known" with "what can be scientifically verified," but left no room for God, the miraculous, the eternal. Stripping the religious from one's vocabulary to replace it only with the secular/scientific created a monstrous vacuum – one we consequently feel today.

Lewis explains in *The Abolition of Man* that such displacement leaves mankind with both grave and significant consequences: "In a sort of ghastly simplicity we remove the organ and demand the function. We make men without chests and expect of them virtue and enterprise. We laugh at honour and are shocked to find traitors in our midst. We castrate and bid the geldings be fruitful."

Sayers too believed that limiting ourselves to the "provable" robs people of meaning. The first time I read Sayers' *The Mind of the Maker,* she convinced me that there's no proof of God's existence or his involvement in our lives that will ever submit to scientific verifiability, because the proof is through personal experience. Admitting this, she goes further by arguing that man *always* understands God in terms of man's own existence. In other words, while science requires us to verify information outside our own experience, such verification must be through objective proof. However, Sayers explains in *Christian Letters to a Post-Christian World*: "To complain that man measures God by his own experience is a waste of time; man measures everything by his own experience; *he has no other yardstick*" (emphasis mine).

Lewis and Sayers help us realize that just because science provides proof, that doesn't mean science provides meaning. Yet it's fair to say that science does not strip mankind of all meaning. As long as a person is a curious being, he or she will find meaning in the pursuit of scientific inquiry. However, strict standards of scientific proof in certain personal areas of life do strip mankind of a meta-narrative – the context for mankind's existence. To clarify, meta-narrative is defined as "a narrative that is common to all." Lewis and Sayers believed that all persons live inside the grand story of God's authorship.

Loving a damn good story

And both authors loved a damn good story, as these colleagues with often colorful language would express it. Story was the center of their lives, especially when it came to their individual abilities to write good fiction. Both succeeded wildly, Lewis in The Chronicles of Narnia (and my favorite Lewis novel, *Till We Have Faces*), Sayers in her Lord Peter Wimsey mysteries.

Both understood the necessity of putting their beloved characters into good narratives. The fact is: story matters. Good characters dwelling in a poor story won't win us over. And similar to fiction, *our* stories matter. Placing mankind in a pointless series of atomic, hapless events kills the characters living in it.

Lewis was devoted to writing stories that would draw us in. His characters are so familiar that we recognize most of them as shadows of ourselves. We find great sympathy with them and their trials. Whether through Eustace or Orual, Lewis takes our deepest struggles and helps us find our way. He walks us off the ledge because he knows that "proof" cannot. I agree that the crises of life are best solved through a good narrative. Our personal questions of identity, purpose, and meaning are the meta-narrative we all live out in God's grand plan. Lewis reminds us of this in every character and plot twist.

Sayers was devoted to writing stories full of characters with relatable struggles. Her detective novels hold up the mirror to her readers as she puts fictional characters through quirky ethical dilemmas. The questions and struggles Sayers' characters experience are deeply relatable to us as humans. I find that her non-fiction works also serve to remind us that we are more than just mud and clay. Through her writings she breathes new life into what it means to be human. While scientism tells us that we are merely atoms in motion, Sayers bids us remember that we are indeed divine. She explains in *Christian Letters to a Post-Christian World* that man is the *imago dei*, the image of God, because he has the ability to "create." She dedicates much of her writing to the definition of work and man's ability for profound artistic creation. Her devotion to the subject must have been a beacon to readers who lived through both world wars, and who didn't buy scientism hook, line, and sinker. By emphasizing people as "creators," Sayers puts the human back in humanity. And she puts humanity back into God's story.

Lewis and Sayers are not always remembered for taking on the scientism-zeitgeist which sprung up in their era. But in my mind, it's their most remarkable connection. Both provided spirited responses – carrying almost a prophetic tone of warning against yielding to such a philosophy. If we restrict the realms of "truth" by criteria that can be "proven," we will indeed be in an empty, desperate state. We will be lost.

In a letter to Arthur Greeves, his lifelong friend in Ireland, Lewis recommends Sayers' book *The Mind of the Maker* while warning against her detective novel *Gaudy Night* (which apparently he "didn't like at all"). Lewis had an affinity and a kinship with Sayers that cannot be denied. Together they shared a desire to fight a trend which still envelops much of the world. But they provided an alternative philosophy that is compelling and continues to be relevant today. They were mutual comrades against the zeitgeist.

I suspect that if they'd ever bumped into one other at The Eagle and Child pub where the Inklings met, Lewis would have acknowledged (welcomed?) his female comrade and invited her to share a pint. I, for one, would have enjoyed seeing the same battle of wits displayed in their letters, but this time during a face-to-face conversation… and over a damn good beer.

. . . .

Kasey Macsenti is a graduate of Gutenberg College, Eugene, Oregon, a liberal arts college that offers a degree in The Great Books, a curriculum centering around the most influential ideas of Western civilization. The degree is comprised of the major historical works of science, history, philosophy, theology, and mathematical theory. After graduating from Gutenberg, Kasey continued to pursue her career in the wireless industry as a national director. Recently married, she and her husband live in Portland and attend Imago Dei Community Church where she teaches philosophy at Imago's School of Theology.

SECTION FIVE

Lewis, the mentor – how his views on women impact mine

Walter Hooper notes that C.S. Lewis' first reference to Mrs Moore as a mother figure was in his letter to Sister Penelope on 9 November 1941. Lewis and the nun for whom he would write the Introduction to her 1944 book, *St. Athanasius on the Incarnation*, established a professional relationship and a personal friendship marked by the frankness seen in their letter-writing. He asks Sister Penelope to "Pray for Jane… She is the old lady I call my mother and live with (she is really the mother of a friend) – an unbeliever, ill, old, frightened, full of charity in the sense of alms, but full of uncharity in several other senses. And I can do so little for her." By then Mrs Moore was in her late sixties, crippled, often in great pain, and in need of almost constant care. Lewis continued to be what he described as her nurse and domestic servant. Hooper writes that Lewis was clearly "worn out," yet he continued to be attentive, devoted, and kind to a woman some considered irascible.

This respectful attitude toward Mrs Moore illustrates well what Owen Barfield said about Lewis – that what he thought about everything was secretly present in what he said about anything. In short, Lewis was authentic. As a deeply committed Christian who read the Bible daily and explained the walk of faith in a way that's still being read fifty years after his death, it's not surprising that he would call for more people like himself: Christian writers who could write good and compelling stories, non-fiction, and essays – but with their faith woven naturally through their work. The word he used in his 1945 paper entitled simply "Christian

Apologetics," was "latent," and he emphasized it with italics. Today we might say "organic," meaning that such a writer's thoughts and opinions, even fictional plots, grow naturally from how their hearts have been changed. "What we want is not more little books about Christianity, but more little books by Christians on other subjects – with their Christianity *latent*."

It seems that C.S. Lewis has called people to do even more than write.

* * *

Section Five provides three detailed accounts of people whom Lewis inspired to take action regarding gender issues. Randy Alcorn shares his personal story of discovering C.S. Lewis, who helped him to find the passionate voice with which he speaks out on twenty-first century cultural debates through his Eternal Perspectives Ministry and his numerous fiction and non-fiction books. He provides our first chapter, "Lewis inspired me to speak out for women."

Second, "On being the father of immortals: Lessons from 'The Weight of Glory'" is by John Stonestreet, ministry leader, radio commentator, book author and – his best-loved role – father to daughters, which is the basis and inspiration for his chapter.

Fittingly, a woman has the last word in our five contributor sections. Christin Ditchfield provides our third chapter, "More than a fairy princess: what Narnia teaches about being strong, courageous women." As do the others in Section Five and in our Conclusion which follows, she speaks from her heart.

CHAPTER ONE

Lewis inspired me to speak out for women

Randy Alcorn

As a teenager, new in my faith, I was hungry for truth. I went several times a week to a nearby Christian bookstore, where I found a book called *The Problem of Pain*. It was the first time I'd seen the name C.S. Lewis.

I was stunned by his discernment and clarity. Like me, he remembered what it was like not to know God. I returned to the bookstore and discovered Lewis' *Out of the Silent Planet, Perelandra,* and *That Hideous Strength*. I'd thought I would have to leave science fiction behind me now that I knew Jesus, but I devoured The Space Trilogy's deep theology. Then I read The Chronicles of Narnia. One among a thousand insights that gripped me:

> "You come of the Lord Adam and the Lady Eve," said Aslan. "And that is both honour enough to erect the head of the poorest beggar, and shame enough to bow the shoulders of the greatest emperor on earth."

That one quote from *Prince Caspian* encompassed the doctrine of man created in God's image, and fallen from greatness to sin – a hundred pages' worth of theology in less than forty words. And Lewis did that time and again.

Lewis proved that one person could write both good non-fiction and fiction, and emboldened me to try. His mentorship and impact on my life, and indirectly on my ministry, has been profound. *Mere Christianity* plays a major role in the conversion of the protagonist in my novel *Deadline*. In my novel *Dominion*, Lewis, in Heaven, is one of the characters. The Narnia books also play a role in that storyline.

Lewis is not an idol, but a treasured companion. I learned long ago what Lewis knew – that an author can become a friend, someone you can rejoin at will and pick up right where you left off. I look forward to meeting Jack Lewis, and exploring the New Earth together in the presence of the Fountainhead of Joy, the Maker of Friendship.

Lewis' high view of women

Lewis wrote admiringly of "the English Evangelicals who abolished the Slave Trade," and just as he advocated equal rights for all races, I have no doubt he would fully advocate women's rights, though his calling wasn't one of a crusader. I cringe whenever I see Lewis called a misogynist. Certainly, to the degree that most of us are, he was a creature of his day and culture – indeed, he called himself a dinosaur – but in many ways, in the deeply respectful tone in which he speaks about women, he seems more ahead of his time than behind it. He was a true complementarian, one who saw women as God's image-bearers with fully equal value to men, even if sometimes intended for different roles, something he celebrated.

As the father of two daughters, I love seeing Lewis' tenderness toward girls. In his *Letters to Children*, he treats young girls with great respect and never talks down to them.

In 1949, Lewis sent his thirteen-year-old god-daughter, Lucy Barfield, the completed manuscript of *The Lion, the Witch and the Wardrobe* with a letter saying, "I wrote this story for you," which later became the dedication in the printed book. The way he portrays Lucy, as the most spiritually perceptive and good-hearted of the children, is itself a compliment to females – no male character in The Chronicles compares to Lucy in her love for Aslan, nor does Aslan love any character more than Lucy.

Many don't know that the actual inspiration for Narnia's Lucy was June "Jill" Flewett (later Jill Freud), a London girl who at age sixteen, during World War II, was evacuated to Lewis' house in Oxford to escape the bombings. Lewis wrote, "I never appreciated children till the war brought them to me." In his letters Lewis praised Jill as a "bright spot" in the home and "the most selfless person" he'd ever known.

Children often have a way of sensing an adult's true nature, so I was interested to read a 2005 interview with then seventy-eight-year-old Jill Freud in *The Telegraph*. When asked her first impressions of Lewis, she said, "Oh, I loved him." She said Lewis was like an adoptive parent to her. "He influenced me hugely... He did think I was bright."

Lewis paid for her to go to the Royal Academy of Dramatic Art, where she began a successful career as an actress.

Her assessment of Jack Lewis? "I thought he was wonderful." Not the assessment that a girl or young woman would make of a misogynist!

Lewis developed a good friendship with Ruth Pitter, an accomplished poet. Lewis admired her poetry. His correspondence, including his critique of her work, demonstrates great respect for her intellect and artistic gifts.

Lewis deeply respected and appreciated his friend Dorothy L. Sayers, one of the greatest British intellectuals of her time, as well as a popular playwright and writer of mysteries. At Sayers' funeral in 1957, Lewis' warm eulogy spoke of the extraordinary craftsmanship displayed in her radio plays on the life of Christ, *The Man Born to Be King*. He said he had read it "every Holy Week since it first appeared, and never re-read it without being deeply moved." Sayers was an outspoken woman with a forceful intellect, some of the same qualities Lewis would admire in his future wife, Joy.

Jack and Joy: a partnership of equals

Lewis developed a close friendship with Joy Davidman Gresham before they married. He loved her deeply and after her death, writing *A Grief Observed* under a pseudonym, he called Joy "a splendid thing; a soul straight, bright, and tempered like a sword." If some of Lewis' earlier books seem occasionally condescending or stereotypical concerning women, his later writings show strong respect, and toward Joy, deep admiration.

Lewis met few men who were his intellectual equal, but he was delighted to meet and eventually marry a woman who had two of his own qualities: a photographic memory and a love for debate. Joy's son, Doug Gresham, confirms that theirs was a marriage of equals, with a mutual depth of respect.

It is impossible to separate how Jack Lewis viewed women, later in life, from how he viewed Joy, the woman with whom he shared his dreams, pleasures, and sorrows. How brilliant was Joy? She entered college at age fourteen. By twenty, she had an MA with honors from Columbia. Her poetry was published in the most prestigious magazines. At age eight, she read H.G. Wells' *Outline of History* and declared that she was an atheist. (Many years later she credited the books of Lewis with bringing her to Christ.) Her brother recalled that she could read a page of Shakespeare once and memorize it instantly. Her IQ tests were literally off the charts. (Some of the claims about her intellect may seem overstated, but Doug Gresham, when I asked him, confirmed their truth.) Any man who was insecure around capable women would surely stay away from Joy, who was so brilliant and prone toward debate!

Warren Lewis, Jack's brother, wrote: "For Jack the attraction was at first undoubtedly intellectual. Joy was the only woman whom he had met... who had a brain which matched his own in suppleness, in width of interest, and in analytical grasp, and above all in humour and a sense of fun."

Paul Ford points out that the female characters in the four Chronicles of Narnia written prior to *The Horse and His Boy* are more old-fashioned, while afterward the women become more modern, intellectual, and self-sufficient. It's no coincidence that *The Horse and His Boy*, dedicated to Joy's sons, David and Doug, was the first one written after Lewis had gotten to know Joy. In his last novel, *Till We Have Faces*, Lewis' favorite, he writes from the point of view of Orual, a woman. Joy collaborated with him on this book, which he dedicated to her. At Doug Gresham's home, I've seen and admired the typewriter used by his mother, on which she typed the final manuscript. Many believe that Orual, in many respects, reflects Joy's persona. Theirs was a true partnership of equals.

Without his understanding of women that came through his relationship with Joy, *The Four Loves* might not have been written, and certainly would not be as rich and perceptive.

After Davidman's death from cancer in 1960, Lewis wrote in *A Grief Observed*: "She was my daughter and my mother, my pupil and my teacher, my subject and my sovereign; and always, holding all these in solution, my trusty comrade, friend, shipmate, fellow-soldier. ...If we had never fallen in love we should have none the less always been together."

My wife Nanci and I were very touched, many years ago, to view Joy's memorial epitaph in Headington, near Oxford, with the words written by her loving husband Jack Lewis. He could not have expressed such deep affection for one woman without embracing a high regard for womanhood:

> *Here the whole world (stars, water, air,*
> *And field, and forest, as they were*
> *Reflected in a single mind)*
> *Like cast off clothes was left behind*
> *In ashes, yet with hopes that she,*
> *Re-born from holy poverty,*
> *In lenten lands, hereafter may*
> *Resume them on her Easter Day.*

Lewis inspired me to speak out for women

Nanci and I raised two daughters whom I respect deeply. When the first was born, the Christian doctor said to me in the delivery room, "Sorry, Dad. It's a girl." I looked at him without appreciation and said, "I prayed we'd have a girl." I've never had a moment's regret that God gave us girls instead of boys.

Lewis' writing and focus on Heaven powerfully reminds us to live our lives seeking to please Christ. His emphasis on eternity helps us to become the kind of Christians who actively reach out to others in Jesus' name, addressing both their physical and spiritual needs. Many of the most materially needy and emotionally abused people in the world are women.

Nanci's and my book *Help for Women Under Stress* was written to give hope, encouragement, and practical assistance to women facing life's challenges. We encourage women to embrace their worth but recognize their limits. Their energy is perishable, but can and should be daily replenished. Most important, we remind readers that God will wipe away all their tears in an eternal world of rest, refreshment, thriving relationships, and unending adventure. This eternal perspective emerges in both Lewis' fiction and non-fiction, and it's something all of us need to consider.

My books *ProLife Answers to ProChoice Arguments* and *Why ProLife?* were born out of a deep concern both for the unborn and for their mothers. A little more than half of aborted children are female, and in some cultures prenatal testing is done to identify females and kill them before they are born. This is anti-women on the most basic level.

Because I've been outspoken in my support of women, it was a particularly hard blow years ago to be pigeonholed as "anti-women" because I publicly opposed abortion. In fact, my concern about abortion didn't start with a burden for children, but a burden for women who struggled due to their past abortions. I believe abortion not only kills children, but deeply hurts women.

It was during this time of public criticism that I began daily to think about God as "the Audience of One." Lewis helped me remember that eternal realities alone, not temporary ones (including other people's opinions of us), are truly important. When Jack Lewis met his Savior, I believe he heard, "Well done, my good and faithful servant; enter into your Master's happiness." When that day comes for all of us, we will know instantly that the one opinion that really mattered all along was his.

Randy Alcorn *is the founder and director of Eternal Perspective Ministries and a* New York Times *best-selling author of more than forty books including* Heaven *(more than one million sold),* If God is Good, *The Treasure* Principle, *and Gold Medallion winner* Safely Home. *His books sold exceed eight million copies and have been translated into more than fifty languages. He lives in Gresham, Oregon, with his wife, Nanci. They have two married daughters and five grandsons. Randy enjoys hanging out with his family, biking, tennis, research, and reading.*

Chapter Two

On being the father of immortals: lessons from "The Weight of Glory"

John Stonestreet

I've often thought that if Blaise Pascal's idea was correct, that all of us have a "God-shaped" vacuum in our hearts only God himself can fill, it would be a thought almost too good to be true. Could it be that God made us with an internal GPS of sorts that would point us in his direction? Pascal thought so.

Paul also believed in God's relentless self-revelation. Speaking to the Epicurean and Stoic philosophers of Athens, he suggested God also uses our time and place to nudge our divine investigations. God determined when and where his image-bearers would live, so that "they should seek God, and perhaps feel their way toward him and find him..." (Acts 17:27, ESV).

Though I believe each to be true, I struggle to understand how my personal longings and the current priorities of my Western culture could possibly work together toward these good ends. I want my desires to lead me in the right direction, but I often find them working as spoiled and misdirected accomplices with the worst of my culture to lead me astray. Our inherent awareness for the transcendent is easily taken captive by false promises of immediate gratification.

It concerns me more to see this tension in my children. Each of my girls, though young (ages five, seven, and nine), expresses remarkable curiosity about God. And they reflect the inherent longing that's in all of us to know and be known and, at the end of the day, to matter to others.

Yet, I also see how often their active imaginations are tempted to that small view of life for which far too many Westerners settle. I fear they will begin to believe, as they absorb constant marketing pitches aiming for their affections and pocketbooks, that they are what they buy; that the hole in their being is stuff-shaped rather than God-shaped; that fame is more important than significance; that life is best understood in temporal rather than eternal categories. Don't get me wrong: I will do all I can to prevent their deception, but I'm also all too aware of the tug-of-war in my own heart; and, frankly, most days I doubt whether my meager voice can compete with million-dollar messaging.

And so I find myself asking: is it even possible, in light of our culture's very attractive appeals to perpetual shortsightedness, that the longings of our heart can serve their God-given purpose? Can our desires be properly cultivated and not inevitably corrupted? Are we better off suppressing longings lest they fall victim to what Aldous Huxley called our "almost infinite appetite for distraction"?[1] How, as a father, might I assist my daughters to find truth, identity, and meaning in their time and place?

Rescuing desires

Lewis wrestled with questions of meaning and longing in a number of places, but nowhere like he did in "The Weight of Glory," a sermon preached in June 1941 at Oxford University's Church of St Mary the Virgin. In it, Lewis suggests that desire can be rescued only by being properly understood. "If you asked twenty good men today what they thought the highest of the virtues," Lewis began, "nineteen of them would reply, Unselfishness."[2] And before reading "The Weight of Glory," I might have answered that way, too.

It's easy to get the impression that following Christ is wholly incompatible with our desires, which we should give up "for his glory." Frequent altar calls to surrender one's life to foreign missions or "full-time Christian service" reinforced this for me. I remember thinking that if God did indeed "call" me to his service, I hoped it wouldn't be to some jungle tribe or underdeveloped country. But I also had this nagging feeling that I had best not say (or even think) that out loud, because God would send me there – not out of spite, but to teach me a lesson. Even more terrifying, I'd heard that God calls some to singleness. And I certainly didn't want to risk that.

But as Lewis rightly notes, our desires are described throughout the Scriptures as proper motivations for virtuous living, which also promises *us* glory. Further, Lewis thought that to wrestle with one's desires is to, in fact, wrestle with God himself. He's the one, after all, who made desire so central to our individual and collective humanity. And by doing so, Lewis thought, God was really up to something.

In Lewis' intentionally twisted analysis of the Enemy's perspective, the elderly demon Screwtape warns his protégé Wormwood to never forget "that when we are dealing with any pleasure in its healthy and normal and satisfying form, we are, in a sense, on the Enemy's ground."

> *Though the demons have used pleasure as a lure to damn many souls, still it is His invention, not ours. He made the pleasures: all our research so far has not enabled us to produce one. All we can do is to encourage the humans to take the pleasures which our Enemy has produced, at times, or in ways, or in degrees, which He has forbidden... All those fasts and vigils and stakes and crosses are only a façade. Or only like foam on the seashore. Out at sea, out in His seas, there is pleasure, and more pleasure.*[3]

God is, Screwtape describes, a "hedonist at heart" who has "filled His world full of pleasures." Thus, he concludes despondently,

"Everything has to be twisted before it's any use to us. We fight under cruel disadvantages."[4]

Lewis understood that it is the direction our desires take and not the desires themselves that are the problem. Rightly ordered, human longings point us to answers about life and its meaning. Ultimately, they point us to God, the only source for knowing our true selves. Our capacity for desire is *good*.

The mistake many make about desires, Lewis thought, is confusing means for ends. We all know how pursuing desire as an end in and of itself results in a treadmill of personal disillusionment and relational carnage. Fulfillment remains perpetually just beyond reach for those who treat pleasure as the destination rather than as joys of the journey.

On the other hand, those who suppress desire to achieve holiness have embraced an idea that owes itself "to Kant and to the Stoics"[5] but not to Christianity. In fact, as they try to honor God they will miss him, since he created our capacity for pleasure in a world full of it, to point our hearts to higher things.

> ...it would seem that Our Lord finds our desires, not too strong, but too weak. We are half-hearted creatures, fooling about with drink and sex and ambition when infinite joy is offered us, like an ignorant child who wants to go on making mud pies in a slum because he cannot imagine what is meant by the offer of a holiday at sea. We are far too easily pleased.[6]

Redeeming and re-embracing desire

How might desire be reclaimed? Only, Lewis believes, by allowing it to at least partially explain our full identity as human beings. Yes, we are promised that "we shall be with Christ" and also that "we shall be like him," but, Lewis notes, via "an enormous wealth of imagery," promises of "glory," of feasting and enjoyment, and "some sort of official position in the universe – ruling cities, judging angels, being pillars of God's temple."[7]

This is no gnostic vision of a disembodied rescue from the evil of our beings. This is sheer bliss, the abundant life promised by our Lord (John 10:10, ESV).

Undergirding the truth of Lewis' observation is the biblical endorsement of the goodness of humanity when restored from brokenness by sin to fullness in Christ. We are, Lewis thought, something we cannot yet be, and so our reunion with God in Christ is also a reunion to our true selves. As Thomas Howard wrote:

> *He did not come to thin out human life. He came to set it free. All the dancing and feasting and processing and singing and building and sculpting and baking and merrymaking that belong to us, and that were stolen away into the service of false gods, are returned to us in the gospel.*[8]

How marvelous to think that in Christ, my girls (and I) are not saved from our humanness but, in fact, *to* it.

And yet this is just one of the ways our desires point to a greater reality that though we can now imagine, we cannot yet see. Lewis' imagery for this is a door. We stand on this side, sensing something fuller on the other side. It's an image Lewis uses to open and close his children's series, The Chronicles of Narnia.

In *The Last Battle*, the Narnia inside the stable door is larger than the Narnia outside the door. As they wonder how that could be, Queen Lucy remarks, "In our world too, a stable once had something inside it that was bigger than the whole world." Soon, they realize that the Narnia they thought to be real was actually only a copy. "It's all in Plato, all in Plato: bless me, what *do* they teach them at these schools?" the professor asks.

And yet, the vision of the "real" Narnia differs from Platonism in a very important sense: it's not a disembodied place. "Aslan's world is, you could say, more *material* than ours: its sensory delights more intense."[9] Yet, these sensory delights do nothing to diminish the reality of life in the Narnia they knew and loved.

So it is with us, Lewis thought. "Some day, God willing, we shall get *in*," Lewis says,[10] but our eternal longings do not diminish the legitimate pleasures we experience now. They are real, and they are good.

I'm learning to help my daughters look for theirs, and when they find them, to cultivate them and protect them. Lewis has taught me to praise the curiosity that drives my oldest daughter to seek answers, even if she gets it wrong. And, because of Lewis, I know why a paintbrush or a craft brings remarkable focus to my usually all-over-the-place middle daughter. And I see the weight of glory in the laugh that takes over my youngest daughter's entire person when she's delivering an impression of one of us.

Lewis closes his sermon with a final thought on cultivating and protecting: we do so best as we think much of others. We live, and therefore desire, in community, not alone. As we do, we push one another either towards or away from the God-given ends for their desires. Thus, we must take each other seriously. After all, "There are no *ordinary* people. You've never talked to a mere mortal... it is immortals whom we joke with, work with, marry, snub, and exploit – immortal horrors or everlasting splendours."[11]

My daughters can, moment by moment, resemble either. So can I. I suppose my wife and I have our work cut out for us.

. . . .

John Stonestreet *is a Speaker and Fellow of the Chuck Colson Center for Christian Worldview. He communicates on faith and culture, theology, worldview, education, and apologetics, and speaks at conferences, colleges, churches, schools, etc. John is the co-host with Eric Metaxas of* Breakpoint, *the Christian worldview radio program founded by the late Chuck Colson, and the voice of the* Point, *a daily national radio feature on worldview,*

apologetics, and cultural issues. He also serves as Senior Content Advisor for Summit Ministries in Manitou Springs, Colorado. John holds degrees from Trinity Evangelical Divinity School (Illinois) and Bryan College (Tennessee). He is co-author of Restoring All Things *(Baker Books, 2015),* Same-Sex Marriage *(Baker Books, 2014), and* Making Sense of Your World: A Biblical Worldview *(Sheffield Press, 2007). He and his wife Sarah have three daughters and a dog, and live in Colorado Springs, Colorado. Connect with John at ThePointRadio.org.*

More than a fairy princess: what Narnia teaches about being strong, courageous women

Christin Ditchfield

I was seven when my aunt gave me my first copy of *The Lion, the Witch and the Wardrobe*. Little did I know that The Chronicles of Narnia would have such a profound and lasting impact on my life! I was immediately captivated by the adventures of the four young children who tumble through the door of a mysterious wardrobe, finding themselves in Narnia – an enchanted world of talking beasts, fauns, dwarfs, giants, and other creatures. I soon devoured the entire Narnia series, reading each of the seven books more than a dozen times, until they literally fell apart. Every time I read the books, I loved them more. They became a part of me.

I discovered – as millions have – that there's far more to The Chronicles of Narnia than meets the eye. They have stories within the stories. Each book is full of hidden truths and spiritual treasures.

C.S. Lewis insisted that The Chronicles are not allegories, and technically speaking, that's true. In an allegory, every character and event symbolizes something else. Many characters and events in Narnia do not represent anything in particular – they're simply elements of the wonderful and fantastic adventures Lewis created. But many characters and events *do* represent something else: truths from the spiritual realm. And although Lewis did not initially intend to write stories to illustrate the most vital truths of the Christian faith, that's essentially what he did.

Jesus said, "Out of the abundance of the heart, the mouth speaks" (Matthew 12:34). Consciously, and perhaps, at times, even unconsciously, Lewis wound powerful biblical truths through every chapter, every scene in The Chronicles. His deeply rooted faith naturally found its expression in everything he wrote.

My own spiritual life as a child and as an adult has been profoundly influenced by echoes of Scripture resounding through Lewis' stories, and as an author and speaker, I love sharing these truths with audiences of all ages. But these classic novels have inspired me in many other ways – and on many other levels. I've really gotten to know Polly, Lucy, Susan, Aravis, and Jill, the young women who play such important roles in The Chronicles. And I've learned a lot from them.

Lewis' high view of women

Lewis writes his female characters from a perspective scholars refer to as a "high view" of women. Sometimes it's described as "chivalrous" – in the medieval fairy-tale sense. Others might simply call it "biblical" – women are not only of equal value and worth to God as men are, but women are a true reflection of God's nature and character (created in his image), and an integral part of God's plans and purposes for humanity.

Like our male counterparts, women have extraordinary potential to do amazing things in God's power and strength. And just like our male counterparts, women also have the ability (in our flesh) to make colossal mistakes!

There's something inherent in womanhood, in femininity – a special grace, a unique and incomparable beauty – that should be honored and admired and respected. In Narnia, as in our world, Lewis asserts that some activities are beneath a woman to do. Some tasks, some battles, some responsibilities are not ours to face. Not because women are incapable, unable or unwilling – but because those tasks have been appointed to others. And because women's strengths and skills are better suited to other equally vital tasks.

In Narnia, women don't run from the battle. Women don't hide and women certainly don't stay behind in the camp, cooking for the men! But women do use different strategies in the battle – such as fighting with different (but equally lethal) weapons and sometimes going behind enemy lines on other critical missions instead.

The Chronicles of Narnia teach us...

Women can be strong and bold and courageous. Like Lucy, we can stand up for ourselves and what we believe in, even if no one else believes in us. Women can embrace the spirit of adventure. Like Aravis, we can dare to dream of a different life – and risk everything to make the dream come true. We can rule justly, we can right wrongs, we can rescue the oppressed, we can protect and defend ourselves, our families, our country. We can take down witches or wicked queens, Telmarines or Calormenes. And we can take the initiative, leading by example, when the courage of men fails.

Women can be the voice of reason. We can be blessed with a great deal of wisdom and common sense. Sometimes, like Susan or Polly, we get grief for having tunnel vision, being too practical, too focused on ordinary, supposedly boring details. But we don't shut ourselves in wardrobes or get lost in the "Wood between Worlds" or leave our coats and shoes (which we'll later need) back on the beach. Yes, we know... you men can thank us later.

Women can show great compassion and tenderness, kindness and consideration for others. We can be loyal and dedicated and devoted. Our sensitivity can be a great gift. Because of it, we sometimes experience Aslan in ways our brothers may not. We may be more aware of Aslan's presence – in moments that others miss. Lucy especially exemplifies this, but Susan and Polly and Aravis and Jill have their own special encounters – deep and meaningful conversations with Aslan that draw them closer to him.

Women can be just as frail and flawed, just as blind, just as selfish and stubborn, and just as proud as their male counterparts. But we can also be quick to repent; quick to forgive and to be forgiven. Lucy and Aravis and Jill, in particular, show us that we don't have to stay the same. We can learn from our mistakes. We can change. We can grow in every kind of grace.

Women can be more than our culture dictates, more than society expects. We don't have to be an empty stereotype. Shallow or giddy or vain. Envious. Materialistic. Self-obsessed. Our lives can – and should – be about so much more than celebrity gossip and fashion trends, "nylons and lipstick," and parties and boys. There is something far more real and precious – a deeper life, a greater purpose. We can choose to be part of it. We can answer Aslan's call.

As Polly, Lucy, Susan, Aravis, and Jill discover, it's not always easy to follow Jesus. But it's an amazing journey, full of wonder and adventure.

What C.S. Lewis has given the world in the young women of Narnia is extraordinary. They are extraordinary. And they teach us that we can be too.

. . . .

Christin Ditchfield *is the best-selling author of* A Family Guide to Narnia: Biblical Truths in C.S. Lewis' The Chronicles of Narnia, *which has sold more than 55,000 copies and been translated into half a dozen languages. A popular conference speaker and syndicated radio host, she has written sixty-six other books, including several literature curriculum guides introducing thousands of elementary school children to the world of Narnia. She holds a BA in Christian Leadership and an MA in Biblical Theology.*

What do Lewis' life and literature reveal for today's culture?

Carolyn Curtis

At the end of the day – and this book – do we think C.S. Lewis was sexist, or even a misogynist? Or did he take what literary scholars call a high view of women in his writing? What about his life? Did girls and women have an impact on Lewis, his thinking, his work? Let's break this down and apply what we've read.

We think of Lucy, memorable for her bravery and being the one who recognized Aslan for who he was. We have Lewis' fantasy/sci-fi character, Jane Studdock, a brilliant scholar pursuing her doctorate degree while juggling what she regards as her high calling as a wife and mother. We have Orual in *Till We Have Faces*, Lewis' opportunity to speak with great truths and meaning through the voice of a woman, an ugly woman at that, a leap of literary achievement and a critical risk by a man of his reputation in the 1950s. And we have Lewis' selection of brilliant and accomplished women friends, Ruth Pitter and Dorothy L. Sayers to name two, culminating in his late-in-life romance and marriage to Joy Davidman Gresham. She was a woman of intestinal fortitude (read: guts) and professional achievements, whose thinking Jack described as "muscular," a decisive compliment about her capabilities resulting from her richly developed mind, heart, and soul. (Orual's wisdom and literary voice were doubtless inspired by Joy, described by her son, Doug Gresham, as the unacknowledged co-author of *Faces*.)

Yet, as a leader in the Inklings, why didn't Lewis insist on including women? A product of his times, perhaps. Or maybe Lewis was prudent, knowing that women meeting in private settings with men (some married) had a downside potential worth avoiding. Were women authors held back by not being part of this inner circle? Were the all-male Inklings poorer in their creativity and literary output because they lacked the thinking and critique of women?

And, turning to his relationships, what do we make of a man who lived with a woman who was not his wife and who eventually married a woman with whom he did not (at first) live?

Finding the trajectory of his attitudes

Lewis' mother, Flora, was a brilliant intellectual – but she died when he was a boy. And young Jack felt abandoned again when his father sent him from Ireland to England for schooling, although the experience ultimately led to educational opportunities, high academic achievements, and employment in his chosen profession, university teaching. Yet he longed for a woman, specifically a mother figure.

One stepped in briefly, a Miss Cowie, matron at one of his English boarding schools. Though motherly in her affections, she filled the boy's head with ideas about the occult. (According to George Sayers' biography of Lewis, *Jack*, Miss Cowie was sacked by the school.) Her influence and other factors sent him into a dark period, a turn to materialism and a spell of winter for his intellectual, imaginative development.

Then came a time of learning with the Great Knock and a time of mourning with the Great War.

Enter Mrs Moore. Leaving aside the debate about whether they had a sexual relationship, she certainly had an impact on his life. He was not really free to marry. As a non-intellectual, she may have influenced his opinion of women as companions, the memory of his brilliant mother perhaps seeming like an anomaly.

It was after the relationship with Mrs Moore began that his attention turned to spiritual matters. Lewis had long clung to atheism. But friendships with several Christian men, respected and prominent scholars such as Tolkien (an eye-opener for Lewis, no doubt), expanded his mind. A spiritual process occurred, resulting not just in his switch to becoming a Christian but in becoming a man whose faith was truly alive. It was palpable to him... and to those who knew him. Lewis' faith grew, and it changed him. Among other things, it brought him out of his winter of darkness, famously connecting his imagination and intellect – and his work began to flourish.

It's interesting that as his faith grew, his dependence on the companionship of Mrs Moore faded (though he continued his commitment to care for her, with daily visits to her nursing-home bedside even after her mind was gone, until she died). Also, his circle of influence had been growing to include strong, successful women as close friends. Many were female correspondents whose letters he answered as faithfully as those from males. They influenced him both personally and professionally.

As to his work, for some years Lewis had been writing and speaking on "apologetics," explanations of the Christian way of life. And – although he experienced what today we call "workplace discrimination" for his outspokenness about faith in the hallowed halls of Oxford – his countrymen called on him in the greatest crisis of their generation, World War II. The BBC invited Lewis to address the nation, and he did – along with Winston Churchill – Lewis on faith that sustains, Churchill on their cherished freedom. Together they inspired not only a nation but all who were fighting for freedom.

Reluctance to mix "politics" with "religion"

Later, when Churchill offered Lewis a CBE (Commander of the British Empire), Lewis declined, fearing that acceptance might appear to mix "politics" with "religion." If he were alive today, would Lewis join voices denouncing cultures that deny school-age girls access to education? Would he speak against thinking that denies women equal cultural, economic, and societal privileges accorded to men? Would he lift his voice against the abuse and degradation of women in pornography and sex trafficking?

Or would he – as he did so effectively during his lifetime – point to the Bible as his source of truth, recommending it to others (perhaps the highest form of activism), working alongside patriots, as he did with Churchill, to achieve freedom and dignity for all? No one can be certain, but we can look to his early life for clues.

Although C.S. Lewis later denounced whatever childhood faith he may have developed before his mother's tragic death, he saw and knew faith in action from his earliest years. For starters, his grandfather was a prominent minister in Belfast. On her deathbed, his mother Flora was advising her nurse to settle down with a good Christian husband like her own Albert. Her final gift to Jack and Warnie was a Bible for each boy. (Before his adult conversion, Jack avoided for years the Scriptures his mother so wanted him to know, but his stepson, Doug, reported decades later that he never knew a day when his stepfather did not read his Bible.)

Likewise, Lewis' father was a man of faith. Early in his career, he was known as an effective orator, often quoting the Bible. After Albert's sons were grown and gone (having served in World War I), and Jack was struggling to find an academic job despite proving to be a highly successful scholar, Albert one day was called to the phone at his home in Belfast. Taking it, he learned of a telegram waiting for him. "Read it," he said. The next words he heard were: "Elected Fellow Magdalen. Jack." Albert ended the call and climbed the stairs to his son's bedroom, where he burst into tears. He knelt by the bed and thanked God. His diary entry for that day ends, "My prayers have been heard and answered."

So seeds of faith were sown in Lewis' earliest home. But disappointment that God did not answer his prayers to save his mother's life (Jack's childhood understanding of God's answer) led to his embrace of atheism and, at least, figurative embrace of an older woman and mother figure, who was less than supportive of his newfound faith when he claimed it as an adult. Nevertheless, C.S. Lewis' welcome embrace of Christ's offer of grace led to some of the most influential writing of the twentieth century. On that, few – if any – critics disagree. What disagreement there is focuses on Lewis' views of the female gender, the subject of this book.

Lewis' high view of women

We conclude that both Lewis' life choices and his writings take a high view of women, noting that the direction of his attitudes about women continues higher as his life goes on. Said differently, as he aged and matured, he grew in faith. Likewise, as he aged and matured, his views of women grew "higher."

In addition to his well-known male friends, he opened himself up to women as friends – strong, accomplished, intellectual women (Sister Penelope, Dorothy L. Sayers, Ruth Pitter, his numerous women correspondents, to name a few) – although he occasionally navigated some relationships in ways that were less than tidy. If we can forgive those instances, we can remember that he actively supported their work, relished their deep thinking, and enjoyed their lively companionship.

Enter Joy Davidman Gresham. (Her first name is the word Lewis used all his life for a longing he felt, even in childhood, of something so wonderful it was almost unattainable – what he eventually recognized as an understanding of the divine, of God, of what and whom he must choose to believe in for himself.)

Joy is perhaps the high point in his trajectory, the direction or course of his attitudes. Besides marrying a woman of Joy's intellect and achievements while in his fifties, Lewis wrote the novel he most valued not only with her by his side but with her in his heart. So *Till We Have Faces* becomes another "data point" as we track his evolving attitudes on women.

It's interesting that – even after Joy's death and in Lewis' last years on earth – he tidied up another matter that bears scrutiny when examining his views on women. A scholar named Elizabeth Anscombe had debated with Lewis in 1948. A formidable intellect, Anscombe criticized material in the third chapter of Lewis' book, *Miracles*. Many who were present for the debate believed Anscombe bested Lewis – apparently including Lewis himself, considering he rewrote the chapter according to Anscombe's comments when the book was republished in 1960. (He also recommended a woman to succeed him as president of the Socratic Club, which hosted the debate.)

Does it matter whether a writer as influential as C.S. Lewis had a high view of women?

We think it does matter, which is why we assembled the group of contributors to *Women and C.S. Lewis* to write their opinions. Not all of them agree in the same way. And not all of them agree, period.

Some wrote on ways Lewis' life and literature have undergirded their personal and professional development, even their actions, in a culture that can be affected by the views of people who freely admit Lewis helped to shape their minds and hearts.

Making a difference in today's culture

It seems fitting to end with additional examples of people who provide real-life applications of Lewis' influence and mentorship of them – and thus Lewis' impact into the twenty-first century. These people are making a significant difference in the world today. They see the lostness of our culture. But they understand the power of words, actions, and truth to influence change. They also recognize that issues affecting women affect men, too.

We begin with **Dr Carol M. Swain**, Professor of Political Science and Law at Vanderbilt University in Tennessee. Frequently quoting C.S. Lewis, she is passionate about empowering others to raise their voices in the public square. As a recognized authority on political science, law, race, and immigration, she is a frequent guest on American and British television and radio. A prolific author, Swain's *Black Faces, Black Interests: The Representation of African Americans in Congress* (Harvard University Press, 1993) has been cited by US Supreme Court justices in several decisions. Cambridge University Press published her books examining white nationalism and immigration in America. Swain's most recent book is *Be the People: A Call to Reclaim America's Faith and Promise* (Thomas Nelson, 2011), her title playing on the opening words of the United States of America Constitution.

Carol Swain has lived the American Dream. Long before she was influenced by C.S. Lewis and others, she was one of twelve children being raised in extreme rural poverty, even without running water. She has risen from being a high school dropout who went on to earn a GED to an acclaimed university professor known for her courageous defense of Judeo-Christian values and her work to apply them to issues affecting women and men. In *Be the People* (93), she writes, "Higher poverty rates among blacks and Hispanics relate directly to higher rates of children in households that are headed by females."

Does Swain see Lewis as relevant in the twenty-first century? "Yes," she says. "I like what Lewis had to say about marriage and societal progress." In *Be the People* (108) she quotes from the Christian Marriage chapter of *Mere Christianity* – Lewis' views on "two distinct kinds of marriage: one governed by the State with rules enforced on all citizens, the other governed by the Church with rules enforced by its own members. The distinction ought to be quite sharp…" In quoting Lewis, Swain writes that he "offered words of wisdom about marriage and divorce that apply well to the debate over same-sex marriages."

Randy Singer, a Virginia-based lawyer, pastor, and author of award-winning legal thrillers, was inspired to try his hand at writing in the voices of women protagonists, as C.S. Lewis famously did in *Till We Have Faces*. He calls Lewis one of his literary heroes and personal mentors.

Singer says he tries "to create strong female leads as both protagonists and antagonists, allowing those leads to work against stereotypes. As a male novelist, one of the great dangers in writing female leads is the temptation to cram them into one of several boxes that our culture has created to define the way women are perceived. In reality, each woman is unique, multi-faceted, and unpredictable."

He does not flinch when placing female characters into harm's way, a cultural reality. His first novel begins with the vicious attack by terrorists of a missionary serving God with her husband in a country where the Christian faith is not welcomed. Written before September 11, 2001, the book was *Directed Verdict* and won for Randy Singer the first-place Christy Award in the Suspense category.

Eager to shine light on violence, abuse, and humiliation of women, he says, "I've been especially intrigued by the influence and unbreakable spirit of women, even in societies where they are treated as second-class citizens."

Lancia E. Smith of Colorado is a photographer, writer, gardener, business owner – and mother and grandmother. But like C.S. Lewis' character Sarah Smith in *The Great Divorce*, Lancia Smith seems to have "many children," because she shares her love and wisdom with numerous people whose younger years included abandonment, abuse, addiction, and other problems which derailed her life before she found her way. She calls Lewis her spiritual and intellectual father, saying, "God dressed himself up in Lewis' words and put them on so I could have a trail to follow in the dark."

Among Smith's professional ventures is her website, *Cultivating the Good, the True, & the Beautiful*, which she describes as "an exploration of how to identify and intentionally develop what is of eternal value amidst the real pressures of our daily lives... [and living out] the values that will outlive us."

She recalls her condition when she discovered Lewis. "I can only describe it as being a kind of emotional feral child... learning what many people do without a second thought: live as a human being with others, the life of community. Lewis left wide open a window on his life, and his transparency has allowed millions of us to learn from him not just the value of literature but the value of a life submitted to God."

As Smith climbed out of the mire of her difficult early years, some of it foisted on her by abusers and some of it caused by her choices, she discovered from Lewis her worth as a female, particularly through his fiction. "He is one of the best and clearest examples of a writer giving glory and a sense of value to women and effectively conveying how powerful that expression of redemption and empowerment can be."

With intentionality, she shares these lessons freely with others, both women and men, including employees at her company, visitors to her website, and friends and soon-to-be friends she encounters along her path.

David Holland of London is the author of *Paying for Sex* and director of Explicit Freedom, a ministry for people struggling to overcome sexual addiction and achieve a lasting breakthrough. His book explores spiritual "costs" to people and society at large in today's sex-drenched culture, such as degradation of women – and of men, a newer attitude for his generation, including younger Christians.

As a writer, broadcaster, and blogger, Holland's heart is to help create fully developed disciples of Jesus through his message about sex, freedom, and intimacy with God. He serves on the core leadership team of his growing church in the heart of London.

He finds much in the writings of C.S. Lewis addressing issues of sexuality and its misuse – thinking which Holland says addresses the twenty-first century. He quotes from *Surprised by Joy* on Lewis' views about the dangers of exaggerating Eros, from *Reflections on the Psalms* on intimacy addiction, and *The Screwtape Letters* on wrestling personal demons. Holland uses a quote from Lewis' 1942 sermon, "The Weight of Glory": "Our Lord finds our desires not too strong but too weak. We are half-hearted creatures, fooling about with drink and sex and ambition when infinite joy is offered us, like an ignorant child who wants to go on making mud pies in a slum, because he cannot imagine what is meant by the offer of a holiday at the sea. We are far too easily pleased."

Candid about his journey to sexual freedom and respectful attitudes between women and men, Holland writes, "We settle for sin at the expense of the glory that God would offer us in his presence. Pornography, masturbation, premarital and extramarital sex are the mud pies that we favour instead. I could have had intimacy with God, but instead I chose nudity, rebellion, and sin."

Lisa Ledri-Aguilar is heartbroken to discover so many women selling their bodies (or being abducted into sexual slavery), many of them Mexican nationals near where she teaches college in Southern California. For Ledri-Aguilar, walks on the beach overlooking the Pacific Ocean are spoiled by the realization that many couples she encounters are in an exploitive "relationship," an arrangement that degrades the women (and, truth be told, the men too).

It's a subject close to the heart of this mentor, educator, and professor, who was awarded the California Association of Teachers Excellence Award for college-level teaching, the highest award granted by a state-level organization.

"Most people are outraged at the idea of slavery," says Ledri-Aguilar. "Even after all the human rights documents, protests and unilateral agreements, slavery has re-emerged in the form of human trafficking throughout the world. In this multicultural, multilingual, multi-sexual world, why is slavery even remotely tolerated? Why are we not doing more as a global community to stop this grievous crime against so many men, women, and children from all nations?"

She quotes Lewis' 1943 book, *The Abolition of Man* (73), saying he makes a clear argument for the necessity of a shared

Moral Law. "A dogmatic belief in objective value is necessary to the very idea of a rule which is not tyranny or an obedience which is not slavery." Lisa Ledri-Aguilar believes that all people with an understanding of the Moral Law should be engaged in this fight against modern slavery.

Is C.S. Lewis relevant today? You decide.

Questions for Reflection and Discussion

1. C.S. Lewis used the term "joy" to describe which early experiences and emotions in his life? In what ways can you relate?

2. Think about his relationship with Mrs Moore. What do we know about it and what does it tell us about Lewis?

3. Lewis' life was marked by a number of losses, hardships, disappointments, and upheavals. How did he handle these?

4. Think about his friendships with both men and women. How did his friendships seem to influence his life, his thinking, his work?

5. Lewis said that George MacDonald's book *Phantastes* baptized his imagination. What did he mean by this? What books by Lewis or other authors have done the same for you?

6. In his youth and as a young man, he dabbled in the occult and considered himself an atheist. What circumstances and people might have fueled these ideas in him?

7. Lewis placed a high value on the combination of intellect and imagination, especially their point of intersection. How do they affect you?

8. Lewis took a spiritual journey that led him to the Christian faith. How did that struggle and his ultimate decision to trust God impact his life and his work?

9. Think about Joy Davidman, her accomplishments and her life's journey. How do you think the relationship between Joy and Jack affected each of them?

10. Consider Lewis' life and body of work. From what sources did his moral compass come and how did that play out in his personal and professional choices?

11. Some critics have said that Lewis was a sexist, that he did not have a high view of women and girls based on his life and literature. What do you say to that claim?

12. Contributors to *Women and C.S. Lewis* have shared from their hearts as well as their extraordinary minds. What did you learn that can apply to today's culture?

Endnotes

Introduction: Not mere mortals
Dr Mary Pomroy Key

1   Como, James, ed. 2005. *Remembering C.S. Lewis: Recollections of Those Who Knew Him*. San Francisco: Ignatius Press.
2   C.S. Lewis College motto "Pursuing truth in the company of friends." Borrowed, with permission, from Page Smith, the Founding Provost of the University of California, Santa Cruz.
3   Lewis, C.S., "The Weight of Glory".
4   Fondly based on the Inklings, the "Sprinklings" are a loose-knit group of writers who meet together to read original works and solicit critique and encouragement at conference events sponsored by the C.S. Lewis Foundation.
5   Harwood, Laurence. 2007. *C.S. Lewis, My Godfather: Letters, Photos and Recollections*. Downer's Grove, IL: Intervarsity Press, p. 124.

Section One, Chapter One: The enduring influence of Flora Lewis
Dr Crystal Hurd

1   Smith, Sandy. *C.S. Lewis and the Island of His Birth*. Derry-Londonderry: Lagan Press. 2013. 83.
2   Lewis, *Surprised by Joy: The Shape of my Early Life*. San Diego: Harvest. 1955. 3.
3   Smith, *C.S. Lewis and the Island of His Birth*. 71.
4   Smith. *C.S. Lewis and the Island of His Birth*. 61–62.
5   *The Lewis Papers*, Vol. 2. 251.
6   Smith. *C.S. Lewis and the Island of His Birth*. 74.
7   *The Lewis Papers*. Vol. 2. 248.
8   *The Lewis Papers*, Vol. 3. 389, 450.
9   Smith. *C.S. Lewis and the Island of His Birth*.143–48.
10 Sayer, George. *Jack: C.S. Lewis and His Times*. San Francisco: Harper & Row. 1988. 6. Later editions of Sayer's biography published by Crossway were titled *Jack: A Life of C.S. Lewis*.
11 Myers, Christine. "Academic Student Life." *University Coeducation in the Victorian Era: Inclusion in the United States and the United Kingdom*. New York: Palgrave Macmillan (2010). 70.

12 The May 25, 2009 issue of *Italy* magazine reports that Walter Hooper, Lewis' secretary and biographer, gave author Giuseppe Fortunati a copy of a Latin atlas of Italy that belonged to Lewis in which the author of The Chronicles of Narnia had underlined the Latin word *Narni*. Lewis was fascinated with Roman history. According to *Italy*, Hooper said Lewis told him he had been inspired by it for his Chronicles.

13 Sayer, *Jack: C.S. Lewis and His Times*. 4., *The Lewis Papers*, Vol. 2, 220.

14 *The Lewis Papers*. Vol. 3. 119.

15 Sayer. *Jack: C.S. Lewis and His Times*. 22

16 Smith *C.S. Lewis and the Island of His Birth*. 37–38, 104.

17 *The Collected Letters of C.S. Lewis*, Vol. 3. Ed. Walter Hooper. San Francisco: Harper. 2007. 398.

Section One, Chapter Five: The Divine Comedy of C.S. Lewis and Dorothy L. Sayers
Dr Crystal L. Downing

1 Diana Glyer, *The Company They Keep: C.S. Lewis and J.R.R. Tolkien as Writers in Community* (Kent, OH: Kent State Univ. Press, 2007), 23, nt21.

2 *The Letters of Dorothy L. Sayers*, vols. II–IV, ed. Barbara Reynolds (Cambridge, GB: Carole Green, 1997–2000), III.45. All subsequent quotations from Sayers can be found in these volumes, keyed to the date.

3 *The Collected Letters of C.S. Lewis*, vols. II & III, ed. Walter Hooper (San Francisco: HarperSanFrancisco, 2004, 2007), III.1400. All subsequent quotations from Lewis can be found in these volumes, keyed to the date.

4 Dec. 1945 (II. 682).

5 Scholars endorse Walter Hooper's suggestion that Sayers' comment on miracles was "the encouragement Lewis needed" to write his 1947 book (*Letters II*. 573 nt103). The Beatrice metaphor, of course, is my own.

6 Mary Stewart Van Leeuwen, *A Sword between the Sexes? C.S. Lewis and the Gender Debates* (Grand Rapids, MI: Brazos, 2010), 107.

7 These words were part of an essay Sayers sent to the Bishop of Coventry in June 1944 (*Letters III*. 29).

8   The first phrase is from a letter to Margaret Gray, dated 9 May 1961 (*Letters III*. 1265); the second is in a letter to Edward T. Dell, dated 25 Oct. 1949 (*Letters II*. 989).

9   Barbara Reynolds, *The Passionate Intellect: Dorothy L. Sayers' Encounter with Dante* (Kent, OH: Kent State University Press, 1989), 24.

Section Two, Chapter Four: The Pilgrim's Paradox: Female characters in *The Pilgrim's Regress*
Dr David C. Downing

Works cited

Lewis, C.S. *The Pilgrim's Regress: An Allegorical Apology for Christianity, Reason, and Romantism*. Originally published by J.M. Dent in 1933.

Lewis, C.S. *All My Road Before Me: The Diary of C.S. Lewis, 1922–1927*. Ed. by Walter Hooper. San Diego: Harcourt Brace Jovanovich, 1991.

Lewis, C.S. *The Collected Letters of C.S. Lewis, Volume 1: Family Letters 1905–1931*. Ed. by Walter Hooper. London: HarperCollins, 2000.

Lewis, C.S. *The Collected Letters of C.S. Lewis, Volume 2: Books, Broadcasts, and the War, 1931–1949*. Ed. by Walter Hooper. London: HarperCollins, 2004.

Lewis, C.S. *The Collected Letters of C.S. Lewis, Volume 3: Narnia, Cambridge, and Joy*. Ed. by Walter Hooper. London: HarperCollins, 2007.

Downing, David C. *The Pilgrim's Regress: The Wade Center Annotated Edition* by C.S. Lewis and edited by David C. Downing. Grand Rapids, Michigan: Eerdmans, 2014.

Lewis, C.S. *Perelandra*. London: The Bodley Head, 1943.

Lewis, C.S. *Surprised by Joy: The Shape of My Early Life*. New York: Harcourt Brace Jovanovich, 1955.

Hilder, Monika B. *The Gender Dance: Ironic Subversion in C.S. Lewis' Cosmic Trilogy*. New York: Peter Lang, 2013.

Section Four, Chapter One: Jack, the "old woman" of Oxford: sexist or seer?
Dr Monika B. Hilder

1   Along with his idea that wives were prone to "fidgetiness," Lewis had the idea that males, unfortunately, were naturally lazy. In *The*

Screwtape Letters, he points to male reluctance to take proper trouble for others (142); in *The Four Loves*, he speaks of the male tendency to abdicate leadership in marriage (98); privately he speaks of male laziness as opposed to female fidgetiness (*Letters II* 507).

2   See C.S. Lewis, "The Necessity of Chivalry" 13.

3   See my endnote 1.

4   Mary Stewart Van Leeuwen believes that Lewis overused the "either/or" rhetorical strategy, thereby eliminating additional possibilities, and points to this discussion in other critics (44–45, 37n). Chad Walsh, however, while he points to the either/or strategy, states that in this he has taken the "role as Devil's advocate" in "mak[ing] the case stronger than [he] actually consider[s] it to be" (*Literary Legacy* 205–206), and states, "It is always possible, though not necessarily true in every controversy, that God can count beyond two" (207). Walsh also notes Lewis' "modesty"; "Sometimes he confesses that he cannot make up his mind between two viewpoints, and offers them both. When he ventures an opinion on some controverted point of orthodox theology, he usually prefaces it with a warning that this is merely what he thinks and he may be wrong" (*C.S. Lewis* 154).

5   See Alan Jacobs' (232–33) and Alister McGrath's (252–59) discussions.

6   In "Imagination and Thought in the Middle Ages," Lewis speaks of intuitive reason as angelic and discursive reason as a necessary and "laborious process" that is indicative of "our [human] inferiority" (53). See my discussion of discursive and intuitive reason in *The Gender Dance: Ironic Subversion in C.S. Lewis' Cosmic Trilogy* 68–70.

Works cited

Barfield, Owen. *Owen Barfield on C.S. Lewis.* Ed. G.B. Tennyson. Middletown, CT: Wesleyan UP, 1989.

Barkman, Adam. "'All is Righteousness and there is no Equality': C.S. Lewis on Gender and Justice." *Christian Scholar's Review* 36.4 (Summer 2007): 415–36.

Bayley, Peter. "From Master to Colleague." *Remembering C.S. Lewis: Recollections of Those Who Knew Him.* Ed. James T. Como. San Francisco: Ignatius, 2005. 164–76.

The Bible. King James Version.

Ezard, John. "Narnia books attacked as racist and sexist." *The Guardian* June 3, 2002. Web. 15 July 2011. <http://www.guardian.co.uk/uk/2002/jun/03/gender.hayfestival 2002>.

Filmer, Kath. *The Fiction of C.S. Lewis: Mask and Mirror*. London: Macmillan, 1993.

Fredrick, Candice and Sam McBride. *Women Among the Inklings: Gender, C.S. Lewis, J.R.R. Tolkien, and Charles Williams*. Westport, CT: Greenwood, 2001.

Green, Roger Lancelyn and Walter Hooper. *C.S. Lewis: A Biography*. London: William Collins, 1974.

Grossman, Lev. "J.K. Rowling Hogwarts and All." *TIME* July 17, 2005: 38–43. Print.

Hilder, Monika B. *The Gender Dance: Ironic Subversion in C.S. Lewis' Cosmic Trilogy*. New York: Peter Lang, 2013.

Hooper, Walter. "C.S. Lewis and C.S. Lewises." *G.K. Chesterton and C.S. Lewis: The Riddle of Joy*. Eds Michael H. Macdonald and Andrew A. Tadie. London: Collins, 1989. 33–52.

Jacobs, Alan. *The Narnian: The Life and Imagination of C.S. Lewis*. New York: HarperCollins, 2005.

Lewis, C.S. "Christianity and Culture." 1940. *Christian Reflections*. Ed. Walter Hooper. Grand Rapids, MI: Eerdmans, 1975. 12–36.

Lewis, C.S. "Christianity and Literature." 1939. *Christian Reflections*. Ed. Walter Hooper. Grand Rapids, MI: Eerdmans, 1975. 1–11.

Lewis, C.S. *The Collected Letters of C.S. Lewis, Volume I (Family Letters, 1905–1931); Volume II (Books, Broadcasts, and the War, 1931–1949); Volume III (Narnia, Cambridge, and Joy, 1950–1963)*. Ed. Walter Hooper. New York: HarperCollins, 2004, 2007.

Lewis, C.S. *The Discarded Image: An Introduction to Medieval and Renaissance Literature*. 1964. Cambridge: Cambridge UP, 1978.

Lewis, C.S. *Dymer*. 1926. *Narrative Poems*. Ed. Walter Hooper. New York: Harcourt Brace Jovanovich, 1979. 7–91.

Lewis, C.S. *English Literature in the Sixteenth Century, Excluding Drama*. 1954. Oxford: Clarendon, 1968.

Lewis, C.S. "Equality." 1943. *Present Concerns*. Ed. Walter Hooper. San Diego, CA: Harcourt Brace Jovanovich, 1986. 17–20.

Lewis, C.S. *The Four Loves*. 1960. London: Collins, 1974.

Lewis, C.S. *A Grief Observed*. 1961. New York: Bantam, 1976.

Lewis, C.S. *That Hideous Strength: A Modern Fairy-Tale for Grown-Ups.* 1945. New York: Scribner, 2003.

Lewis, C.S. "Imagination and Thought in the Middle Ages." 1956. *Studies in Medieval and Renaissance Literature.* Ed. Walter Hooper. Cambridge: Cambridge UP, 1966. 41–63.

Lewis, C.S. *The Last Battle.* 1956. Harmondsworth: Puffin, 1975.

Lewis, C.S. *The Lion, the Witch and the Wardrobe.* 1950. Harmondsworth: Puffin, 1975.

Lewis, C.S. *The Magician's Nephew.* 1955. Harmondsworth: Puffin, 1975.

Lewis, C.S. *Mere Christianity.* 1952. London: Collins, 1974.

Lewis, C.S. *Miracles.* 1947. London: Macmillan. Revised Fontana 1960.

Lewis, C.S. "Modern Man and his Categories of Thought." 1946 MS. *Present Concerns.* Ed. Walter Hooper. San Diego, CA: Harcourt Brace Jovanovich, 1986. 61–66.

Lewis, C.S. "The Necessity of Chivalry." 1940. *Present Concerns.* Ed. Walter Hooper. San Diego, CA: Harcourt Brace Jovanovich, 1986. 13–16.

Lewis, C.S. "On the Reading of Old Books." 1944. *God in the Dock: Essays on Theology and Ethics.* Ed. Walter Hooper. Grand Rapids, MI: Eerdmans, 1976. 200–207.

Lewis, C.S. *Perelandra.* 1943. New York: Scribner, 2003.

Lewis, C.S. *Prayer: Letters to Malcolm.* 1964. London: HarperCollins, 1977.

Lewis, C.S. "Preface." *George MacDonald: An Anthology.* Ed. C.S. Lewis. 1946. London: Fount, 1990. 21–35.

Lewis, C.S. "Priestesses in the Church?" 1948. *God in the Dock: Essays on Theology and Ethics.* Ed. Walter Hooper. Grand Rapids, MI: Eerdmans, 1976. 234–39.

Lewis, C.S. *The Problem of Pain.* 1940. London: Collins, 1975.

Lewis, C.S. *The Screwtape Letters.* 1942. New York: HarperCollins, 2001.

Lewis, C.S. *Till We Have Faces: A Myth Retold.* 1956. New York: Harcourt Brace Jovanovich, 1984.

Lewis, W.H. "Memoir of C.S. Lewis." *Letters of C.S. Lewis.* Ed. W.H. Lewis. London: Geoffrey Bles, 1966. 1–26.

Lindskoog, Kathryn. "Sex." *The C.S. Lewis Readers' Encyclopedia.* Eds Jeffrey D. Schultz and John G. West, Jr. Grand Rapids, MI: Zondervan, 1998. 370–71.

McGrath, Alister. *C.S. Lewis - A Life: Eccentric Genius, Reluctant Prophet*. Carol Stream, IL: Tyndale, 2013.

Milton, John. *Paradise Lost*. 1667. Ed. Merritt Y. Hughes. Indianapolis: Odyssey, 1976.

Milton, John. *Paradise Regained*. 1671. *John Milton: Complete Works and Major Prose*. Ed. Merritt Y. Hughes. Indianapolis: Odyssey, 1976. 483–530.

Nietzsche, Friedrich. *Beyond Good and Evil*. 1886. Trans. and Ed. Marion Faber. Oxford: Oxford UP, 1998.

Pullman, Philip. "The Darkside of Narnia." *The Guardian* October 1, 1998. Web. 15 July 2011. <http://dedulysses.wordpress.com/2006/07/15/the-darkside-of-narnia-by-pullman/>.

Sayer, George. *Jack: C.S. Lewis and His Times*. New York, NY: Harper & Row, 1988.

Shaw, George Bernard. *Man and Superman*. 1903. New York: Brentano's, MCMV.

Van Leeuwen, Mary Stewart. *A Sword between the Sexes? C.S. Lewis and the Gender Debates*. Grand Rapids, MI: Brazos Press, 2010.

Walsh, Chad. *C.S. Lewis: Apostle to the Skeptics*. 1949. Folcroft, PA: Folcroft, 1974.

Walsh, Chad. *The Literary Legacy of C.S. Lewis*. London: Sheldon, 1979.

Wollstonecraft, Mary. 1792. *A Vindication of the Rights of Woman*. London: Penguin, 1992.

Wordsworth, William. *The Prelude*. 1850. *William Wordsworth: Selected Poems and Prefaces*. Ed. Jack Stillinger. Boston: Houghton Mifflin, 1965. 193–366.

Section Four, Chapter Three: From feminist to mere Christian
Dr Mary Poplin

1   C.S. Lewis, Foreword in Joy Davidman, *Smoke on the Mountain: An Interpretation of the Ten Commandments*. Philadelphia, PA: The Westminster Press, 1953.

2   Douglas Gresham, Introduction to C.S. Lewis, *A Grief Observed*, NY: Harper Collins, 1994, p. xxviii.

3   Lewis in Davidman, p. 7.

4   Lewis in *A Grief Observed*, pp. 4–5.

5   Lewis in Davidman, p. 9.

6   C.S. Lewis, *A Grief Observed*, pp. 47–48.

7   In addition to the play and her letters and detective novels, Sayers wrote other significant works: *Creed or Chaos, Letters to a Diminished Church, The Mind of the Maker* and *Are Women Human?*

8   Adam Schwartz, "The Mind of the Maker: An Introduction to the Thought of Dorothy L. Sayers through Her Letters." *Touchstone*, May 2000.

9   Joy Davidman, *Smoke on the Mountain*, pp. 23–25.

10 C.S. Lewis, *The Weight of Glory and Other Addresses* (Revised and Expanded Edition by Walter Hooper), (in the essay on Transposition), NY: Collier Books, 1980, p. 72.

Section Four, Chapter Four: Lewis as teacher and servant… and my respectful disagreement on women as priests
Revd Dr Jeanette Sears

1   C.S. Lewis, "Priestesses in the Church?" was published originally in *Time and Tide* August 1948 and reprinted in Walter Hooper (ed.), *God in the Dock* (Grand Rapids, Michigan: Eerdmans, 1970).

2   Lewis' letter of 13 July 1948 to Sayers can be seen in Walter Hooper (ed.), *The Collected Letters of C.S. Lewis*, vol. 2 (HarperCollins, London, 2009), and her response of 19 July 1948 in Barbara Reynolds (ed.), *The Letters of Dorothy L. Sayers*, vol. 3 (Dorothy L. Sayers Society, 1999).

3   See, for example, Mary Hayter, *The New Eve in Christ* (London: SPCK, 1987), and Mary Stewart Van Leeuwen, *A Sword between the Sexes? C.S. Lewis and the Gender Debates* (Grand Rapids, Michigan: Brazos Press, 2010). (Note that I don't agree with Van Leeuwen's idea of Lewis being Arian concerning essence and hierarchy in the Trinity in his early thought.) The arguments around women priests and bishops in the Church of England can be seen in *Women Bishops in the Church of England? A Report of the House of Bishops' Working Party on Women in the Episcopate* (London: Church House Publishing, 2004) or www. churchofengland.org/media/38523/gs1557.pdf.

4   Dorothy L. Sayers, op.cit., to Mrs Robert Darby on 31 May 1948 – Sayers is defending Lewis against the charge of intellectual arrogance, but adds: "…I do admit that he is apt to write shocking nonsense about women and marriage. (That, however, is not because he is

a bad theologian but because he is a rather frightened bachelor.)" In her letter to John Wren-Lewis on Good Friday, March 1954 she refers to Lewis as an excellent apologist but one who sometimes writes outside of his range and in particular is "hopelessly unsafe on sex", getting his hierarchical view of the genders from Milton.

5   C.S. Lewis, *A Grief Observed* (London: Faber and Faber, 1961), p.17.

6   Jean-Pierre de Caussade, *Abandonment to Divine Providence*, first published in 1861 and available at www.ccel.org/ccel/decaussade/abandonment.toc.html.

Section Four, Chapter Six: C.S. Lewis on love and sex
Dr Holly Ordway

1   "Christian Apologetics." In *God in the Dock: Essays on Theology and Ethics* (New York: Eerdmans, 1971), 101.

2   *The Abolition of Man* (New York: HarperOne, 2009), 70.

3   *The Four Loves* (New York: Mariner, 2012), 102.

4   *Mere Christianity* (New York: HarperSanFrancisco, 2009), 95.

5   *Abolition of Man* 77.

6   *The Four Loves* (New York: Mariner, 2012), 94.

7   *The Four Loves* 113.

8   *The Four Loves* 9.

9   *The Four Loves* 113.

10 *The Four Loves* 81.

Section Four, Chapter Seven: Mistress for pleasure or wife for fruit?
Dr Michael Ward

1   For more on this point, see John Finnis, "C.S. Lewis and Test-Tube Babies" in his *Human Rights and the Common Good: Collected Essays Volume III* (Oxford: Oxford University Press, 2011).

2   For more on this theme, see Arthur Mastrolia, *C.S. Lewis and the Blessed Virgin Mary: Uncovering a "Marian Attitude"* (Lima, OH: Fairway Press, 2000); cf. Jason Lepojärvi, "Worship, veneration and idolatry: observations from C.S. Lewis" in *Religious Studies* (November 2014) pp. 1–20.

3   A phrase derived from Martin Buber's *I and Thou*, which Lewis read in 1942, not long before the completion of *That Hideous Strength*. Buber writes: "The *Thou* meets me. But I step into direct relation with it. Hence the relation means being chosen and choosing, suffering and action in one; just as any action of the whole being, which means the suspension of all partial actions and consequently of all sensations of actions grounded only in their particular limitation, is bound to resemble suffering."

4   For more on Jane's ancestry and her role in bringing to birth the heir of Jupiter, the new Pendragon, see my *Planet Narnia*, pp. 52–53, 174–75; cf. 183–86.

5   I discuss this scene in further detail in "Voyage to Venus: Lewis' Imaginative Path to *Perelandra*" in Judith Wolfe & Brendan Wolfe (eds), *C.S. Lewis' Perelandra: Reshaping the Image of the Cosmos* (Kent, OH: Kent State University Press, 2013).

Section Five, Chapter Two: On being the father of immortals: lessons from "The Weight of Glory"
John Stonestreet

1   *Brave New World Revisited* (New York: RosettaBooks, 2000), 35.

2   *The Weight of Glory and Other Addresses*, (San Francisco: HarperSanFrancisco, 2001), 25.

3   *The Screwtape Letters* (New York: Macmillan, 1970), 41.

4   *The Screwtape Letters*, 101–102.

5   *The Weight of Glory and Other Addresses*, "The Weight of Glory," 26.

6   "The Weight of Glory," 26.

7   "The Weight of Glory," 34.

8   Thomas Howard, *Evangelical is Not Enough: Worship of God in Liturgy and Sacrament* (San Francisco: Ignatius Press, 1984), 38.

9   Rowan Williams, *The Lion's World: A Journey into the Heart of Narnia* (Oxford: Oxford University Press, 2013), 117.

10 *The Weight of Glory and Other Addresses*, "The Weight of Glory," 43.

11 "The Weight of Glory," 46.